SPORTS AFIELD
FRESHWATER
FISHING

SPORTS AFIELD
FRESHWATER
FISHING

Edited by Frank S. Golad

HEARST BOOKS
New York

Inquiries should be addressed to Permissions Department,
William Morrow and Company, Inc., 1350 Avenue of the
Americas, New York, N.Y. 10019.

It is the policy of William Morrow and Company, Inc., and its
imprints and affiliates, recognizing the importance of preserving
what has been written, to print the books we publish on acid-free
paper, and we exert our best efforts to that end.

Library of Congress Catalog Card Number:
ISBN 0-688-11538-1

Printed in the United States
First U.S. Edition

1 2 3 4 5 6 7 8 9 10

Designed by Dirk Kaufman
Edited by Susan E. Davis
Produced by Smallwood and Stewart, Inc.
New York City

Contents

INTRODUCTION

Why fish?

Think about what fishing really is: A human being—the supposed pinnacle of evolution on this planet—attempting to fool a slimy, cold-blooded vertebrate, with a brain the size of a pea, into eating something attached to the end of a line.

Is that difficult?

It certainly can be, at times. But it's also a lot of fun. That's the essence of fishing.

Something must be mighty attractive about this sport, because we live in a nation of anglers. The latest estimate of the number of people who pursue fish in the United States is in the neighborhood of 60 million. The makeup of these anglers crosses all boundaries of age, sex, and income. And the figure continues to grow every year.

Because you bought this book, you're ready to join the ranks. Perhaps you've already fished once or twice and want to learn a little more about it. Maybe you've never fished at all and need to know the basics before starting out. Possibly you've done a fair amount of fishing, but want to brush up on the rudimentary skills and pick up a new tactic or two.

In any case, you've made a good choice. Billions of words have been written on the subject of fishing, and more are being written every day. Unfortunately for the beginner, many books and articles deal with one particular aspect of fishing, or focus on one particular species. That's why this book has been purposefully compiled of nothing but information about fishing *basics*: what you need to know about the fish, the tackle, and the techniques to get started properly. It covers all realms of freshwater fishing, from the best size of earthworm to use for catching bluegills to the proper type of casts to employ when presenting a dry fly to an ultra-wary brown trout. You'll learn the difference between a pike and a pickerel, and the best fishing tactics for each. You'll find out why a baitcasting reel offers certain advantages over a spinning reel, and then you'll learn how to use one. You'll find out which parts of a stream are likely to hold fish—and which parts you should avoid.

Much of the material contained in this book has been gathered from the pages of *Sports Afield* magazine. Frank S. Golad, a long-time editorial staff member at *Sports Afield*, surveyed hundreds of past issues to find articles, departments, and features that introduce fish and fishing to a beginner. All those pieces were written by experts in the field: Anthony Acerrano, Gerald Almy, Homer Circle, among others. Then Frank determined which sections would be of the most help to a new angler and organized them into a simple format. Note that a cross-referencing system is included in the text to aid the reader; wherever additional material can be found on the same subject, the Roman numeral for that chapter is provided.

The result is in your hands: a book dedicated to the new angler. Congratulations and welcome.

Tom Paugh
Editor in Chief, *Sports Afield*

CHAPTER I

THE FISH'S WORLD

No fisherman had ever laid eyes on the trout. Twenty-five inches long, easily 5 pounds, it was one of the biggest trout in Little Flat Brook, definitely the biggest one in that half-mile stretch of gurgling riffles and serene pools.

The trophy trout rarely left its lair among the submerged roots of a towering streamside oak tree. Only at night-time, or on those days when the river ran high and muddy from a recent storm, did the big brown venture out into the closest pool. He did so to feed—on large minnows and crayfish, usually, but also on frogs, mice, and the occasional small hatchery trout stocked regularly each spring. The big trout could quickly fill its belly on such siz-able forage and return to the safety of the root system under the bank.

One spring evening, just at sunset, an old man stood on the bank just upstream from the big oak. Rod in hand, the man looked closely at the stream, muddied by an afternoon rain.

As the sun dipped below the horizon, the old man carefully hooked a soft-shelled crayfish onto his line. He quietly entered the water and slowly waded to a position just up- and across-stream from the big oak. He cast the crayfish into the current, knowing the bait would drift in front of the roots.

The line dipped suddenly, and the old man quickly raised his rod tip, set-ting the hook into the big trout's jaw. The fight was on.

The old man eventually landed that trout. But he never could have done so without a good knowledge of fish behavior. Remember, no one—includ-ing the old man—had ever seen that big trout. But our angler knew something about how brown trout, especially big ones, behave.

Our angler knew that a submerged root system would make a perfect lie for a trophy fish. He also knew that any big trout would take advantage of such a variety of forage in the stream—even before nightfall—and that the muddy color of the water would pro-vide concealment. And he knew that crayfish were a preferred trout food at that time of year. So the old man wasn't all that surprised to see that huge brown trout leap out of the water after he set the hook.

Well, maybe a little surprised.

This chapter outlines the basic aspects of fish behavior, or at least what we know now about it. Fish behavior will always be an imperfect science, but the more you understand how fish act and react to various stimuli, the better chance you stand of putting a fish on the end of your line.

How Fish Behave

No two fish behave exactly alike. Different fish have different needs, and it's important to recognize the various behavioral patterns exhibited by the fish you want to catch. Think about it: If all fish acted and reacted the same way to the same stimuli, it'd be relatively easy to hook all the fish you wanted.

For example, the motivation of a fish to strike at a bait or lure isn't always hunger [II]. Cast a small spinner near a bluegill nest and a male bluegill—guarding the eggs from predators—will probably strike at the lure out of defense. Compare this behavior to that of the American shad, which, on its spring spawning run in freshwater rivers, will often hit at shad "darts," tiny lead-bodied lures popular with shad anglers. But cut open the belly of a spawning shad, and you'll find it empty. Shad don't eat during their migration, yet will strike a properly drifted dart out of reflex or frustration.

The location of fish in a body of water varies from species to species and is often keyed to protection, food availability, and oxygen content. You'll seldom spot fish swimming out in the open. Fish conceal themselves in a

number of places: weeds, rocks and other bottom debris, submerged trees, or the darkness of a creek pool or lake bottom.

Fishing for lake trout in mid-summer calls for heavy—sometimes wire-cored—line, stout rods, and beefy reels, because the lakers will locate at or near the bottom of lakes, and heavy tackle is needed to bring the large, flashy spoons down deep [III, V]. Contrast this with the flyfisherman floating a dry fly, no bigger than the nail on your little finger, over a wary brown trout feeding on spent mayflies in the surface film. Fooling such a fish means quiet wading, delicate casts, and a hair-fine leader at the end of your flyline.

Naturally, the location of a fish will dictate the presentation of the bait or lure. Just tossing a worm-baited hook into a "bassy"-looking farm pond won't guarantee that a hungry largemouth will find it. Cast the worm into the sun-dappled shallows, and you'll soon have pesky sunfish picking away at it. If you add a lot of weight to your line and plunk the worm down into the deepest section of the pond, you stand a very good chance of hooking a catfish. To catch a bass, you must put the worm where the bass are: along the edge of that steep drop-off on the opposite bank, say, or just inside that bed of lily pads over by the old dock.

Want to catch a big bass? Fish that same farm pond later in the evening. Largemouths, especially the heavyweights, typically feed freely throughout the nighttime hours. And forget the worms—still-fish a big shiner or cast out and slowly retrieve a hefty crankbait. Truly big bass rarely expend their energy chasing after what amounts to an appetizer, like a little garden worm. They want a meal.

Probably the most important factor affecting fish behavior is temperature. Some fish, like brook trout, require cold water to survive—clear mountain streams, with plenty of shade trees and spring-fed holes. On the other hand, some like it surprisingly warm. Largemouth bass don't feed much in the dead of winter, but come into their own once spring returns. Yet other species, like chain pickerel, can tolerate a range of water temperatures. You can catch "chainsides" during a heatwave in July or through the ice on the coldest day of the year—at the same lake.

But this doesn't mean pickerel thrive in any temperature. The pickerel you caught out of that weedy back bay in July certainly won't remain there when ice starts forming on the surface. Opportunistic feeders, pickerel will move out into deeper water come winter, where they'll find plenty of forage fish to satisfy their hunger. With a covering of ice on the lake, the concealment that weeds provide is no longer a factor anyway.

Water quality also impacts upon fish. The carp—an Asian species introduced from Europe years ago, spurned by the majority of sportfishermen but revered by a few—has infiltrated millions of lakes and rivers in the United States because it can tolerate almost every type of water, even those severely polluted. Carp don't demand waters with a high oxygen content, as do the trouts. The limit of acceptability ranges from species to species, but all demand some level of oxygen to survive.

Lunar and atmospheric cycles have a definite effect on fish, although they're not fully understood. Some anglers swear that fish bite best just before a major storm; others are convinced there's no better time to fish than right after a rain. The same goes for cold fronts, warm fronts, and moon phases.

But don't let all these factors complicate your fishing plans. Just use common sense and try to "think like a fish" before making that first cast. Most anglers don't—and that's why many of them don't catch fish.

The Wind and Fish
The effect of wind on fishing—often underestimated or ignored by anglers—can be seen in this example. During a hot August in western New York, Lake Ontario shoreline fishing was excellent when strong north winds blew in cold offshore water from the depths. The temperature change drew smallmouth bass and jumbo yellow perch into water 3' to 5' deep only a short cast from the beach. Salmon and brown trout that had been at the 90' and 100' level for weeks moved to 30' depths when the winds brought in 54°F water. Two days later, offshore breezes pushed the cold water out, replacing it with 70°F water. The fish disappeared. Wind can matter even when the water temperature remains unchanged.

The Sound Effect

The world of a fish is so fraught with peril that only about 1 in 1,000 lives to maturity. A fish can do without sight, smell, taste, and physical touch, but take away its hearing and it would never survive. Thus a fish is especially wary of unusual sounds in its environment. Knowing this can make you a more efficient fisherman.

You must always think "sounds and hearing" as you pursue a wily creature. It's helpful to know how a fish hears. A fish does not have ears appended to the sides of its head as we do, nor does it have eardrums. Instead, it has internal and external sound sensors.

Its internal detectors consist of a rudimentary apparatus that detects vibrations transmitted through skull bones. Tests show that these inner sound devices are used for long-range hearing of sounds of up to 7,000 vibrations per second. (Humans, in comparison, can hear up to 20,000 vibrations per second.) Such sounds are caused by pressure waves that force water molecules to vibrate without making any movement of the water. They travel about 1 mile a second, or some 5 times faster than sound travels through air.

The external hearing system comprises two lateral lines found on each side of the fish's body. Each line, which resembles a finely stitched thread, consists of minute openings that contain neuromasts, or tiny nerve endings. These nerves detect nearby vibrations created when water molecules are displaced by strong pressure waves. These waves are usually given off by objects less than 50' away, something such as a swimming creature or a wiggling lure.

Equipped with this dual-range hearing ability, a fish can first detect your lure's sounds at a great distance through its inner hearing. Alerted, it can then wait for the lure to approach within range of its external hearing system. Even if the fish is blind, it can determine the direction of the lure and intercept it.

The sounds you make can either help you catch fish or cause you to lose them. For instance, sounds that travel farthest and sharpest usually come from a tacklebox scraped over a boat bottom or bumped against the side of a boat. In fact, a boat will amplify any sharp sound made in it. Other sharp sounds include intermittent oar or paddle movements, as well as scraping or squeaking; revving an outboard or electric fishing motor; leather shoes kicking the bottom or sides of the boat; and anchors being plopped overboard and thudding onto a hard bottom.

Other Senses

Fish smell. They have noses that can smell food, return to their place of origin by following scents (like salmon), and react to sex signals, the body odor of other fish and to odors of alarm. A fish also has a talent for tasting. Taste buds on the body and barbels of fish unerringly locate food. Finally, fish speak. If you submerge an underwater microphone you will hear grunts, rattles, snaps, and honks.

Metal boats should have carpeting to deaden sounds. Modern flotation boats have built-in sound insulation, such as foamed compartments and double-hull construction, but reasonable silence should still be maintained when you're moving things around.

Though some sounds can hurt your fishing, others can help it. Many popular lures have built-in noisemakers that vary from a buzz to a loud clatter. Though these should be used with discretion, there are times when a loud rattle attracts bass, such as when the fish's visibility is limited to a few feet or inches. However, a rattle can repel fish in clear water.

Some fishermen have made trolling tests in clear water, using the same lures on equal-test lines set the same distance behind the boat. One lure is rigged with a noisemaker and one without. The results show conclusively that in water with exceptional clarity, such as 20' visibility, a lure without the noisemaker is more efficient.

When working a top-water lure, keep in mind that at times fish appear supersensitive to a great deal of commotion. A loud popping or chugging noise might spook them. But if you let that lure lie quietly, barely nudging life into it every half minute or so, you can trigger some strikes.

Conversely, there are times—such as during the dog days of summer—when a surface lure jerked violently will goad fish into vicious smashes. This paradox cannot be explained; just remember to try it. In general, the clearer the water, the quieter you and your lure should be. In most fishing situations, it's best to approach your chosen spot so quietly that the only sound a fish hears is that of your lure falling into the water.

Taking the Temperature

Many of us have heard that water temperature is the factor governing where fish will be and how they will behave, yet we tend to ignore it.

Because fish are cold-blooded, physiological processes, such as respiration and digestion, and their general level of activity fluctuate with the surrounding water temperatures. Each species has upper and lower temperature limits and a comfort zone in the middle that prompts them to feed more aggressively. If you know this and look for it, you're going to be more successful on stream, lake, estuary, or river.

Researchers have proved that fish can detect temperature variations of less than 1°F. Humans don't have a sensory system that sophisticated. We don't need it, but fish do. That fact tells you how important

After Ice Out
Anglers will find that after a long winter under the ice, fish are not finicky about what they eat. In the spring, warm water is where you find the fishing action. Shallower lakes and shallow places in lakes warm first. Good places to find most warm-water species— largemouth bass, crappies, and bluegills—are sheltered channels, backwaters, and bays. Choose those with no outlet (they create currents that carry off warm water) and lots of sunlight. Cool-water species such as walleyes and pike will usually be near spawning areas, marshes and bays for pike, inlet streams and sand/gravel flats or marshes for walleyes. Both species normally spawn before or at ice out.

Fishing in
Cold Waters
If waters are cold early in the trout season, consider trying for brookies rather than browns and rainbows. They feed in cold water and are often quite active when browns and rainbows are still lethargic.

temperature can be when you're attempting to locate your mark.

Bass fishermen, for instance, realize that the first large-mouths of spring will be in the shallow waters at the back ends of coves. That's because these areas warm faster, and the fish will start to feed sooner. During the middle of summer, the same fish could be in deep water that remains relatively cool, foraging along the shoreline at daybreak and dusk. On many Southern lakes, in fact, summer bassing becomes a nighttime operation. Water temperature holds the key to success.

Freshwater species are usually confined to a specific body of water and move from the depths to the shallows or vice versa only when seeking a comfortable area. By knowing

the limits for the species you seek, you can search for waters of the correct temperature before you even start to fish.

The reading on your thermometer also tells you how to fish and the technique to use. In cold water, fish are going to be more sluggish and will generally feed close to the bottom. They will be looking for natural baits that they can take slowly and without much effort. Retrieves must be exceptionally slow. These fish cannot move very quickly, and they are not about to chase a fast-moving offering over a long distance.

Lure selection should also be tailored to the reading on the thermometer [III]. When the water is cold, that's the time to let a nymph drift along the bottom or inch a plastic worm in front of a

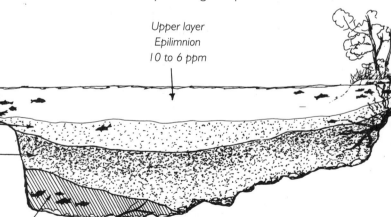

Upper layer
Epilimnion
10 to 6 ppm

Middle layer
Thermocline
4.5 to 3 ppm
Lower layer
Hypolimnion
3 to 0 ppm

Oxygen inversion
8 to 12 ppm

The phenomenon of oxygen inversion sometimes occurs in deep lakes and ponds, trapping fish at the bottom of drop-offs. Look for fish at the lower edge of the epilimnion and within the oxygen inversion itself. The hypolimnion, which is devoid of oxygen, won't hold fish.

bass. If you are not a purist, consider natural baits early and late in the year.

Veteran anglers find that lighter lines and smaller lures often catch more fish when the water is cold in the spring. One reason is that most gamefish feed on easier-to-catch small baitfish at this time. Another lies in the fact that a thinner-diameter line or leader gives a lure or bait more enticing action, and that can make all the difference.

In a stream or shallow water, you can get by with a hand-held thermometer. Even on lakes, surface water temperature can be an important measurement. Many boats are equipped with gauges that take these readings continuously. However, serious anglers also try to determine the temperature at various depths. Some fishermen use units that are attached to a downrigger and lowered to the required depth. They then send a signal back to a meter on the boat. Or attach a thermistor and wire to a sinker, then lower that instrument to any reasonable depth and take readings along the way.

If you don't have a thermometer with you, you can always put your hand in the water. You won't be able to detect minor differences, but you can tell whether the water is warm or cold. That's better than having no infor-

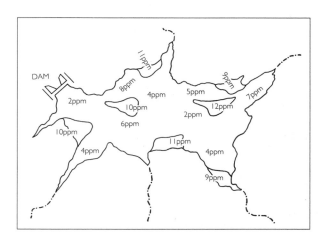

No oxygen means no fish, so rule out those area of lakes that contain less than 5 parts per million (ppm) of dissolved oxygen. Also avoid highly oxygenated waters—those higher than 13 ppm. Fish will concentrate in areas of 9 to 11 ppm of oxygen.

mation about the temperature at all.

Once you begin using a thermometer, keep a log of your daily findings. Note the water temperature, how you fished, the baits or lures you used, all observations, and your results. This data will help you the next time you find similar conditions. The more entries you have in your log, the more valuable it becomes and the easier it is to detect patterns found under certain circumstances.

When you see and catch fish, there's a reason. When they seem to have disappeared, there's also a reason. If you do some probing with your thermometer, you'll usually find that water temperature is the determining factor.

Rising Temperature
Some of the best striper fishing of the year takes place in late winter and early spring, when the water temperature rises. Stripers will start biting as soon as it reaches into the mid-40s. They begin feeding avidly once the temperature approaches the 50°F mark.

CHECK THE WEEDS TO FIND THE FISH

There are scores of plants that live in or near streams, ponds, and lakes, and some of them can be your key to finding fish. Illustrated are a few of the more common varieties that provide shelter and food sources for smaller fish, which in turn are preyed on by larger gamefish.

Take time to scout out and familiarize yourself with subsurface masses and standing patches of plants and weeds. Troll past or cast to the edges to tease the game fish out of their lairs and hit your lure or bait.

Large Duckweed

Freefloating leaves, 1/3" long, either single or in clumps, green on top, with purple undersides. Usually found on the surface of still or stagnant water.

White Water Lily

Glossy leaves, up to 1' across with a large notch extending to the stem. Blossoms 6" across are white with yellow stamens. Floating on the surface with stems rooted to the bottom. Found in coves of lakes, ponds, and slow-moving streams.

American Bulrush

Unmistakable freestanding plant with woody stems up to 8' long. Grows along edges of ponds, lakes, and stream margins. In ponds and lakes can grow from the shore out to water that is several feet deep.

Long-Leaved Pondweed

Two types of freefloating leaves, mature surface leaves 4" long and 2" wide; submerged leaves thin and long. Found in ponds, lakes, and slow-moving streams.

American Lotus

Large, shield-like leaves up to 2' across. Floating leaves with stems rooted to the bottom. Flowers pale yellow, up to 10" across, whose centers become hard, circular pods that contain seeds in separate compartments. Grows in muddy marshes, ponds, and sheltered shallows of lakes.

Arrowhead

Freestanding plant with a unique large leaf, up to 3' in height with 4" to 6" leaves. Grows in clumps in the shallow margins of marshes, ponds, lakes, and slow-moving streams.

Water Willow

Opposing narrow leaves are 6" long on smooth woody stems. Grows bushlike along waterways and in wet places. Usually in clumps no higher than 6'.

Cattails

Two types: broad-leaved and narrow-leaved. Both grow up to 6' in height and prefer marshes and still waters.

Curly Pondweed

Weak-stemmed plants with wavy-margined, fine-toothed leaves. Prefer hard or brackish water; often a sign that water is polluted.

Water-Smart Weed

Stems are about 20" long, with 4" leaves on or below the surface. Found along edges of ponds, streams, and marshes rooted in oozes.

Water Buttercup

Submerged plant with weak, flexible stems. Found in shallow water, forms dense masses, even in swift-moving water of brooks and streams.

Spiked-Water Milfoil

Another soft, weak-stemmed plant. Leaves are whorled in groups of four or five. Grows to long lengths, forming dense masses below the surface.

Cabomba

A subsurface plant that grows several feet in length. Leaves, alternate and opposite, arranged like fans. Prefers ponds and slow streams.

Hornwort

Can be 8' long, with leaves in whorls of five to twelve resembling a coontail. Habitat is either ponds or slow streams.

Stone Wort or Chara

An algae with a clump of fine, bristly filaments that is coarse and prickly to the touch due to its high lime content. Common in springs and ponds with hard water.

Elodea

Long plant with 1/2" leaves attached to a soft, weak stem. Roots quickly and forms dense masses over mucky bottoms.

TIPS FOR APPLYING THESE PRINCIPLES TO REAL SITUATIONS

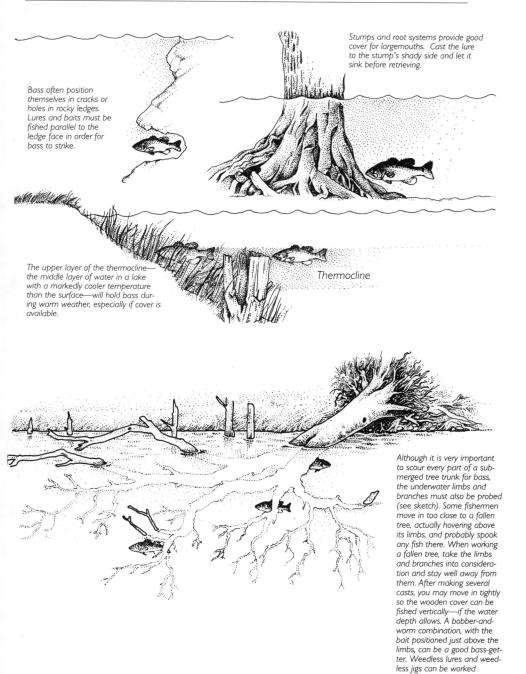

Stumps and root systems provide good cover for largemouths. Cast the lure to the stump's shady side and let it sink before retrieving.

Bass often position themselves in cracks or holes in rocky ledges. Lures and baits must be fished parallel to the ledge face in order for bass to strike.

The upper layer of the thermocline— the middle layer of water in a lake with a markedly cooler temperature than the surface—will hold bass during warm weather, especially if cover is available.

Thermocline

Although it is very important to scour every part of a submerged tree trunk for bass, the underwater limbs and branches must also be probed (see sketch). Some fishermen move in too close to a fallen tree, actually hovering above its limbs, and probably spook any fish there. When working a fallen tree, take the limbs and branches into consideration and stay well away from them. After making several casts, you may move in tightly so the wooden cover can be fished vertically—if the water depth allows. A bobber-and-worm combination, with the bait positioned just above the limbs, can be a good bass-getter. Weedless lures and weedless jigs can be worked through the branches.

CHAPTER II

FISH SPECIES

When is a bass not a bass? When it's a largemouth bass. This prolific and widespread gamefish—the most popular species among American fishermen from coast to coast—is actually a member of the sunfish family.

Then there's the poor, misaligned walleye. For many years, fishermen referred to this gamefish as a "walleyed pike," meaning, of course, a northern pike with large eyes. But not only is the walleye totally unrelated to the pike, it doesn't even look like one.

Plenty of other fish go by wrong names, or at least improper ones. But let's leave those headaches to fish taxonimists, the scientists responsible for the official naming and classification of all species. Instead, we should concern ourselves with catching a fish.

In this chapter you'll learn all about the habits, habitats, and characteristics of the most common and popular gamefish in the United States, along with some specialized methods of catching them. You may be tempted just to gloss over the profiles of each species—the range of each fish within the country, its preferred environment and water temperature, average size, and so on—and go directly to the sections that tell you how to catch them. Don't! Truly good fishermen, the kind who catch fish even when most others can't buy a nibble, know their quarry intimately.

Being a successful angler means much more than just knowing which lure to use for, say, Delaware River smallmouth bass in the spring. It means knowing that the best smallmouth lure in the world won't catch a bass if it's fished in any of the slow, mud-bottomed stretches of this big waterway. Smallmouths' favorite foods at this time of year are hellgrammites, crayfish, and stonecats, and they also prefer clear, highly oxygenated water with a good percentage of riffles.

In the Delaware, both the favored foods and the preferred water types are concentrated in the rock-filled, fast-water stretches, which are located in the narrower sections of the river and areas where the elevation drops a bit. So the savvy smallmouth angler may spend as much time traveling from riffle to riffle as he does actually fishing them. But chances are good that he'll catch more smallmouths than the fisherman who just walks down to the river and starts casting.

So read these species profiles, and keep the facts in mind the next time you go fishing. You may not be able to pronounce *Micropterus dolomieui*, but when a pair of them are sizzling in your frying pan, who cares?

Basses

Family: Centrarchidae

Bass Action

If you want to score on bass, work points systematically. Start far back, working the 15' to 30' depths where a point drops off into the main lake. Use worms and jigs here. Then move to shallower areas, probing both sides of the point with crankbaits and spinnerbaits, gradually working all the way up to the shoreline.

Although these fish are commonly referred to as "black basses," they're actually members of the sunfish family. There are at least 11 black bass species and subspecies, but the largemouth, smallmouth, and spotted are the most common and widespread. The largemouth bass, indigenous to many Eastern and Southern waters, is now found in almost every state. It tolerates a fairly wide range of water temperatures and qualities, including brackish water. The largemouth's availability and usual willingness to hit anglers' lures have made it the favorite gamefish of millions of fishermen. The smallmouth bass, originally found only in the Lake Ontario and Ohio River drainages, has also been introduced across the United States. It generally prefers water cleaner than that the largemouth inhabits, and it is one of the scrappiest fighters in fresh water. The spotted bass, sometimes referred to as the Kentucky bass, shares many characteristics of the largemouth and smallmouth. It ranges from the Mississippi drainage south to the Gulf of Mexico and west to Texas.

The Time for Bass

In early June, seek waters where the temperature is in the 65° to 75°F range. Bass are gregarious and have a pecking order; the bigger ones rule the group and stay farther back in heavy cover, while smaller, less wary bass cruise the fringes [V]. Securely hidden, they lie in ambush and pounce on passing food fish.

A bass fisherman should have three outfits rigged and ready with fresh line [III]. One has a plastic worm because it's weedless and can be fished anywhere; the second has a deep-diving crank lure that sinks to bottom fast; and the third has a slim-minnow lure that floats at rest and runs shallow when retrieved.

This provides you with three diverse action/depth lures at the ready. Now lay out these additional lures: (1) an overhead spinner, (2) a weedless spoon with a pork frog, and (3) a jig-and-eel combination. Here's where and how to use them.

Shore Cover. Find weeds, reeds, or brush that borders deeper, darker water. Always begin with a plastic worm (the 6 1/4" size in blue or purple works best) and a 3/8-ounce

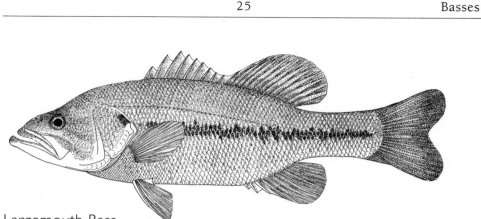

Largemouth Bass

(*Micropterus salmoides*). Introduced into streams and ponds all over the United States. Is the gamefish most popular with and most sought by anglers.

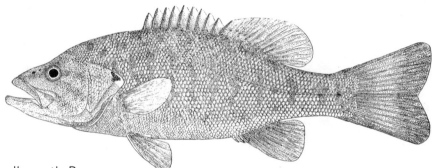

Smallmouth Bass

(*Micropterus dolomieui*) Has been introduced widely in this country and abroad. Prefers to nest on a firm gravel bottom.

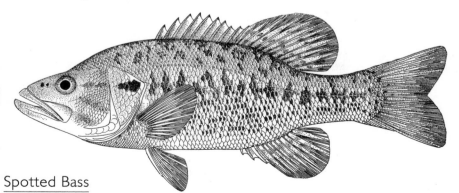

Spotted Bass

(*Micropterus punctulatus*) Ranges from upper Mississippi Valley south and east to the Gulf. Survives adverse conditions better than either smallmouth or largemouth.

Fishing with Lures

When fishing for bass with floater-diver lures, try twitching them gently, as if they were surface lures, instead of reeling them in. Jerk the plug lightly so that rings spread out; then allow them to dissipate. Twitch again, then pause. If no strikes come, reel in fast, cast to the next piece of cover, and repeat.

Fishing with Plastic Worms

If you have trouble connecting with bass on 6" and 8" plastic worms, try switching to 4" or 5," or change to worms with double hooks rigged through the body.

slip-sinker, rigged weedless. Cast into the fringe, pockets, and down alleys [IV]. Let the worm settle to the bottom and work it back slowly, always maintaining tension in your line.

Keep your mind on that worm as it sinks; get accustomed to the feel as it takes the line to the bottom. If you notice any change at all, reel the slack out of your line and set the hook as fast as you can.

If nothing happens on the initial cast and a slack line tells you the sinker is on the bottom, gently reel the slack out of your line with your rod tip low over the water and pointed toward the worm. Then raise your rod tip sharply to an overhead position; hold it there.

You'll notice your line move slowly toward you because the sinker is swinging over the bottom, like a pendulum, until it comes to rest again. Repeat until the worm is directly below your boat.

When a bass sucks in the worm, you'll feel it all the way up and down the line to your rod handle. At that moment set your hook hard and fast; that bass can blow out the worm just as fast as he sucked it in.

Make no more than 10 casts with the plastic worm; then switch to the deep-diving crankbait outfit. Coast close to shore cover and begin reeling the instant the lure touches down. Continue for 10 casts.

If you get no offers, pick up the outfit rigged with the slim-minnow lure and cast it close to the cover. Let it smack down to get the bass's attention; then allow it to lie motionless for a few seconds. Twitch it ever so slightly, as if the minnow is stunned and trying to regain its strength to escape. Repeat twitches for about 6', then hurry it back.

For the next 10 casts repeat the twitches close to the cover; then retrieve the lure just fast enough to make it wiggle below the surface, creating a V wake that is both audible and visible to the bass below.

Making Points. If you've determined that the weedy cover doesn't hold any bass, head for the points—any finger of land that runs downhill and disappears into the lake. Points can be weedy, rocky, brushy, or timbered, all excellent bass hangouts.

Use the same tactics mentioned for shore cover, only try the overhead spinner for 10 casts as well. Work this lure as if you were using the plastic worm; it covers the bottom similarly, only with more flash and vibration.

Glean the Streams. If you haven't located bass around shore cover or points, head for inflowing streams. Food fish gather here to feed on inflowing plankton. Once you see a cluster of lily pads, tie on that weedless-spoon/pork-chunk combo. Cast it back into the pads. Crawl and wiggle it slowly over, around, and under the pads. When you get a strike, don't give the hook a hair trigger; pause and then set it.

Stalk the Docks. Every smart dock owner has planted a brushpile to attract fish. Here, use wiggling lures that resemble minnows, such as crankbaits and slim minnows, plus that plastic 'worm. Keep changing lures after 10 casts.

Strategies for Smallmouths

The smallmouth bass may well be the ultimate North American gamefish. It is found throughout much of the country and is available over long stretches of the season. It's susceptible to a wide variety of angling methods, from chucking bait to drifting flies. And the bronzeback is also a wild fish, supported throughout its vast range exclusively by natural reproduction rather than by stocking from hatcheries.

Smallmouths are bold and aggressive. If analogies are to be made, the smallmouth might better be compared with the trout—in particular the brown trout—than with the largemouth.

Where to Fish. The places where stream smallmouths hang out are obvious to the eyes of experienced anglers [V]. You'll soon learn to recog-

nize them, too. Here are features to look for: undercut banks, rocky drop-offs, fallen trees, debris pileups, runs where dark currents rub against rocky shores, tops of big boulders in deep water, midstream channels, matted roots, rocky bluffs, gravel flats bordering deep water, rocky points disappearing into dark water, and eddy slots below rapids or falls. Rocks and smallmouths go together like cold hands and mittens—wherever you see a concentration of rocky outcroppings in water depths of 6' and more.

You must also determine the depth at which bronzebacks can be found. Time of day is one important factor. Low light in early morning and evening, plus hatching insects and foraging crayfish, entice smallmouths to feed in thin water, even during summer. Bright midday conditions, however, send them scurrying back to deep holes near such structures as reefs, ledges, and drop-offs.

Finally, clouds can also influence where you find bass. During overcast or rainy weather, bronzebacks may remain in the shallows all day, even during the heart of summer, unless the water temperatures become unbearably warm for them—above 75°F.

What to Use. Because average smallmouth waters are usually clearer, today's lighter rigs and smaller lures

Summer Waters
As summer waters become hot and river levels fall, look for smallmouths in riffly areas. There's plenty of oxygen here, and the bass will hold in pockets behind ledges and rocks. Work a spinnerbait, floating minnow plug, or popper through the bubbly water, and you should find quick action.

Surface Lures

When fishing surface lures, start your retrieve before the lure touches down; have it moving as soon as it hits the water. This trick often results in quick, instinctive strikes from gamefish that might not hit if you let the lure sit before retrieving.

Try a Bigger Offering

If you are catching fish on a particular lure and the action dies suddenly, try a larger one. Sometimes the bigger offering will turn the fish on.

are more effective [III]. A 5' to 6', light-action graphite rod, medium-size reel filled with 6-pound mono, and lures mostly in the 1/4- to 3/8-ounce range will serve most needs. And lighter tackle also enhances the in-fighting.

Productive lures include both the live and the artificial kind, and there are days when one outfishes the other, so it pays to offer both. Hellgrammites, leeches, frogs, crayfish, and minnows make up the bulk of their natural diet.

Artificial lures tend to run smaller for smallmouth than for largemouth bass. For surface action try the steady performance of slim-minnow types made of balsa, which has more bounce.

Choose natural-scale patterns over chrome backgrounds for both appeal and flash.

Crankbaits should include both shallow and deep runners, again in natural, flashing patterns, and lipless crankbaits in small and medium sizes, both floaters and sinkers.

In-line spinners hold an edge over the overhead type. Try these with pork-frog trailers and curly-tail grubs in assorted colors. Small spoons can also be very effective.

But the deadliest lure is a jig-and-pig combination, fished slowly enough to maintain bottom contact. Darker colors, in natural greens and browns, are very dependable. Also try tube lures and small

plastic worms fished on 1/4-ounce jig heads.

Here's How. Fishing from an anchored boat calls for proper positioning in order to work the lure best, which is usually parallel to the deepest hole or run. Wet wading in warm weather is also a fun way to work the water.

There are holes where the water is flat on nonwindy days. Fish with slim-minnow lures on the surface, working with both gentle and sharp twitches [IV]. Also, add enough weight to sink the lure slowly and work it in just over the bottom.

Use jig-head tube lures and worms along undercut banks, rocky dropoffs, and midstream channels. Smallmouths hang in the quiet eddy water and dash out to grab food fish in the current. But to catch the biggest smallmouth in any steam, the one lure that seems to have a special appeal is the jig head with a small pork frog attached. The more slowly you drag this combo over the bottom, the more enticing it is to the eye of whopper smallmouths.

One Final Tip. Don't be in too much of a hurry to set the hook when bottom fishing with jigs. Smallmouths suck in their food and crush it before swallowing. Set the hook too soon, and you'll jerk the lure out of the bass's mouth. Wait until you feel a steady tension on the line, then bury the barb.

White Basses
Family: Percichthyidae

North American basses that live in or enter fresh water in order to spawn are a subfamily of the sea bass family. Two species, the yellow bass and white bass, live strictly in fresh water, and two, the striped bass and white perch, live in the ocean or brackish waters or are land-locked in freshwater. There are two other species that live along the coast and in the rivers of Western Europe.

These basses live in a variety of habitats: yellow bass usually in rivers, white bass in lakes, white perch in brackish bays, and striped bass along coasts, usually close to the shore. All the species move around a great deal.

All basses eat any kind of animal food of suitable size.

Where to Find Them
In spring look for stripers near the headwaters of lakes, where they often congregate before staging spawning runs up major tributaries.

White Perch

(*Morone americana*) This fish ranges from Nova Scotia to Georgia in coastal waters, bays, and rivermouths. They are often landlocked and introduced into inland lakes and reservoirs. They are common in Lake Ontario. White perch live in shallow water, wandering from place to place in small schools. In spring they may migrate into streams to spawn, but some of them spawn in shoal areas in brackish or salt water. They commonly grow to a length of 10" and a weight of 1 pound, but some reach over 4 pounds.

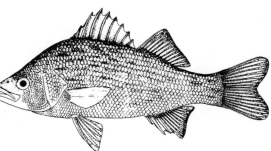

White Bass

(*Morone chrysops*) This fish ranges from the Great Lakes to the Mississippi Valley, and across Texas and the Southwest. The white bass does exceptionally well in many big, multiple-use impoundments and has been widely planted. This species is gregarious, often schooling at the surface. White bass are very prolific, grow rapidly, and mature early. They are good to eat and easy to catch with minnows, grubs, or worms. Sometimes they will rise to a fly. They average 3 to 4 pounds and can go over 5 pounds.

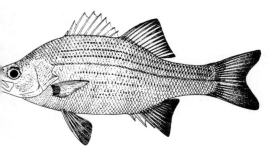

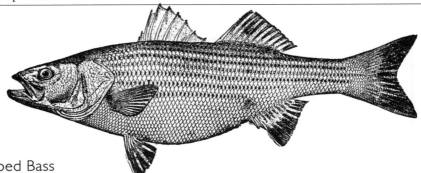

Striped Bass

(*Morone saxatilis*) This fish ranges along the Atlantic Coast from New Brunswick to Florida and on the Gulf Coast from Texas to Alabama. Introduced into San Francisco Bay in 1879, the striped bass now ranges from southern California to Washington. In coastal areas striped bass are anadromous, living in salt water and migrating into fresh water to spawn. Now they have been widely introduced in inland freshwater systems. Striped bass may live 16 to 19 years. Some grow to a very large size. A fish 36" in length can weigh up to 18 pounds, but lengths of 4' to 5' and weights of 50 to nearly 100 pounds are on record.

Tackle for Stripers

The best tackle to use for striped bass depends upon the specific fishing technique. For live-bait fishing, vertical jigging, and plug casting, use a 5 1/2' to 6 1/2' spinning or baitcasting outfit with 10- to 14-pound-test line. Trolling calls for a sturdy 6' to 7 1/2' rod, level wind reel, and 12- to 20-pound-test line. Flyfishermen should go with an 8 1/2' or 9' rod rated for 7- to 10-weight line. If very large stripers are a possibility, use tackle at the heavier end of these ranges.

Small basses eat small shrimp and other crustaceans, as well as squids, worms, and insect larvae. Larger basses eat larger shrimp, squids, and worms, and in addition a considerable proportion of their food is small fishes, minnows, and the fry of larger fishes.

The basses of this group, particularly the white perch and the striped bass, are important commercial fish as well as popular sportfish.

White Bass Tactics

Pound for pound, the white bass is the hardest hitter among America's freshwater game-fishes. With this species you never have to guess if it's a fish or a snag. One of the greatest values of the white bass as a gamefish is its availability during extremely hot or cold spells when other sporting species are hard to come by.

How to Find Them. White bass feed on threadfin shad and juvenile gizzard shad, and at times they are the easiest fish to locate because you can see and hear them feeding on the surface at great distances. You will usually discover them on the bottom in 20' to 50' of water. Sonars and trial-and-error luring will help reveal exact locations. Once you find a number of places they frequent, try various lures from top to bottom.

How to Catch Them. Catching white bass can be wildly active or frustratingly slow. The important point to keep in mind is variety, both in lures and retrieves [III]. Your selection of lures should include jigs in 1/4- to 3/8-ounce sizes; flat lures, all sinking; floating, minnow-shaped lures; and metal spoons that sink quickly in the 1/4- to 3/8-ounce range.

There are two main types of water you'll be fishing: rivers and reservoirs [V]. River fishing is usually simpler because the hangouts are easier to read. Drift and cast to the banks in early spring, right after ice out up North, and in March or April down South. Below dams where the water flowage creates eddies is also a good bet; go for the "slot" where the current flowing downstream rubs against back currents flowing upstream.

In reservoirs you may notice a time period that's especially productive for catching white bass, especially during early summer through the dog days. Be afloat at dawn and hang in there until dusk. Make notes of the times you catch white bass and also remember the areas, since they may form a pattern.

A seek-and-catch approach is fairly effective. If there is no wind, stand up and scan the lake for telltale splashes of a feeding frenzy. Rush to the fish and don't crowd the frenzied school; stay an easy cast distant. Cast ahead of the school in the direction it is working; if you get too close, the fish will sound. Floater/diver lures, surface spinners, and shallow runners are best here.

When surface action ceases, seek out deepwater areas where streams flow into the lake, along the riprap, close to pilings, and in deep bays. Use sinking lures and let them settle

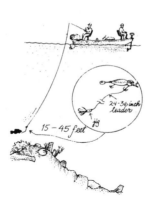

Trolling Tactics
Use a plug-and-jig combination when trolling for stripers in spring and early fall. Focus on submerged humps and points.

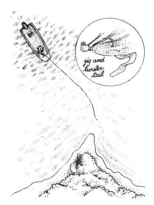

Casting
A white bucktail jig is deadly on stripers. Cast to points and steep banks; retrieve steadily.

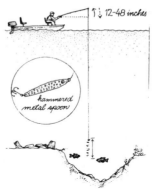

Jigging
When striped bass are deep, try jigging them up with a spoon. Jig vertically, with 1' to 4' lifts.

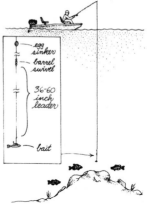

Baitfishing
If you can spot stripers on your depthfinder, lower them a live shad. Use a bait rig, as illustrated, for best results.

to the bottom. Be alert for strikes as they sink because white bass stratify at middle levels at times. Spoons, jigs, and weighted spinners are especially effective.

TROUTS
Family: Salmonidae

Authorities are not certain how many species or subspecies of trout there are in North America. This is partly because isolated populations vary in color, body form, and other characteristics. Changing conditions have resulted in some species becoming extinct or hybridizing to such an extent that the original groups can no longer be distinguished.

The trouts may be divided into two groups. First are the chars (genus *Salvelinus*), including the arctic char, brook, Sunapee, lake, and Dolly Varden trouts—all with the color characteristic of light spots on a darker background. These fish spawn in autumn. The other group (genus *Salmo*), including the rainbows, cutthroats, and brown trout, has dark spots on a lighter background. These fish spawn from early spring to early summer. All have one or several closely related species. No fewer than eight are closely related to the rainbow, 10 have branched off from the cutthroat stock, and four have evolved from the brook trout ancestral form. Several species or subspecies are known to be extinct.

Like other members of this family (the salmon and white-fishes), trouts are found over the northern parts of the world, generally north of latitude 40. They have succeeded in penetrating more southern regions only by taking advantage of cool or cold water found in high mountain conditions.

Flyfishing for Trout

There are many ways to get started in flyfishing, but for practical purposes, let's narrow them down into two broad categories: attending a flyfishing school or learning on your own.

Going to a school is perhaps the easier of the two. Most schools offer two- to four-day courses during the week or on weekends for fees of $150 to $400.

If you're hesitant to learn on your own, don't be. It's easy to outfit yourself with enough gear to fish effectively, and you'll find that the more you practice with that gear, the better flyfisherman you'll become.

Flies. Perhaps the most difficult part of assembling flyfishing tackle is deciding which flies to use [III]. Basically, you will want to acquire a good cross-section of flies that fall within three major aquatic insect orders: mayflies, caddisflies, and stoneflies. Ask your

Brook Trout

(*Salvelinus fontinalis*) Originally distributed from Labrador to Saskatchewan and from Maine to Alabama west to Minnesota, brookies can remain landlocked in lakes, rivers, and brooks where summer temperatures are not much greater than 65°F. In northern regions some races habitually go to sea, returning to small streams to spawn. Large individuals can go over 14 pounds.

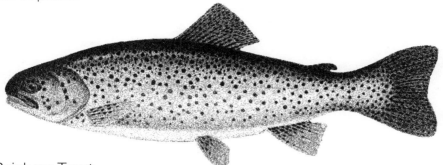

Rainbow Trout

(*Salmo gairdneri*) Likely the most important anglers' fish in western North America, where it is native, and in many other swift, cold waters where it has been introduced, sea-run rainbows are called steelheads; they are known to reach a weight of 40 pounds.

Brown Trout

(*Salmo trutta*) Introduced from Europe in 1883 or 1885, brown trout are now wide-spread. They can tolerate warmer water (up to 75° or 80°F) than native trouts, which increases stocking value in marginal trout waters. Their size varies widely: Maximum average weight is between 5 and 15 pounds; the largest is around 35 pounds.

Cutthroat Trout

(*Salmo clarki*) Distributed from northern California to Alaska, the coastal stream variety of trout sometimes migrates to salt water, where it reaches a weight of 20 pounds; the largest on record is 41 pounds. In mountain regions they may average 5 pounds. Cutthroats are known by the two red streaks on the lower jaw.

Lake Trout

(*Salvelinus namaycush*) Living in deep lakes, these trout were originally distributed from Labrador to Alaska and south through New England and the Great Lakes; now they have been introduced in the West. Lake trout weighing more than 100 pounds have been reported, but the accepted record is 65 pounds.

Golden Trout

(*Salmo aguabonita*) Originally living only in tributaries of the South Fork of the Kern River in California at elevations of 10,000' or more, golden trout have been planted in many other high-altitude lakes and streams of the Sierras and Rockies. Golden trout seldom exceed lengths of 14" and weights of 1 pound in streams, but elsewhere they often grow to a size of 4 to 6 pounds, the largest reaching 11 pounds.

local tackleshop dealer for advice on specific patterns, but try to get a variety of dry flies, which imitate adult insects, and wet flies and nymphs, which mimic immature, swimming insect stages. Also get streamers and backtails, which resemble minnows, dace, and other small baitfish, and terrestrials, which imitate land-based insects.

Choosing the correct hook size for these flies is also important. For medium-length trout (8" to 16") in average-sized trout streams, a good selection of Size 12 (medium) to Size 24 (tiny) flies would be advised. In large, brawny, windswept waters with big fish, you'll need larger offerings that may range up to Size 6 or even 1 (the largest).

Lines. The line you'll be using can be divided into a number of sections. The 2' or 3' section of nylon monofilament tied directly to the fly, with an improved clinch knot, is called the tippet. The tippet, in turn, is tied to a slightly heavier, longer piece of monofilament called the leader. Use a blood knot or surgeon's knot for this connection. The flyline itself—which comes in a variety of sinking and floating models, depending upon whether dry or wet flies will be used in fast or slow water, and in windy or still conditions—is attached to the leader with a nail knot. Finally, use a tube knot to

attach the flyline to your 100 yards of 20-pound-test braided Dacron backing, which is attached to the reel.

The concept of all this is simple: You've got a thin, nearly invisible combination of tippet and leader, which the fish can't see and which will allow your fly to alight delicately on the water; a heavier flyline, whose bulk allows it to sink or float and to be waved back and forth in the air—cast—with relative ease; and backing in case a big fish should make a long run up or downstream.

When choosing your flyline, remember that the weight of the line is measured in grains over the first 30' length, excluding the front taper. A Weight 2 flyline is the lightest available, and Weight 13 the heaviest. Most trout anglers opt for a Weight 5, 6, or 7, depending upon the size of the water and weather conditions. Leaders should be 9' to 12' long and taper down to 4X, 5X, 6X, or even 7X. Buy spools of tippet material in these sizes to add to the leader after you've cut it back a bit while changing flies. The 5X size (which equals about 2.4-pound test) is a good universal size, and you'll have to use the thin 7X size (1.1-pound test) only when you're fishing for trout selectively feeding on small No. 24-size insects. (Pound test, by the

Midsummer Trout
In midsummer, trout seek areas in a stream that are cooler and have more oxygen. At such times it is advisable to fish the rapids and heads of pools where there is fast water.

Casting at Night
Casting a trout fly on a black night can pose problems. One solution lies in marking your flyline so you know the exact distance past the tiptop of the rod. Take the measurements in the daytime, and then either make a nail knot with monofilament around the flyline at the precise spot or mark it with dental floss. When your fingers feel this projection, you know you're ready to make the cast.

way, indicates the relative strength of the line.)

Reels and Rods. Flyreels are used primarily for line storage, although a smooth, capable drag is also important, especially if you're fishing for large trout. Make sure that the reel you choose will accommodate the weight line you plan to fish with and be compatible with the type of flyrod you select.

Rod choice is a slightly more complicated matter. Rod weight must match line weight if you are to cast effectively. If you're going to be fishing with a No. 6 floating flyline, for example, you should purchase a No. 6-weight rod. Flyrods for trout fishing should be 7 1/2' to 9' long, unless you plan to fish small, brush-choked streams. Then a shorter rod, even down to 5 1/2', is the only way to go.

Bamboo is the traditional material for flyrods. When drafted by an expert, a bamboo rod can cost $650 or more—not the sort of fragile gem a beginner should learn on. It's better to buy an inexpensive fiberglass rod (about $25 for a serviceable one) or, if you want something that will still suit you as your casting improves, a graphite or boron/graphite rod. Graphite rods are the ones most people choose today: They cost less than $100, are easy to cast and light in weight, and offer

good action. Boron/graphite rods cost a bit more, with a marginal increase in effectiveness.

Extra Gear. Other gear you'll eventually need includes waders; a flyvest with pockets for storing all your paraphernalia; landing net; wading staff for wading in slippery situations; polarized sunglasses, which cut the glare on the water and help you see fish; hemostats for removing hooks from trout; fly flotant for dabbing on dry flies to help them float; flyboxes for storing your many flies; extra leader and tippet material; a creel, if you intend to keep your catch; nail clippers, for cutting line; a cap; insect repellent; and suntan lotion. Also bring along a thermometer. Trout are most active and most catchable when water temperatures are around 60°F. If it's too hot or too cold, they become sluggish, and you may as well find a different spot to fish.

Casting. Now you're ready to go fishing. But first, you should try some practice casting in the backyard with a hookless fly. See Chapter IV for detailed instructions on various useful casting techniques.

Finding a Trout Stream. Where to go is the next question [V]. If you don't know any good streams near your home, ask. Ask in tackleshops; call your local chapter of the

Pack Rods

If you fly to any of your fishing destinations, consider investing in one or two pack rods. Advancements in manufacturing techniques have allowed companies to build three- and four-piece pack rods that have actions virtually indistinguishable from those of two-piece rods. So good are the new pack rods that some anglers use them exclusively. Having one or two pack rods you can stash in a small duffel and carry aboard an airplane is a smart idea. That way, you'll always have them as backup rods in case your checked luggage is lost. In addition to the rods, always carry your lures, flies, and a change of clothing in your carry-on bag. Pack rods are also great if you do backpacking into remote areas because of the ease of carrying and packing them. Costs for such outfits range from $100 to $300.

Trout Unlimited organization; read the outdoor column in your local newspaper. Unless you live in an extremely warm part of the world, you should be able to find trout fishing near your home. If not, adapt the flyrod to the species in your area.

Catching Trout. When you arrive at the stream, approach it slowly and cautiously. Trout are extremely wary and will often be spooked by unnatural shadows or movements along the shore. Deep pools will hold trout, and the beginner is best off casting to such stretches of water first. Trout almost always face upstream to watch for food floating by and to breathe oxygen. A dry-flyfisherman should work a pool from the downstream part up. Work the tail end of a pool first, then gradually lengthen your casts to cover the whole pool. This strategy will ensure that you don't scare all the fish right away with a long cast across the entire pool.

As you slowly wade and cast your way upstream, keep your eyes open for any place where a trout could be lurking. Undercut banks are favored hideouts, as are eddies at the base of riffles. Any obstruction that breaks the current flow—logjams, boulders, underwater ledges—and provides trout with a resting place with easy access to food flowing by should be cast to.

When fishing dry flies, cast upstream of the obstruction and let the fly float naturally into the area. If a trout should strike your fly, quickly pull in line and yank back on the rod to hook the fish.

If fish don't seem to be feeding on surface insects, it may pay to tie on a nymph, wet fly, or streamer, put on your sinking line, and try the subsurface approach. Look for the same basic holding areas you would while dry-flyfishing, but instead work downstream, letting the current drift your submerged offering into likely trout hangouts. Mend or pull in line as your fly floats downstream, thus giving it a drag-free (natural) drift. Strikes often come as the flyline and leader straighten out at the end of the drift.

Depending upon circumstances, you can fish a dry fly downstream or a nymph or wet fly upstream. That, in fact, is another challenge of flyfishing. If you can adapt to different stream conditions, you'll catch more fish than will the follow-the-rulebook angler.

Flyfishing has always had a mysterious aura for the beginner. Actually, it's simple, fun, and readily learned with a minimum of practice. If there is any secret to the technique, it centers on the selection of a rod and line that work in harmony. Choose the right outfit, learn how to use it, and you will soon be catching trout.

Increase Your Catch
Trout streams have an "easy" side from which most anglers approach. You can often increase your catch by crossing over and coming at the stream from the opposite shore.

Dapping
If you spy a trout ensconced beneath an overhanging bush or against a bank where a traditional cast can't be delivered, try dapping. Sneak slowly up to within rod's reach of the trout on hands and knees, then gently reach out and place the fly on to the water over the fish. Chances are good a slurping take will result.

Stealthy Approach
To reach trout in the low waters of summer, use a stealthy approach. Keep a hunchbacked profile, or get down on your hands and knees and creep into final casting range. Wade only as a last resort.

Waders

When fishing small streams, you may find yourself staying on the bank for the entire day without getting your feet wet. In summer it may also be warm enough to wet-wade in old trousers and sneakers or canvas wading shoes. But for most situations, waders are vital for keeping you warm, dry, and clean.

Hip boots can be used in small, shallow trout streams. Chest waders are preferable for most medium-size and larger rivers. Thin, lightweight versions are excellent for hot weather when you don't have to walk through lots of brush and stickers or rough country, which could snag and tear them. For other fishing needs, neoprene waders are hard to top. Bootfoot and stockingfoot models both have their proponents, with many anglers preferring bootfoots because of their convenience, warmth, and ease of getting in and out of. Be sure to buy waders that are large enough so you can wear several pairs of socks in cold weather. A good pair of hip boots will cost $30 to $75; chest waders range from $100 to $250.

Terrestrials for Trout

It might seem odd that creatures living on dry ground would figure as significant trout foods, but the fact is that terrestrial insects enter streams and lakes by the thousands over the course of a single day. Some fall in, others are washed in by rain, some get blown in by gusts, others attempt to fly over a river or lake and make it only halfway across. Once they fall into the water, these insects are held firmly by the surface tension between air and water. Few are able to escape, and trout eagerly feed on the helpless insects.

By imitating this important food source for trout, you can enjoy some of the most consistent dry-fly sport of the season. For unlike mayflies and caddis, whose hatches occur only during certain time frames of the season and at certain times of day, terrestrials are always on the water, from dawn to dusk, spring through fall.

A common misconception is that terrestrials are strictly summer insects. In reality, some land-based insects are active along streams as early as April and as late as November in most regions. Summer and early fall are particularly choice times to fish these flies, however, because this is when the land insects are most abundant and trout are keyed to feed on them. Trout take them in all types of flowing waters— meadow and forest, freestone and limestone—as well as in lakes and ponds.

●

Quick Wader Repair
Carry a jar of rubber cement in your fishing vest for quick wader repair. Let the waders dry, then brush a thick coat of cement over the tear or hole from the outside. Allow this coat to dry for several minutes, then add several more layers. In short order you will have leakless waders.

Seven major orders of land-dwelling insects are important to the fisherman. These include the *Hymenoptera* (ants, bees, wasps); *Coleoptera* (beetles); *Orthoptera* (grasshoppers, crickets, roaches); *Lepidoptera* (butterflies, moths); *Homoptera* (leafhoppers, treehoppers, cicadas); *Hemiptera* (true bugs); and *Diptera* (true flies). Dedicated flyfishermen will want to stock several patterns for imitating the major insects in each of these orders. If your interest in terrestrials is more casual, a basic starter selection would include: black and either cinnamon or orange ants, Sizes 14 to 22; black beetles, Sizes 10 to 18; hoppers and crickets, Sizes 8 to 14; leafhoppers, Sizes 18 to 22; bees, Sizes 8 to 12; and caterpillars, Sizes 8 to 12.

Standard trout flyfishing tackle works for presenting all these flies: an 8' to 9' rod, Weight 4 to 6 weight-forward or double-taper line, and an 8' to 12' leader tapering to a 3X to 7X tippet. This will vary depending on the size fly being used and the heft of trout being sought.

It's not crucial, but you can't hurt your chances by trying to figure out which type of terrestrials the trout are feeding on before tying a pattern to the tippet. Walk slowly along the bank and stoop to examine any insects you come across. Carry a fine-mesh net and check out what's floating in the stream's surface film. If one land insect is particularly abundant, this gives you the obvious choice of fly.

You can also make an educated guess regarding which fly to use by accounting for the time of day and season, type of streamside habitat (wooded, brushy, grassy), and your experiences on the water. Since so many land-based insects tumble into the stream over the course of a day, you seldom face a situation in which only one fly will work.

Rarely will you kill trout, but if you did, you'd find most have a hodgepodge of beetles, ants, true bugs, leafhoppers, and sundry other creatures in their stomachs. Trout are opportunists and seldom focus on one land insect during summer and fall. Rather, they'll sip in a few ants that float by, swim over and nab a beetle that plops in, scarf down a few more ants, then top them off with a cricket.

Thus the specific fly you choose may not be critical. However, your approach to the fish and your presentation of the fly are. In summer, many streams have shriveled to trickles compared with spring's freshets. The trout are more exposed in the thin flats and shrunken pools, and they know it. They're extremely skittish. Furthermore, since many terrestrials dribble in from the streambanks, trout are often found

Windward Bank
Most anglers try to get out of the wind, but the optimum oxygen levels and water temperatures for gamefish are often found on the windward bank. Wind can also blow insects and baitfish into these areas.

Light-Shy Brown Trout
Big brown trout are light shy. Fish for them in the first and last hour or two of daylight and after dark.

hovering right next to land, in very shallow water.

Delivery of terrestrial patterns should mimic the way naturals enter the stream. Lightweight insects such as leafhoppers, small ants, true flies, and tiny beetles settle on to the stream as fluffs of dandelion might. They seldom make enough noise on impact to draw the trout's attention. Because of this, the fish use sight as their primary sense when feeding on these bantam-weight insects. The angler should take his cue from this, delivering imitations of these tiny insects (Sizes 18 to 24) as delicately as possible and allowing them to drift drag-free over the trout. When you see fish rising to what appear to be bits of nothing on the surface, this is likely the presentation that will pay off.

You'll experience another kind of terrestrial angling when trout are feeding on big, heavy-bodied creatures such as hoppers, crickets, chunky beetles, caterpillars, carpenter ants, and bees. These insects make a distinct splat when they land on the stream's surface—and this sound often attracts trout in the area. Heavy, boiling rises are usually the result.

Mimicking these big terrestrials' clumsy entry into the water can yield some spectacular fishing. Flies used to imitate these insects are often

made of dense materials such as packed deerhair, cork, or balsa wood, so just driving them into the water with a slightly overpowered forward stroke creates the splat you want. If a trout is close enough to hear or sense the fly's entrance, a broad wake will likely furrow the water as the fish swims over to examine your offering.

Some of the best fishing with these large insects, using a sound cast [IV], comes on slow, glass-smooth pools and thin runs near shaded banks, and where brush and branches lean out over the water. If possible, try to spot the fish before casting, so you can deliver the fly just where you want it—usually behind or to the side of the trout. By presenting the fly this way, you keep your leader out of view and also catch the trout by surprise, often eliciting a quick turnaround and instinctive strike before the fish's sense of caution has a chance to take over. If you can't see a trout but an area looks promising, the sound cast is a great way to prospect.

Whether you delicately drift a No. 24 leafhopper over a dimpling trout or plop a chunky deerhair beetle down with a hearty splat, don't overlook the terrestrials. They can provide some of the most reliable and satisfying dry-flyfishing of the year.

Driving Trout Wild

In spring a great way to take trout is to row a boat slowly around the lake a short way offshore, trolling wet flies or small streamers. Use a few split-shot for weight and either ultralight spin or fly tackle. There's something about the steady action of the flies being dragged behind the boat that drives trout wild at that time of year.

SPINNING FOR TROUT

Rods

When you're selecting a trout spinning rod, the first thing you can do to narrow your choice is to eliminate anything heavier than "light action." Light or ultralight is the way to go. For most small- and medium-size streams, ultralight is the better choice. These rods have the finesse to let you detect delicate strikes and the bend necessary to protect the light lines you'll be using. They also provide the best sport when battling fish that in most parts of the country average 8" to 16". If you're going after unusually large fish such as rainbows in Alaska, steelhead and brookies in Canada, or the large trout sometimes found in tailwaters such as the White and Norfolk rivers in Arkansas, a light-action rod should get the nod over ultralight.

Material for the rod can be limited to one choice: graphite. Rods with at least some graphite (the more the better) offer greater sensitivity and lighter weight than fiberglass rods. Prices have come down enough so that a good graphite trout spinning rod can be purchased for $35 to $100.

The length of the rod should match the type of fishing you'll be doing. For small mountain streams with thick tree growth and bushes right along the banks, 5' to 5 1/2' is perfect. You'll seldom need to cast far, and the small rod is easy to maneuver in tight quarters. For medium streams, a 5 1/2' to 6 1/2' rod is a good choice. Drifting spawn bags for steelhead is best accomplished with an even longer rod—something in the 7 1/2' to 9 1/2' category—so you can keep lots of line off the water and remain in close contact with the offering as it tumbles along the streambottom. If you choose to go after large fish such as steelies with the line in the 2- or 4-pound class, you may want to use the superlong "noodle rods" of 10' to 12'. These extremely soft-action rods provide a tremendous cushioning effect to protect the gossamer monofilament.

Reels

A quality closed-face spinning reel works well for trout, but most fishermen prefer open-face ultralight or light models in the 5- to 8-ounce range. The reel should be small enough to balance well with the lightweight rod you'll be using, yet big enough to hold sufficient line for the fish you're going after.

For typical trout fishing, the smallest reels are perfect.

Natural Bait

Natural bait is deadly for taking trout, but don't confine yourself to the standards—worms, salmon eggs, and so on. Try such offerings as small live minnows, hellgrammites, large mayfly nymphs, caterpillars, grasshoppers, and crickets. Fish them on fine-wire hooks, with just a tiny split-shot or two for weight and 2- or 4-pound-test line.

Even a 3- or 4-pound fish will never strip all the line from such spools. If you're tackling big sea- or lake-run steelies, opt for a larger reel, something that will hold 150 yards or more of 6-pound line. Whatever size you settle on, be sure the reel has a smooth drag so it doesn't balk when a fish makes a sudden run or diving lunge. The price for a good trout spinning reel will run approximately $25 to $60.

Line

Monofilament line in the 2- to 6-pound class will cover virtually all your trout fishing needs, with the appropriate size varying with the heft of the fish you're likely to encounter, the weight of the lures used, and the clarity of the water. For high, murky conditions after rains and during spring runoff, you can get by with a line that's heavier than one you'd use in midsummer, when river levels are low and streams clear.

Besides pound test, consider the color of the line and its thinness compared with those of other brands of the same rating. The less conspicuous the line, the better it is for trout fishing. Clear or neutral shades are more productive than bright, fluorescent ones, and fine-diameter mono can produce more strikes than thicker line.

Tackleboxes

One of the nice things about stream and river trout fishing is that you don't need to carry a large assortment of tackle. A good selection of the lures and accessories described at right can easily be toted in a few clear, 4" to 8" compartmentalized plastic boxes that fit nicely in a fishing vest, coat pocket, or light canvas bag. This is much more efficient than having one large tacklebox you must lug around and sort through.

Lures

Lures can run the gamut from chunky 1-ounce spoons to tiny 1/32-ounce spinners used for native brookies in headwater streams. It's always a good idea to talk with locals and proprietors of nearby tackleshops to find out what the favorite offerings are in the area. But it is possible to make an all-around selection of lures that will enable you to catch trout virtually anywhere they are found.

Jigs with feather, hair, or rubber bodies can be excellent trout lures. Sizes from 1/32- to 1/8-ounce are useful, depending on the depth and speed of the current where the trout are holding and on their size. Spinners should be in every trout fisherman's tacklebox, as should small wobbling spoons.

Small crankbaits are excellent on tailwater streams where larger trout are common. Thin floating/diving plugs are also good on these waters. The Flatfish is a lure that has produced well on trout for decades; other wobbling plugs are favored by backtrollers working big rivers for steelhead.

Baitfishing Gear

A light or ultralight spinning outfit is the best tackle to use when baitfishing for trout. Other items you'll need for presenting bait include short-shank gold-plated hooks, Sizes 4 to 10, and split-shot in Sizes BB, B, and 1.

SALMONS
Family: Salmonidae

This family includes, in addition to the salmons, the trouts, chars and whitefishes, sheefish and ciscoes. The last three are a subfamily but are considered a separate family by some.

Originally confined to the colder waters of the Northern Hemisphere, the salmons offer valuable game and food qualities that have led to their introduction into favorable places in the Southern Hemisphere as well as lakes and streams of high mountains in tropical latitudes.

All the salmons have a somewhat similar life history. They hatch in fresh water (usually streams), spend some time there, and eventually move down to the seas, where they live and grow for a varying number of years. They return to their home streams to spawn in the autumn. If landlocked, some, such as the Atlantic salmon and sockeye, have been able to adapt and remain in fresh water for generations.

Fishing for Salmon

Here is all you really need to know to become a successful Atlantic salmon fisherman:

Flybox. All famous salmon fly patterns have taken salmon at certain times and places. A basic rule for selecting which fly to use is "Bright sky, bright fly; dark sky, dark fly." You

Salmon Lairs
After salmon have entered streams on their spawning runs, look for them in deep, dark holes. Porpoising fish will alert you to their hangouts.

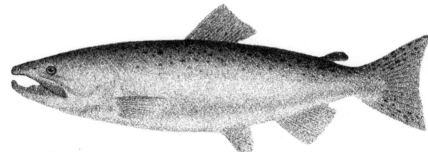

Chinook Salmon

(*Oncorhynchus tshawytscha*) This salmon is often called spring salmon in British Columbia because its spawning runs occur in late spring and early summer. In various other places it is also called king and quinnat. Like the other Pacific salmon, except the sockeye, the chinook ranges from southern California north to Alaska and from there south to Japan. Lengths of nearly 5' and weights up to 126 1/2 pounds have been recorded, but usual size at maturity is between 10 and 50 pounds.

Pink Salmon
(Oncorhynchus gor-
buscha). *Although the
pink salmon is abundant
from the Straits of Juan de
Fuca to Alaska, it is not a
top gamefish there; now it
has been introduced in
eastern Canada and the
Great Lakes. Weights up
to 10 pounds and lengths
up to 30" have been
recorded. The bodies of
breeding males become
distorted between the
head and the dorsal fin,
earning them the name
humpback. The name
Oncorhynchus is a combi-
nation of Greek words
meaning "hooked snout."
The names tshawytscha,
nerka, kisutch, keta, and
gorbuscha are all Russian
common names used for
salmon. They were used
by the Russians for the
same fishes in Alaska.*

need bright and dark flies in small, medium, and large sizes.

45 Degree Casting.
Salmon may lie anywhere the current flows. Start by casting upstream with a dry fly at a 45 degree angle to the current. Make three casts, then take a step forward and cast 3 times again, covering the entire pool. If the dry fly fails, switch to a wet fly and fish back down the pool, repeating a 45 degree cast. Three casts, take a step, repeat. If a salmon comes to the fly but fails to take, wait a minute, then repeat the cast.

Stripping. While stripping, keep your line in the crook of your forefinger so that you can snub the line against the cork grip when tightening on a fish.

The Strike. Salmon take slowly. If you strike too fast, you can pull the fly out of the fish's mouth before it closes its jaws. Delay your strike when one takes by saying, "Good morning, Mr. Salmon." Then

tighten up and let the fish set the hook as it turns to start the fight.

The Fight. When you're fighting a big fish, there is just one rule: "When he pulls, you don't. When he doesn't, you do."

When a salmon is in the air, drop your rod and give a bit of slack. Tighten up again when the fish reenters the water. This keeps the hook from being ripped out when the fish falls on a tight line.

Netting, Tailing. Always net a salmon headfirst so that its last thrust drives it deeper into the net rather than out of it.

If you choose or are required to hand-tail a salmon, grasp it firmly with the palm of your hand around the body and your thumb and forefinger next to the tailbones. Squeezed this way, the tail-bones stiffen and won't slip through your hand. Turning your hand the other way col-lapses the tailbones and allows the fish to slip away.

Chum Salmon

(*Oncorhynchus keta*) The chum salmon is usually the last salmon to appear in migrating groups in the fall. Its weight at maturity is 8 to 18 pounds, but it can go to nearly 30 pounds.

Sockeye Salmon

(*Oncorhynchus nerka*) Although only occasionally taken in salt water by anglers, this is the most prized of the Pacific salmons for canning purposes because of the deep-red color of its flesh. Some sockeyes do not go to sea but remain landlocked. These are called koka-nees. Sockeyes seldom grow larger than 33" and 5 to 7 pounds.

Coho Salmon

(*Oncorhynchus kisutch*) The coho or silver salmon is an important species for anglers. It enters all kinds of rivers and may spawn only a short distance from the sea along the Pacific coast; it has been introduced in the Great Lakes, Maine, Maryland, and Louisiana. The average weight at maturity is 6 to 12 pounds, but weights to 31 pounds have been recorded.

Atlantic Salmon

(*Salmo salar*) This "king of the trouts"—the name comes from the Latin *salire*, meaning "to leap"—ranges the Atlantic from Portugal north to the Arctic and from west Greenland and northern Labrador south to Cape Cod. Fish from 80 to 100 pounds have been caught in Europe; in America 50 pounds is unusual. The average size varies from river to river, but it is likely between 10 and 20 pounds.

PERCHES
Family: Percidae

Winter

Fishing through the ice for yellow perch is one of the greatest ways to shorten a long, cold winter [V]. In fact, some ardent icefishermen are sorry to see the spring thaw come. Return to those bays, reefs, and shores where you caught fish during the other seasons, and cut a hole through the ice. It's easy to tell the good spots because there will be a flock of early birds there ahead of you.

All members of the perch family are carnivorous. As adults, the sauger, walleye, and perch are principally fish-eaters. All are excellent food fishes and are highly regarded as game species. They are distributed throughout Europe, Northern Asia, and east of the Rocky Mountains in the United States and Canada.

The characteristics of a completely divided fin on the back, a spiny portion separate from a soft part, and the presence of only one or two spines in the anal fin distinguish the members of the perch family from the sunfishes and sea basses. There are three subdivisions in the perch family: (1) The walleye, sauger, and their Old World counterparts form one group; (2) the Eurasian and American yellow perches are very similar in color and shape, and with several Old World species make up a second group; and (3) the darters, of which there are 95 species in North America, are mostly small fish, 1" to 3" in overall length, with the exception of the log perch. The members of the darter group do not have a swim bladder, so they are heavier than the water and usually rest on the bottom, braced by their pectoral and ventral fins.

Fishing for Yellow Perch

Most any fishable day you can find anglers standing side by side seeking their favorite and one of the world's finer-tasting fish, the yellow perch.

The usual bait is small minnows because the perch's mouth is tiny [III]. Worms, grubs, larvae, and cut bait are also effective. When fishing tiny jigs or flies, sweeten the hook with a tiny piece of worm or maggot. Once a school is located, it isn't difficult to catch all you care to clean and eat. The real challenge is taking them on artificial lures. A favorite is a 1/64-ounce jig with a white 1" curly-tail body, rigged on an ultralight spincasting outfit with 2-pound monofilament.

Look for perch country [V]: gravel or rock shores that drop off into deep water, reefs bordering open weeds, bays with gravel shores or islands, channels of 10' to 20' depths, cattails or reeds bordering deepening water, and places where small streams enter a lake.

If there is a friendly wind moving you parallel to the shore, put it to work for you. Tie on a tiny jig or spinner, and pay out line until it touches bottom. Then keep it just over the bottom as you drift along.

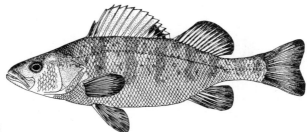

Yellow Perch

(*Perca flavescens*) One of the very best food fishes, the yellow perch has white, firm flesh
of excellent flavor. They are of special importance as a sportfish because anybody can catch
them in all seasons of the year. Perch prefer a diet of minnows and young fish, which they
supplement with aquatic insects. They spawn early, their eggs in adhesive bands that settle
over sticks and water weeds. Perch sometimes reach a length of 13 1/2" and a weight of 1
1/2 pounds, but in most places they run smaller. Their maximum size is around 4 pounds.

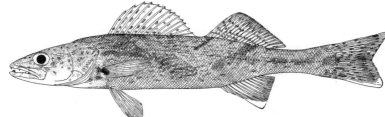

Sauger

(*Stizostedion canadense*) Smaller and more slender than the walleye, the sauger does not
have a dark spot on the dorsal fin. Saugers live in large lakes and large streams but move
into tributary streams or backwater lakes to spawn. Their eggs are scattered and sink to
the bottom. Saugers can tolerate a muddier bottom and more turbid water than the walleye. The largest saugers can go over 8 pounds.

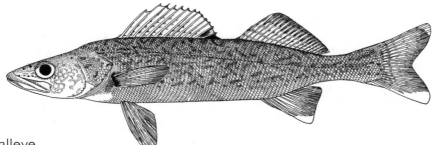

Walleye

(*Stizostedion vitreum*) One of the most important game and food fishes of the United
States and Canada, walleyes have been widely introduced into areas they did not originally
occupy. They usually spawn at night in depths of 1' to 5' over rocky areas, gravel, or sand
bars. The eggs are scattered over the bottom. Walleyes reach a length of over 3' and a
weight of over 24 pounds.

Other Helpful Thoughts

Yellow perch are peculiar. While the intrusion of a boat can send them scurrying, here is a bizarre way to attract them. When fishing a rocky reef (and you catch an occasional perch so you know they're around), try jangling an anchor on the rocks at intervals. Not only can it set off a feeding spree, but it can bring perch from afar.

Trolling at Night

Trolling at night is a great way to take river walleyes. Use medium-diving, narrow-profile crankbaits with a wide wobble or thin floating/diving minnows with weight to take them deep. Troll along ledges and drop-offs where shallow-water falls off into deep water. Start at dusk, and you can fish for several hours.

Keep setting the hook with sharp, short twitches of your rod tip.

When you catch your first perch, have a floating marker handy to toss overboard to pinpoint that spot so you can return to it. The odds say a school of yellow perch is waiting where that perch hit. Anchor over the spot, drop the jig straight down, and retrieve it slowly with intermittent twitches.

Should the wind be offshore, it's good perch-catching weather. Just run in to shore with your outboard, drop your jig to the bottom, and let the wind ease you outward into deepening water as you put the jerk on them. If the wind is inshore, begin in the deep water and drift shoreward. Just keep the marker and anchor handy.

Remember that yellow perch sometimes stratify at certain depths. Keep this in mind and make your wind drifts across bays or between islands and shores. Have a couple of rods with lures down at different depths—say,10' and 15'. You can cover a lot of territory by drifting, and it'll pay off when you discover that magical depth where yellow perch are feeding.

The average yellow perch caught throughout the Great Lakes and the Northeast runs 6" to 10". Jumbo perch are those upwards of 12", and the world record is an awesome 4 pounds 13 ounces! No matter what their size, yellow perch are big on flavor.

Walleye Techniques

Widespread stocking of walleyes has put them into such a broad array of waters that an incredible number of techniques have been developed for various seasons and geographic regions. The following tips—the basics of successful walleye fishing—will help you cash in on the walleye boom going on all across the country today.

Water Temperature. Walleye typically spawn when temperatures reach the 45° to 50°F range [I]. They'll move into shallows at this time, spawning at night either in feeder rivers or in the lake itself over areas of stone rubble and gravel. Walleyes don't feed much during the breeding period itself, but right before and after it are excellent times to fish. Try casting minnow-tipped bucktails or marabou jigs in the 1/8- to 3/8-ounce range and pumping them in slowly across the bottom. Simple lead heads with plastic grub dressings are also deadly.

Wind. Wind is a blessing, not a curse, when walleye fishing. It provides you with locomotion for driftfishing—one of the best ways to present a bait noiselessly to spooky fish. It also oxygenates the water and pushes baitfish schools into tight groups where predatory fish can ambush them. Look for walleyes on the windward side of a lake over points, bars, reefs, and riprap.

Marking Bouys. If you're drifting and catch a walleye, toss a marker buoy overboard immediately. You can then redrift through that area. Walleyes are schooling fish, and there may be others on that spot. If you hook on the second drift through, anchor and cast to the spot. If you don't connect, pick up the buoy and continue drifting.

Jigging. Trollers often use crankbaits, but don't overlook the jig for this method [III]. Tip it with a minnow, or a night-crawler during the summer, and ease the boat along as slowly as it will go to get a crawling presentation. A jig of 1/4 to 1/2 ounce is usually best. This is an especially hot technique for use on Canadian and Midwestern lakes.

Anchoring vs. Trolling. A trolling motor can offer a more flexible way to stay on top of the school since they might be traveling as they swim after bait.

Water Depth. Although walleyes may be found and caught in extremely deep water, most fish hold in water 20' deep or less most of the time.

Rods. A rod for jig-fishing walleyes should be 5 1/2' to 6' long and stiff in action, with just a slight flexibility in the tip section so you won't throw off bait that's often used to tip the jig. Rods of a medium or medium-heavy action are best suited for this type of fishing, but keep in mind that they should be lightweight graphite models.

Lures, Baits, and Rigs for Walleye

Driftfishing. Driftfishing with a live-bait rig and slip-sinker is a great way to take walleyes in spring and summer. Fasten a No. 4 to No. 8 hook to a 24" to 48", 4- to 8-pound-test leader, then attach this to a barrel swivel. Thread an egg or Lindy sinker on the main line from the rod and attack it to the swivel. Bait can be a nightcrawler, leech, min-now, or crayfish. Adjust the size of the sinker according to the depth of the water and speed of drift so you periodi-cally bump bottom. Sizes of 1/8 to1/2 ounce are usually best. When a fish nibbles, feed line for several seconds, then set the hook. Reefs, gravel bars, points, weedbed edges, and sunken islands are all good driftfishing spots.

Jigs. Jigs with marabou or bucktail dressings are popular for walleyes, but a simple lead head with a soft-plastic body and tail will often pro-duce even better. Stock mod-els with both stubby, stiff tails

Depthfinders
Downrigger trolling is most effective when used with a depthfinder and topographic map. Watch for suspended schools of bait or gamefish on the sonar, and use your topo and depthfinder to troll such likely locations as dropoffs, the edges of humps and reefs, deep points, sandbars, and gravel edges. Move the boat in a weaving pat-tern at a slow-to-moder-ate trolling speed. When you find a productive area, mark it on your map for later reference.

Feeder Rivers
One of the hottest spots in spring for walleyes is the deep hole where a river feeds into a lake. The fish hang here in the depths, then move up into the current of the river to feed and spawn in the evening and during the night.

●

Slip-Bobbers

Slip-bobber rigs are great for catching walleyes positioned on or near a reef, hump, point, gravel bar, or other structure that can be pinpointed. This setup consists of a bobber, hook, and split-shot. The only difference between this rig and a basic bobber rig is that a bobber stop is tied or slipped on the line and adjusted to block the free-moving float when it slides up to the appropriate position for the depth you want to fish. When walleyes are deeper than 5', this is the only efficient way to cast and use a float. Minnows, leeches, and nightcrawlers all work well with slip-bobbers.

and long, thin fluttering ones—walleyes can be picky. Purple, black, chartreuse, white, and yellow are top colors. Jig weights should be 1/8 to 5/8 ounce. Plain lead heads or painted jig heads work.

Thin-Minnow Plugs. Thin-minnow plugs work very well in the spring. Use 3" to 6" versions in silver or gold with black backs. If you need extra weight to get the lure deeper, crimp a few split-shot on the line a foot or so above the lure. Reel these in with an ultra-slow retrieve. Use them at night, too; big walleyes often prowl the shallow bays and tops of reefs after dark, looking for minnows. Again, retrieve at a crawl.

Spoons. When walleyes move into weedbeds—lily pads, coontail, cabbage, sand grass, and other types of vegetation—in search of food in late spring and summer, one of the best ways to catch them is to jig vertically with 1/2-ounce spoons. Lower the lure to the level at which walleyes show on the depthfinder, or near the edge of the weedbed, then raise the rod sharply 12" to 24". Drop the rod tip back down just slowly enough so that excessive slack doesn't develop in the line as the lure falls. This is usually when fish strike. If you have too much slack in your line, you won't feel them strike or see the

line stop falling as they inhale the spoon.

Drift-Fishing Spoons. While the most popular rig for driftfishing is a slip-sinker/live-bait setup, a spoon is also an excellent choice for drifting, as is a jig tipped with a strip of ripple porkrind, live minnow, or half a nightcrawler. Work these lures with short hops as you float over reefs, points, gravel bars, ledges, and next to riprap.

Seasonal Bait. Minnows are choice offerings early in the year. In summer, leeches and nightcrawlers are good. In fall, turn to minnows again, choosing jumbo specimens to lure big autumn glass-eyes.

Foating Bait. If bottom rigs and bait aren't producing, try switching to a floating jig head instead of a regular bait hook. This will keep the offering up off the bottom, where it's more visible to roving fish. A tiny float can also be used ahead of a regular hook to keep minnows, leeches, and crawlers slightly above the bottom.

Color. Be prepared by stocking your favorite lures in a variety of colors. Always stock a few bright fluorescent hues, too, since these can often turn reluctant fish on, especially in cloudy water.

Weights. If your spoons, jigs, or plugs aren't running deep enough when trolling for walleyes, add weight. Weights of 1/4 to 1 ounce can be useful, depending on water depth.

PIKES
Family: Esocidae

Pikes are fishes of legend throughout northern Europe and northeastern North America. The legends usually arise out of their predaceous habits, voracious appetites, or cunning in avoiding the angler's spoon or plug. Members of this family are all fish-eaters when adult, but also eat birds, snakes, and frogs. They usually live in and around cover such as brush or logs in quiet, clear water, making their feeding forays from this shelter into open waters or deep channels.

Pikes and pickerels spawn in very early spring as soon as the ice has melted, but the muskie waits until later, often until May. All spawn over shallow flooded areas, if available, or onto the shallows of lakes and streams, scattering their eggs widely. After spawning, they return to deeper waters. The young grow rapidly and mature when only 2 to 4 years old.

The pikes frequently hybridize in the wild; in some places the hybrids are nearly as common as the parent species. These hybrids have colors, patterns, or other characteristics that are intermediate between the parents. Hybrids are nearly always sterile, but on rare occasions a fertile one is produced.

Because of the vast numbers of small fishes they consume, pikes and pickerels are very useful in lakes for controlling overpopulation by the prolific smaller panfishes.

Timing Trips
If possible, time your fishing trips for muskies, stripers, or bass to avoid days immediately after a front has passed through. This tends to slow feeding by these gamefish. By the third or fourth day after the front has passed, action will be back on track again.

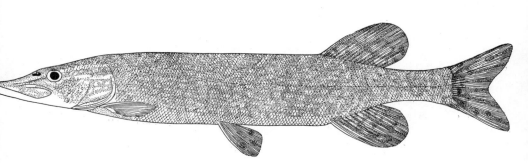

Northern Pike

(Esox lucius) This is the most widely distributed species of strictly freshwater fish ranging across the whole width of northern Eurasia and North America and south to about latitude 39. Young less than 11" have oblique bars on their sides like those marking the little pickerel. The maximum length of the northern is about 6'.

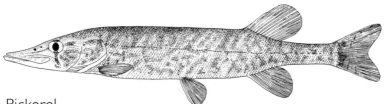

Little Pickerel

(*Esox americanus*) This subspecies is usually found in small streams or sheltered weedy bays of lakes. Little pickerel seldom grow more than 12" long, though some giants reach 15".

Chain Pickerel

(*Esox niger*) This fish is usually found in sluggish waters in the East. The creation of reservoirs by impoundments favors their increase. They remain active all winter, so icefishing for them is a popular sport. Chains reach a length of 36" and a weight of 9 pounds.

Great Lakes Muskellunge

(*Esox masquinongy masquinongy*) Large fish like the Great Lakes muskie need a large body of water for living room. Although these fish are not as abundant as they were before 1900, anglers catch a good many in the Great Lakes each year by spearing or angling through holes in the ice. This muskie also lives in many inland lakes. It reaches a length of over 7' and a weight of nearly 70 pounds.

Ohio Muskellunge

(*Esox masquinongy ohioensis*) This was the original "King of the River" when the Ohio, Cumberland, and Tennessee drainages were used as roadways to the Western frontier. The construction of dams on tributaries and the main rivers, plus increased turbidity of the waters, have greatly reduced its numbers and range.

Pike Fishing

Prime pike habitat can often be described as either a cool lake with a good forage base and shallow weedy or marshy areas available to the fish, or a cool, slow-moving river with quiet backwaters and weedy sloughs out of the current [V].

The Seasons. Pike angling can be divided into two types: (1) summer fishing and (2) spring/fall fishing.

Pike feed sparingly during July, August, and early September. The best bet at these times is to probe deep-water dropoffs, depressions in the lake floor, and areas where springs or feeders enter the lake or river, offering cooler water.

The premier seasons for pike fishing are spring and fall. The locations where you'll find the fish during both these seasons are basically the same. Water depth may range from 2' to 18', though most often the fish will be in 10' or less. Good locations include bays, coves, flats, points, tributary mouths, pools below waterfalls, and sloughs on rivers.

Shallows provide pike with four necessities: cover, warmth, food, and a spawning habitat. Cover will typically take the form of weeds. But if aquatic vegetation has yet to grow up in early spring, or had died out in fall, logs, brushpiles, and even rocks will hold fish.

Shallows heat faster in spring and stay warm longer in fall than the depths do. This warmth and the emerging plankton and insects found there attract smaller food fish such as dace, suckers, chubs, shiners, yellow perch, and ciscoes—and these fish represent a drawing card in the shallows for pike.

Tackle. 10- to 20-pound-test line and a medium to heavy 6' to 7 1/2' rod is ideal [III]. Baitcasting and spinning both work fine. For flyfishing, go with an 8 1/2' to 9 1/2' rod, with a Weight 7 to 10 weight-forward line and a 4' to 8' leader.

Depending on the water you're fishing, the way pike are taking, and the type of offerings you're using, you may or may not need a wire leader. It's often possible to substitute a heavy mono shock leader (25- to 60-pound test) for wire and still land most northerns hooked. If you can get away with this hard-to-see leader, you'll draw more strikes.

Strategies for Pike. In spring or fall start in the shallows. Try fishing flats, points, weedbeds, island edges, beaver dams, brushpiles, and stream outlets and inlets. Next move to sightly deeper creek channel edges, sharply dropping points, submerged islands, and humps in 10' to 18' depths.

Shallow and Fast. Because of the pike's voracious appetite and predatory disposition, large lures and flies featuring

Catching Pike

A red and white spoon is a favorite lure for large pike. When you cast the spoon, don't reel it back immediately. Let it sink just short of the bottom before you start the retrieve. Then lift your rod and let the lure flutter down again.

Flyrod Pike

Aggressive thin-water pike can be taken on the flyrod. Use various red, yellow, and orange tarpon flies and jumbo poppers. Fast, darting presentations seem to tease the fish into striking reflexively. Hit all obvious cover such as weedbed edges, beaver dams, pockets in vegetation, logjams, inlet mouths, and rock piles; also probe open areas.

lots of sparkle, vibration, or wobble often work very well when the fish are in shallow water.

Your aim is to taunt the fish's aggressive disposition. Use retrieves ranging from moderate to ripping. Try both steady and erratic presentations. Bright finishes such as silver, gold, chartreuse, orange, red/white, and red/yellow often draw the best responses. Spinnerbaits, spinners, and spoons can be dressed with plastic twister tails, pork rinds, or minnows. Buzzbaits and plugs are generally fished better clean.

Slow and Deep. If action is still less than impressive on these large, flashy offerings fished slightly slower, it's time to switch to such unobtrusive lures as bucktail jigs or plastic worms.

This is standard operating procedure in summer, when the fish are sulking and off their feed due to high water temperatures. It can also be effective in spring and fall, since pike aren't always in the shallows striking down anything that moves.

One of the deadliest retrieves is smooth and straight, steadily pulling the lure just above bottom; at times, however, a jigging motion works better.

Occasions when subtle lures can work are also excellent times for using live bait. You can dangle a minnow on a hook in likely pike territory as long as is necessary to goad reluctant fish into striking. A variety of baitfish—including suckers, chubs, and shiners—produces well, as long as they are large enough.

Drifting across shoals, flats, and points is an effective way to fish bait. Pinch on just enough split-shot to keep the minnow a few feet below the surface and let out 30' to 50' of line. If the wind is too gentle for drifting, try backtrolling the offering in similar areas and along the edges of weedbeds, logjams, and dropoffs. Another option for fishing bait is to rig a large bobber 3' to 6' feet above the offering and pitch it into pikey-looking cover.

Northerns typically grab minnows sideways, crunching down on the middle of their body. If you impale the baitfish through the back, just under the dorsal, you can usually set up soon after the pike takes, because the hook will already be in its mouth. If you lip-hook the bait, wait until the fish pauses and turns the minnow to swallow before striking. Hook the baitfish through the back and set up quickly—say, 5 to 10 seconds after the strike. This method results in lip-hooked pike and facilitates release [V].

Trolling. A final technique worth trying on pike that won't respond to lures and flies cast in the shallows is trolling. Use heavy spoons,

Tiger Muskellunge

(*Esox masquinongy immaculatus*) Only slightly different from the Great Lakes form, in that it is more distinctly barred, the tiger muskie lives in the lakes of northern Wisconsin, Minnesota, and southwestern Ontario. Its reputation as a fighter has made this muskellunge one of the most prized gamefishes.

minnow-tipped jigs, or diving plugs for water depths of 6' to 28'. If the fish are deeper than that, use downriggers to get thin spoons and floating minnow plugs down to their levels.

Cruise along the edges of weedlines, points, dropoffs, underwater humps, and stream mouths at a slow to moderate speed, following a particular depth contour line. If this level doesn't pay off, move farther out, switching to lures that probe deeper. Make lots of turns and zigzags, since this makes offerings flutter down, then jerk back up as the line draws tight—often prompting pounding hits. Try working one lure 60' or 80' behind the boat and another right up on the prop wash. Sometimes the motor noise actually attracts pike, drawing takes on plugs and spoons pulled right behind the boat. If slow trolling produces no results, try motoring as fast as you can while still getting good action from the lures.

And finally, in case you do latch on to a barrel-chested northern, be sure you have a pair of needle-nosed pliers or hook removers handy. The inside of a pike's mouth is not a place to be tinkering around with unprotected fingers.

Muskie Fishing

Probably the single relevant fact about muskies—aside from their gameness—is their comparative scarcity. Even the best lakes tend to have sparse and scattered populations of adult fish. On even the best of the known lakes and rivers, you'll invest hours hooking each fish.

If you have graduated to the big game of freshwater fish, the muskie, you would be best advised to hire a guide. They are listed in the outdoor magazines and can tell you what you will need in gear and tackle and will work with you to ensure you land your freshwater tiger.

Increase Your Odds
The average number of hours fished per muskie taken is estimated at around 200. You can reduce this considerably if you hire a muskie guide on your first trip, so you'll benefit from his know-how. Also, talk to veteran fishermen to learn the best lures, how to work them, and where to find fish.

Fishing for Pickerel

Esox niger—known region-ally as pike, jack, chainside, and snake—is an energy-charged fish that has salvaged so many late fall and winter fishing trips. Pickerel can be caught in hot weather, but they bite so much better from November through March, when few other fish are stirring—whether you fish the open waters of the South or drill holes in frozen Northern lakes.

They inhabit a broad spec-trum of water types [V], from small natural lakes, ponds, and streams to large tidal rivers.

Pickerel thrive in more acidic water than most game-fish. They're plentiful in black-water ponds stained dark with tannic acid from decaying veg-etation and in tide-influenced rivers that snake through low-lands close to the sea.

While brackish rivers and tannin-stained millponds are consistent pickerel-producers, another type of habitat is the newly impounded lake. Pickerel undergo population explosions in these waters for several years, spreading out and multiplying to fill the fresh, nutrient-rich habitat.

Pickerel Feeding Habits. Pickerel display two distinct feeding modes. One is that of the lone predator that hangs tight to cover, waiting in ambush for prey to swim within striking range. These fish hold near weedbeds, at the edges of dropoffs, in eddies of rivers, and next to docks, bridge pilings, or logs.

The second common feed-ing mode is that of cruising packs of pickerel. These fish rove in loose bands in deeper, open water. Slow pools and backwater sloughs off rivers, lake covers, and deep midsec-tions of ponds are their favored haunts. Pickerel are prime targets for the angler in both feeding situations, though different tactics are required in each.

Tactics. Live baitfish or lures and flies that imitate them are the best offerings [III]. For sheer productivity, it's difficult to top a 2" to 4" shiner wriggling seductively on a No. 1 to 4 hook. If you're icefish-ing, in fact, it's hardly worth bothering with anything other than minnows.

When you're probing for loose schools of pickerel in open water, two minnow-fish-ing methods work well. If the wind is cooperative, driftfish with the bait hooked through both lips. Use just one or two tiny split-shot crimped on the line for weight. Let the min-now swim naturally 30' to 60' behind the boat as you float over deepwater holes, river backwaters, and dropoffs. If there is no wind, cast this same rig out and retrieve it slowly, allowing the minnow to nick bottom occasionally.

For pickerel waiting in ambush next to cover, use one

Casting Live Bait
When casting delicate offerings such as crickets or shrimp, use two hands on the rod and lob the bait gently. If you load the rod in a sharp bend and snap it forward toward the target, soft baits may fall off on the cast.

Water Conditions
When you have a suc-cessful fishing day, take note of water conditions. Is it rough, warm, cold, smooth, clear, or roiled? Chances are that under similar conditions you'll have good fishing.

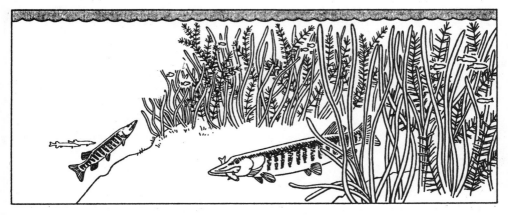

The best place to fish for muskies is along a "food shelf"—a shallow bay or weedbed adjacent to deep water. Muskies move into these areas to feed on the rich array of sunfish and baitfish found there.

small split-shot and the smallest bobber you can that will float the minnow. Fasten the float 2' to 5' above the hook, depending on water depth, and lightly hook the minnow through the back. Cast this rig to structure and wait several minutes. If a pickerel is there, he'll let you know. If no strike comes, retrieve and cast to the next weedbed or blowdown.

Wait 5 to 10 seconds after a strike, then set the hooks. If you let the fish run longer than this, chances are they'll swallow the bait so deep they'll be injured and impossible to release.

Artificials work well on open-water pickerel, but they're particularly useful for fish waiting in ambush near cover. Spoons, spinners, plastic worms, thin-minnow plugs, and jigs can all be deadly.

Though pickerel occasionally wallop muskie-size lures, you'll draw more consistent action by throwing small models. This is particularly true on still days when the surface is smooth and the fish are shallow and skittish. To throw these dainty offerings, you'll need light or ultralight tackle and 4- to 8-pound line.

Spoons, spinners, and spinnerbaits can often be enhanced by adding a strip of porkrind or a tapered chunk of belly meat cut from a crappie or yellow perch. In fact, one of the oldest methods known for catching pickerel, called skittering, consists of dabbling a piece of porkrind or perch belly on a hook through weedbeds with a long, lithe canepole.

No matter if you choose bait, lures, or flies, don't overlook the pickerel this winter. The strikes of these mini-pike can be explosive.

Habits
When the barometric pressure is falling, pickerel often clam up tight. Time of day is also important, with the most consistent action between 9 AM and 4 PM.

PANFISH

Family: Centrarchidae

Attracting Panfish
Here's a good way to attract minnows and panfish to your fishing area: Save breakfast egg shells and take them to the lake. Sprinkle the shells overboard in a circle around the boat. Pieces flutter seductively down through the water and attract both forage and gamefish.

Encouraging Productivity
Planning to build a pond? Here's a way to increase its panfish productivity: Spread driveway-type gravel in a small area in the shallows. The panfish will use this spot for spawning.

The sunfishes are the largest family of freshwater gamefishes in North America and include not only the sunfishes but also the crappies and black basses. There are about 25 species in the family, and their differences in size, habitat preference, food, and habits enable them to flourish in a great variety of waters, both flowing and standing. Not all members of the family reach sufficient size to be of interest to anglers, but the food qualities of the smaller species have led to their classification as "panfish." Several of the smaller species are of great importance as food for the larger crappies and basses.

Sunfishes are relatively easy to transplant, and the balance in numbers established after planting has resulted in widespread introduction into many foreign waters. Originally the family was found only in North America, but now a fisherman may catch sunfishes in foreign countries. The scientific family name of the sunfishes, *Centrarchidae*, means anal spine—from the development of spines in the anal fin. All the family have at least three strong spines in this fin; the crappies, rock bass, Sacramento perch, and several others have more, sometimes as many as eight.

Members of the sunfish family are nesting fishes. The males scoop out a depression where one or more females deposit their eggs. The males guard the eggs and newly hatched young.

Panfishing

Panfishing is the major form of sportfishing in the United States, and probably throughout the world.

Panfish are popular for a number of reasons: They are easy and inexpensive to catch, readily available to most fishermen, scrappy fighters, prolific breeders, simple to manage, and delicious to eat. In addition, they can be taken at any time of the year across the country.

Let's define what we mean by "panfish." Some say they are "any fish that will fit into a frying pan." Because all fish start out small enough to fit into a frying pan, however, it is more accurate to say that panfish are a group of highly desirable freshwater species that are considered too small as adults to be classified as "classic" or "glamour" gamefish. They include all the *Lepomis* genus of sunfish—bluegill, redear, redbreast,

Warmouth

(*Lepomis gulosis*) These are most abundant in quiet waters over mud bottom where there is abundant aquatic vegetation. The warmouth feeds on snails, aquatic insects, and when larger, on small fishes.

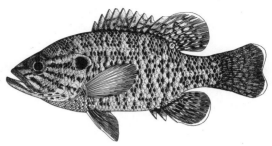

Green Sunfish

(*Lepomis cyanellus*) A small fish, seldom more than 7" long, the green sunfish lives in small creeks, but is adaptable, so it may be found in almost any habitat. It is often mistaken for young bluegill.

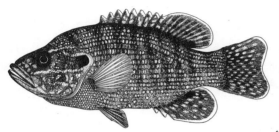

Longear Sunfish

(*Lepomis megalotis*) This fish inhabits the Great Lakes, the Mississippi Basin, and the Gulf states from South Carolina to Mexico. Of small size, the longear sunfish is seldom more than 5".

Redear sunfish

(*Lepomis microlophus*) Located in the Lower Mississippi drainage and from Texas to Florida, this fish was introduced into the Great Lakes and out West. Sometimes the redear sunfish enters brackish water, but it doesn't spawn there.

Pumpkinseed

(*Lepomis gibbosus*) Found in the northern United States, from Colorado to South Carolina, this fish has been planted in many western U.S. waters and abroad.

green, and pumpkinseed—as well as yellow and white perch, black and white crappies, and rock bass. Some anglers also put white bass, whitefish, and small catfish in the category.

Of all the panfish species, the bluegill is king, the classic that best exemplifies the group. Bluegills are found in all states except Alaska, are the most common of the panfish, are great fun to catch, and are delicious to eat. Panfish are both gregarious and prolific creatures. Bluegills, for example, begin spawning activities when the water temperature in the shallows reaches 70° to 80°F.

Bluegill eggs hatch in two to five days. If food and temperature conditions are favorable, growth is rapid for the first three years. As with other panfish species, young bluegills primarily eat microscopic plants and animals. As they grow, their diet changes to aquatic insects, snails, small crayfish, and small fish. The more fertile the water, the more food there is available for the young fish. For that reason, the warm and fertile ponds of the South produce big panfish quickly.

In Northern areas, it takes two or more growing seasons to produce a "keeper" bluegill that measures more than 6" and weighs 4 to 5 ounces.

Perhaps the overriding reason why so many people

catch and eat panfish is that the cost is so little. The most elementary tackle is adequate [III]: A stick, piece of line, and small hook with some worms are frequently all you need to catch a mess of panfish. Recent developments in ultralight spinning and spincasting equipment, improved 4- and 6-pound-test monofilament line, and myriad lightweight spinners, plugs, and spoons have added a great deal of sport to the art of panfishing.

Tips for Panfish

Panfish offer another big advantage: If you carefully pick the waters you visit, you know you'll land at least a few fish, making the day a success [V]. Here are several tips that should help you enjoy panfishing this year.

Lead-Head Jigs. One of the top lures for summer crappies is a 1/16- to 1/64-ounce lead-head jig with a soft-plastic body [III]. Tails can be either the twister type or those with multiple strands. Fish these vertically, using either a canepole or a flyfishing outfit with monofilament line. Plunk the lure next to cover such as deep standing timber or bridge pilings, and watch for a take on the drop. If none comes, hold the jig steadily at the level where you think fish will be hovering—usually from 8'

Catching Bluegills
If tiny jigs, grubs, and spinners aren't producing on bluegills, tip them with tiny porkrind flecks. This sometimes turns on reluctant sunnies.

Fishing Jigs
Whenever fishing jigs vertically for crappie, don't move them sharply. Instead, try to hold the jig as still as you can. The lure will actually be moving slightly, quivering just like a minnow gently finning its pectorals. Crappies find that subtle motion hard to resist.

Bluegill

(*Lepomis macrochirus*) Widespread in
the United States and southern
Canada, this flycaster's favorite and
one of the largest of the sunfishes in
Southern waters averages less than a
pound but can run to over 4 pounds.

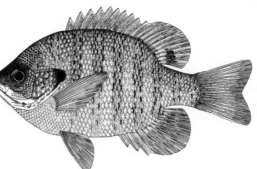

Rock Bass

(*Ambloplites rupestris*) Most often
found in clear waters over gravel or
rocky bottom, this fish tolerates a
wide variety of habitats. It tends to
congregate in deep holes in small
streams.

Black Crappie

(*Pomoxis nigromaculatus*)
This fish nests and lives
in waters 3' to 8' deep
but moves into shallows
at night to feed.

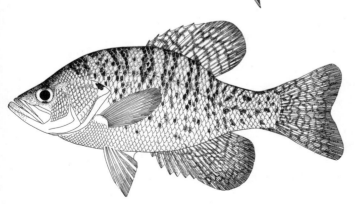

White Crappie

(*Pomoxis annularis*) This
fish prefers shallower
water than the black
crappie; one is usually
more abundant than the
other, the white domi-
nant in the South, the
black in the North.

Panfish Recipe

There are many ways to cook panfish, but one of the most delicious is using a beer batter recipe. Mix 4 parts dry buttermilk pancake mix with 3 parts beer (or ginger ale) to make a batter suitable for coating the fillets. Add lemon juice, salt, pepper, and garlic powder to taste. Dip the fillets in the batter, coating them evenly. Fry in hot oil, browning well on both sides, until done.

Spawning Activity

The bulk of bluegill spawning activity takes place during the few days around the full moon in spring and early summer. Look for the fish in coves and bays. They'll be in groups of a dozen to 100 or more.

to 20' in early and late spring. You don't need to dance or manipulate the lure at all. Just the trembling and natural movement of your hand will make the jig quiver like a real baitfish. If no strike comes, move the lure around to the other side of the cover, hold it there for a minute or two, then move to the next spot.

Leeches. An excellent way to take bluegills and other panfish in deep water during summer is to driftfish with live leeches. Start with a bell sinker weighing between 1/2 and 1 ounce, and attach a pair of Size 6 or 8 hooks a foot or two above the sinker, using dropper loops. Impale a leech on each hook, and drift in deep water near any structure, bridges, dams, or weedbeds. These baits are particularly attractive to jumbo bluegills in the 8" to 11" class.

Spawning Beds. The bluegill spawning bed may be the best place to fish because the males are so aggressive and defensive that they will strike at practically any lure coming near. Some people might criticize the idea of fishing over spawning beds, but you are doing the population a favor by removing some surplus before it enters the system.

Spawning Bed Redear. One of the best ways to catch spawning redear sunfish

or shellcracker is to pole or use an electric motor to move through shallow water (preferably with a sandy bottom), searching for the oval beds the fish make for breeding. If you see fish and they swim off, either note the location and come back later, or simply anchor a short distance away and wait. The spawners will soon return. Toss out a red wriggler or earthworm on a Size 6 or 8 long-shank hook with a tiny split-shot 1' up the line and a bobber adjusted so the bait hangs right in the bed. It won't be long before a redear grabs the worm. Set the hook quickly, since the fish may just carry the worm out of the nest and then drop it.

After the Spawn. After the spawn, look for bluegills in water 8' to 20' deep—areas with sunken brush, weedbeds, or contours such as a hump, dropoff, or long, deep point. Probe these with a small 1/16- to 1/32-ounce rubber-tailed grub in brown, purple, chartreuse, motor oil, or pumpkinseed. Cast out and let the grub sink, then retrieve it ever so slowly just above the bottom, with occasional pauses. Some huge bluegills can be taken with this technique, but you have to have enough patience to reel slowly and keep your lure deep.

Line. For bluegill fishing, use thin-diameter lines, preferably with a clear finish.

Four-pound line is a good standard, but don't hesitate to go to 2-pound test if the water is particularly clear and fish are skittish.

Season and Moon Phases. Do the bulk of your late spring and summer fishing for bluegills and other sunfish during the new- and full-moon periods.

Trout Flies. They don't have to be fancy, and many fishermen like to save flies that trout have chewed up and mangled a bit for use with panfish. Trout nymphs also work well when the fish are deeper. Wet flies such as the Black Gnat or a sinking black ant pattern are deadly on chunky bluegills. Sizes 8 to 14 are best for the small-mouthed panfish.

Cane Poles. The tools are simple, but one of the best ways to catch big bluegills and other panfish is to use a 10' to 14' cane or fiberglass panfish pole and live crickets. Attach from 8' to 12' of 6- to 10-pound line to the end. Then tie on a Size 6 to 10 long-shank hook with a split-shot 1' above it, and a bobber 2' to 4' farther up the line. Work along shoreline cover, dapping and flicking the offering up near brush, weeds, and stumps. Let the cricket sit for a few minutes, then flip it to the next likely spot as you scull along with a light paddle or move under power of an electric motor.

River Redbreast. The redbreast sunfish is a great panfish, particularly when caught in flowing water. Look for redbreasts where the current eases in eddies and pools and near slow undercut banks, rather than out in riffles and rapids. They're particularly fond of clobbering spinnerbaits and traditional spinners crawled in slow and deep, but they'll take wet flies, poppers, and sponge-rubber spiders on a flyrod. Baitfishermen do well with crickets and worms on these feisty, bright-colored fish.

Hooks for Crappie. Use fine-wire gold Aberdeen hooks for crappie fishing, in Size 2, 1, or 1/0, depending on the size of fish present. The fine-wire hooks will readily penetrate a crappie's mouth and hold up during the fight, but they'll bend free if you snag on brush or logs. Since crappies are so often located tight to snags and blowdowns, this will save you lots of expense and time wasted on replacing hooks. Simply bend the hook back into shape after you pull it off a snag with your fingers or a pair of pliers.

Flyfishing Tackle. Flyfishing tackle for bluegills and other sunfish has traditionally meant an 8' rod for a 6-, 7-, or even 8-weight line. You can certainly catch panfish with this tackle, but for the greatest angling pleasure, scale down

Chumming
Try chumming to improve your crappie fishing. Anchor out over a likely location and sprinkle cornmeal around the boat every few minutes. Soon minnows will begin to gather to feed on the chum, and they in turn will attract crappies to your location.

Fishing in Rivers
When fishing for crappies in rivers, look for side sloughs and slack water above and below dams. Concentrate on areas with blowdowns and flooded timber. Use small white, yellow, or chartreuse jigs or live minnows on No. 2 to 6 hooks.

Ultralight Rods

Light-action rods are useful for large crappies and white bass, but for most panfishing, ultralight rigs are the tools of choice. Use a 5' to 6' graphite spinning rod with the smallest reel you can find spooled with 4-pound monofilament.

Light-Action Rods

Light rods are best for panfish, but avoid too-stiff action in the tip. A slightly limber tip keeps bluegills from spitting out the lure as quickly when they feel the tension from the rod and line.

to one of the delightful featherweight flyrods available in the 1- to 4-weight class, combined with a double-taper or weight-forward floating line and a 4' to 9' tapered leader (shorter for wet flies, longer for surface offerings).

Flyfishing for Crappies. Few people flyfish for crappies, but this is a fun and productive way to take these tasty speckled perch. Use a 4- to 6-weight outfit and a weight-forward floating or fast sink-tip line. Tie a 4' to 6' leader tapering down to a 6- to 8-pound tipper, and use a small streamer fly in Sizes 2 to 6. If necessary, crimp a small split-shot on the leader 1' in front of the fly for extra weight. Cast the fly to the edge of weedbeds, along dropoffs, and near deep points, bridge pilings, and flooded timber, and retrieve with short, sharp strips so the fly works at 4' to 12' depths.

Nightfishing. Find stumps, standing timber, or bridges in moderate to deep water, anchor out near them, and set out a lantern along the side of the boat. If you don't want to bother taking a boat out at night, find a dock that extends into deep water and hang a light off the end. The illumination will bring in insects and small baitfish, which in turn will attract crappies. Fish jigs, spinners, or small minnows near the structure.

Bridge Pillings. One of the best places to find crappies in

summer is around bridge pillings. These abutments offer the fish shade and structure, plus a spot to ambush baitfish.

Noise. If action is slow, try slapping and splashing the water with your paddle. This tactic may seem crazy, but the commotion sounds like feeding fish and will often attract nearby crappies to your offerings.

Drift Fishing. Drifting is a great way to locate schools of summer crappies and bluegills. Attach a bell sinker weighing from 1 to 2 ounces on the bottom of your line, then tie off a pair of hooks 12" and 24" above that— Sizes 2 to 1/0 for crappies, 6 to 8 for bluegills. Bait up with minnows for crappies; earthworms, nightcrawlers, or crickets for bluegills. Then drift in coves and feeder creeks of the main lake, as well as deepwater points, flats, channel dropoffs, and the edges of weedbeds. When you catch a fish, throw out a marker buoy and then redrift through that area. You can also try anchoring and casting, but repeated drifting through the payoff spot will usually yield the most strikes.

Weather. Watch weather patterns and try to time your fishing trips for the period just before a front arrives. Panfish of all species tend to feed avidly during the few hours before a storm system or weather change moves in.

CATFISHES
Family: Ictaluridae

There are 24 kinds of catfishes in the United States, but only nine of these are large enough to be of interest to anglers. The blue catfish and flathead catfish are among the largest of freshwater fishes, growing to over 100 pounds. The stonecat and others of the picturesquely named "madtom" group are seldom more than 3" or 4" in length. Originally the North American catfish lived only east of the Rocky Mountains, but the white catfish, bullheads, and channel catfish have been introduced into most of the Western states. The family name *Ictaluridae* is a combination of two Greek words meaning "fish" and "cat."

The North American catfishes all have barbels (whiskers or feelers) around the mouth that enable them to find food by touch and taste. Since most species live in turbid waters and are active at night, these two senses are more important to them than sight. Some biologists say that catfish have super-oral taste, meaning that they can distinguish the flavor, or odor, of food without taking it into their mouths.

Little is known about the sensitivity of pores along the sides of catfish. If a piece of food is brought into contact with either side of a catfish, it will turn and seize it. Juices have the same effect, which means catfish can find food even in muddy water where visibility is nil. Tests have revealed that blindfolded catfish knew each other by smell, but when smell was surgically removed, they became disoriented.

Catfish Facts
- *Many species of catfish can produce vocal noises by contracting their swimming bladders.*
- *The Nile catfish swims upside down to feed on the surface. It has the usual coloration of a catfish, only reversed: Its back is white and its belly dark.*
- *Although catfish are generally associated with sluggish and discolored waters, channel and flathead cats actually prefer clean, clear, swiftly flowing streams and rivers.*
- *Most catfish feed primarily at night.*

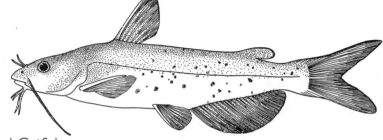

Channel Catfish

(*Ictalurus punctatus*) The channel catfish is the most active of all the catfishes, and this characteristic makes it a prized game as well as food fish. They live in river channels, feeding there during twilight hours and moving into the shallows at night. They ascend small streams to spawn. The maximum length is around 4', and maximum weight is 50 to 60 pounds, but they are usually much smaller.

Spawning takes place in the spring or early summer: April or May in the South, May or June in the North. The habits of the various species are similar, but the kind of site chosen for spawning differs. After spawning, the male drives the female away and assumes the duty of guarding the eggs and young for some time after they leave the nest. Since catfishes have no scales, age is determined by counting the growth rings of the vertebrae, gill cover, or the rings showing in cross sections of the pectoral spines.

Fishing for Catfish

The name catfish may not grab you as do the names bass, rainbow trout, muskie, bluegill, steelhead, salmon, or walleye. Yet it's America's third most popular sportfish.

Catfish are usually caught in the same type of waters throughout the United States [V]. Fish near dams if you're seeking a giant blue, flathead, or channel catfish. Smaller streams, lakes, and ponds yield the other species, including medium- to smaller-size channel catfish.

Catfish find most of their food in deep water. This usually consists of dead fish, crayfish, minnows, crustacea, mollusks, and larvae. Like other deep-dwelling fish, catfish have small eyes, which can withstand increased water pressure.

A great number of catfish are taken on artificial lures [III]. The fact that these fish take artificials indicates they also have a highly developed sense of feel and that both feel and smell enabled them to find those jig-and-porkrind lures that hooked them.

If you want to catch catfish and don't know much about it, seek the advice of veteran catfish anglers. They're everywhere, and most of them are friendly people who enjoy talking about their favorite sport. Read everything you can find about catfish and start a file. Here are some more helpful observations.

Many anglers enjoy flyfishing for catfish. On a flyrod just use monofilament line (20-pound test). Tie on a 2/0 Eagle Claw hook, add a gob of bloody chicken liver, wade into a deep hole, and lob it out. Retrieve slowly over the bottom until a catfish tries to take it away from you.

There are many other ways to catch catfish, such as trotlining, jug fishing, setlining, and noodling (which involves catching the fish with your own hands and a rope). Check the laws in your state to see if these tactics are legal in your area. Also check regulations for the allowable number of hooks.

There is a danger involved when handling catfish: poison. Although not much is known about this toxin, anyone who

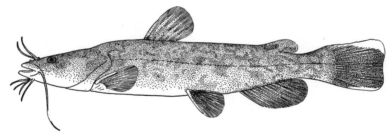

Flathead Catfish

(*Pylodictis olivaris*) This fish lives in large streams, shallow bayous, and overflow polls where it hides in sheltered places. It may be caught at night on a trotline baited with a live minnow or crayfish. The flathead cat reaches a length of 5' and weights up to 100 pounds, but the more usual size is 20 to 30 pounds.

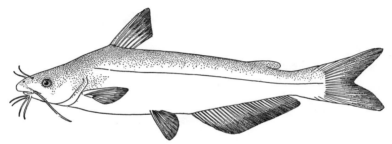

Blue Catfish

(*Ictalurus furcatus*) The blue catfish has been known to reach nearly 100 pounds, but these are rare. Individuals 25 to 30 pounds have been caught, but most are 5 to 15 pounds. Blue catfish move around more than other kinds of catfish, from larger rivers into bayous and backwaters in spring, even ranging into saltwater in Louisiana.
They bite on trotlines baited with small fish and crayfish.

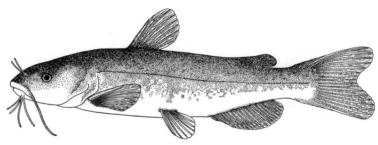

White Catfish

(*Ictalurus catus*) Ranging in coastal streams from New Jersey to Texas, this fish was introduced across the United States. It can reach a weight of around 15 pounds.

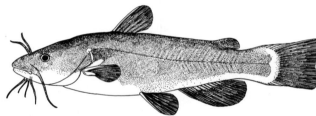

Black Bullhead

(Ictalurus melas) This fish does not reach as large a size as other bullheads; its maximum weight is under 9 pounds. The black bullhead lives well in farm ponds and small streams where there is a soft mud bottom.

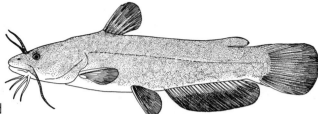

Yellow Bullhead

(Ictalurus natalis) This fish lives in shallow parts of large bays, lakes, ponds, and streams where there is not much current and where the water is clear and water plants are abundant. It reaches a length of 18" to 20" and a weight of 3 pounds.

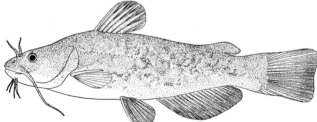

Brown Bullhead

(Ictalurus nebulosus) Their distribution now widespread, brown bullheads are not so tolerant of turbid waters as the other bullheads. The brown bullhead reaches a length of almost 19" and a weight of over 5 pounds.

has been "stung" by a catfish, no matter how small, knows it can bring excruciating pain. When caught, a catfish locks its dorsal and pectoral fins so that the handler actually wounds himself as he tries to squeeze the squirming fish. It's always a good practice to carry a tube of Bacitracin™, an antibiotic, and bandages to treat all outdoor wounds. This immediately nullifies the pain by neutralizing the catfish poison.

There is one common factor among all catfish when they are taken from unpolluted waters. They offer delightful eating whichever way you choose to cook them.

Shad and Rough Fish

The Shad Are Running

Clogging ocean-feeding rivers after the long, cold winter, shad are welcomed by East and West Coast anglers alike. In spring, when shad surge into coastal rivers for their spawning migrations, they offer some of the earliest quality sportfishing of the year.

Shad are fighters to the core. Even after their arduous journey from ocean to spawning grounds, they still store sufficient energy to wage a fierce struggle against light tackle.

Shad are delicious to eat—both the flesh and the roe. Another plus is their easy accessibility. Runs take place on major coastal rivers situated near population centers and millions of anglers [V].

Shad can be caught in most rivers; however, the best action takes place in freshwater reaches, often hundreds of miles up from the mouth.

Anglers pursue two species of shad in spring. White, or American, shad are the most abundant and are found along both coasts. Hickories, the other popular shad, are most common in the Southeast. Bucks of both species are smaller than females. Male white shad average 3 to 4 pounds, with females growing to 4 to 7 pounds. Male hickories weigh about I pound, females I 1/2 to 2 1/2 pounds.

Hickories also have a longer, more projected lower jaw than whites do. The same angling techniques catch both types of fish.

No one really knows why shad strike lures. They don't do it to fill their bellies; that much is certain. During spawning runs, their bodies are so tightly packed with eggs and milt that their stomachs are shrunken. Possible reasons they hit lures anyway include curiosity, aggravation, and reflexive instinct.

Water conditions can vary drastically from the start to the finish of the run and can play an important role in determining how you try to activate the striking instincts in shad. High, cold water is common early in the season, when the fish are sluggish. Lures and flies should consequently be moved slowly and kept deep by using weighted lines, split-shot, twist-on lead, or rubber-core sinkers [III]. As temperatures rise and the river level drops, shad can be taken closer to the surface on smaller, lighter lures and less lead. The warm water also makes the fish more active, and faster presentations can be effective. By the time spawning begins late in the run, fish will be seen splashing on the top near the edges and tails of pools. Evening action can be terrific then on darts and streamers that are fished

Good Times to Fish

The best time of day to fish for shad depends on the type of water. In brackish rivers, the rising tide is best. In freshwater, dawn and dusk are tops; during cloudy, drizzly weather, the fishing can be good all day long. Shad may strike any time the whim hits them.

Fast Retrieve
Many shad fishermen work lures and flies too slowly. True, a crawling retrieve works at times, particularly early in the year when the waters are cool, but in midseason and late season a fast, erratic presentation can often draw crashing strikes from these anadromous gamefish.

just below the surface.

Casting. This method is excellent for the shore or wading fisherman and can also be deadly from a boat [IV]. Use a light-action 6' to 7 1/2' spin rod and 4- to 8-pound line. Shad darts—small, tapered jigs adorned with a tuft of white or yellow bucktail—are the top offering. Dart weights can range from 1/32 to 1/4 ounce, with the heavier ones performing best early in the run, lighter ones later. Red/white and red/yellow darts are most popular, but also stock a few in combinations of green, purple, orange, and black. Small gold and silver spoons can also produce when fished singly or in tandem with a dart.

Cast the dart or spoon across and slightly upstream, then let it sink until it's close to bottom. Begin a slow retrieve. Some anglers favor smooth cranking, but they like to twitch the lure every few seconds. Be especially alert for strikes as the dart swings in an arch in the current. Positioning is critical for this technique. You'll want to be to the side and slightly above where the shad are holding. If strikes are coming slow while you're fishing deep, try a shallower, faster retrieve.

Still-Fishing. This is the most popular way of all to catch shad from a boat. Anchor your craft over the main river channel and, if pos-

sible, 80' or so upstream from a ledge or other obstruction that forces the fish to rise as they move over it, or where a point juts out, concentrating the shad in a smaller area. Cast a dart, spoon, or gold hook with fluorescent beads threaded above it, then let the offering swing down below the boat and hang in the current.

If shad are cruising at a high level or if the water is shallow, no weight may be required. Normally, you'll want one to four split-shot or a 1/4- to 1/2-ounce rubber-core sinker above the lure to keep it deep. Use less lead early and late in the day, more during midday.

Jig the rod occasionally if you like, but most still-fishermen prefer to let the dart just hang in the flow, quivering with the motions of the boat and current. If debris is abundant in the water, check the dart every 10 minutes to make sure the hooks are clean.

Trolling. If you find a secluded stretch of river channel or an area where others use this method, trolling can pay off handsomely. Darts or spoons should be run 75' to 125' behind the boat, with several large split-shot or a rubber-core or bead chain sinker added for extra weight. Twitch the rod tip occasionally as you motor along. Go as slowly as the outboard will allow, trolling both up- and downstream.

Flyfishing. This is a great way to take shad. Use an 8' to

9' rod, a Weight 6 to 8 weight-forward line (full sink or sinking tip), a 3' to 6' leader, and a 4- to 8-pound tippet. Be sure your reel has 100 yards or more of backing on it. This deepwater setup will yield most shad taken on flies.

A variety of commercial shad flies is available, and most will catch fish, though some will doubtless perform better than others on the rivers you fish. Basically, you'll want a simple, brightly colored compact streamer, 1/2" to 1" long. Patterns incorporating red, yellow, orange, white, chartreuse, and silver are particularly good in Sizes 6 to 12.

Flies can be productive when simply cast out and dangled behind a boat in the current as you would with a dart, or you can try wade-fishing. Cast across and upstream, then mend to keep a belly out of the line for the first few seconds of the drift. As the streamer sinks into the strike zone, either allow it to swing around naturally in the flow or pump the rod tip softly to add motion.

Top Shad Rivers. In the East, try the Cape Fear, Connecticut, Delaware, Edisto, Rappahan-nock, and St. Johns. In the West, try the American, Columbia, Feather, Sacramento, and Yuba.

Trash Fish

When the term "trash fish" is used to refer to a nongame species, it's a misstatement because there are sporting qualities in almost all species.

Carp (*Cyprinus carpio*). Ol' Buglemouth is a nickname fishermen hang on this bottom grubber because of its sucker-type mouth. There are two general types: those that are uniformly scaled and those that are not.

Today virtually all states have carp. It's a great species to give a go, especially with a youngster.

How to catch carp: There are three things worth remembering about the carp: (1) it's a bottom feeder; (2) it has an extremely keen sense of smell; and (3) it has a small mouth and thus prefers a small lure [III]. Baits used successfully in many carp holes include fresh shrimp, worms, minnows, grubs, cheese, crayfish tails, mulberries, jelly beans, and scented doughballs. To make a scented doughball, just knead vanilla into several slices of bread. Wad a bean-sized hunk onto a weighted hook, fish along dropoffs in lakes or streams, and you will probably catch some carp.

Bowfin (*Amia calva*). You might know this fish by other names, such as dogfish, grinnel, grindle, spottail, or mudfish. It's a prehistoric throwback, as mean as they come, and strong enough to break tackle if carelessly handled. It's recognizable by the continu-

Migration
Shad begin filtering in from the ocean when river temperatures rise near 50°F. After the run peaks in one area, you can often extend your sport by hopscotching upstream. Studies on the Delaware River have shown that shad migrate just over 4 miles a day, though this speed will vary from river to river.

Carp

(Cyprinus carpio) Carps were introduced into Western Europe from the Near East and then brought to America in 1877. Carps grow to lengths of 3 feet, and weights in excess of 50 pounds have been reported.

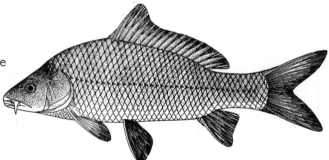

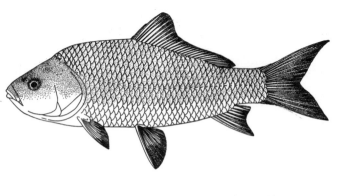

Buffalo

(Ictiobus cyprinellus) This fish lives in larger streams of the Mississippi River system and has been introduced in Arizona and California. Maximum length is 40". Weight can go over 70 pounds, but fish of 30 pounds are common in larger lakes and rivers.

Bowfin

(Amia calva) This primitive fish, of Jurassic ancestry, is located throughout the Mississippi basin, along the southeastern coastal states to Pennsylvania. Growing to over 40", it can be found in sloughs, ponds, swamps, and backwaters of streams.

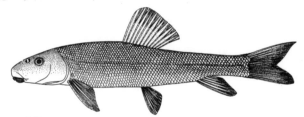

White Sucker

(Catostomus commersonni) The most abundant member of the sucker family living in most streams and lakes east of the Rockies from the Arctic Circle to the northern parts of the Gulf states, white suckers reach a length of 28" to 30" and weight of 6 to 8 pounds.

ous dorsal fin that covers most of the back, plus a distinctive tail spot. The bowfin is found mostly in the eastern United States, especially in the Gulf States and Mississippi River drainage system. It's an air breather and can be located when it surfaces.

How to catch bowfin: The best tactic is to fish shore cover until you find one [V]. This ferocious predator always seems to be hungry enough to attack anything that moves. Regular bass lures will work well, and live minnows are surefire [III]. Just cast out, reel in, and be ready. You will especially enjoy watching a bowfin hit a surface lure. Habitually it will trail the lure, slash at it, and deliberately miss repeatedly. But when it's ready, it will make a vicious attack.

Buffalo *(Ictiobus cyprinellus)*. The bigmouth buffalo (there is also a smallmouth buffalo) is found throughout the Plains states and eastward. The bigmouth, a member of the sucker family, frequently hits the 10- to 20-pound mark. The largest catch reported, an 80-pounder, came from Iowa. Buffalo can be caught on worms, grubs, crickets, and cut bait, and most are snagged during spring [III]. Some anglers use a long canepole and drag a string of single hooks tied closely together through a school.

Others use a weighted treble hook, snatched vigorously through the water with a stout casting rod.

How to catch bigmouth buffalo: During the spring spawning run, buffalo congregate in riffles [V]. This is when native anglers will be wading and "snatching." If snagging goes against your grain, try drifting a gob of worms into a deep hole at the foot of a riffle. A big buffalo will wear you down.

Sucker *(Catostomus commersoni)*. This is the white sucker found throughout the Great Lakes region and down the Mississippi River valley. These fish make annual upstream spring spawning runs and, as onlookers say, "They're so thick you can almost walk across on their backs."

How to catch white suckers: Because suckers have the turned-down mouth of a bottom feeder, you'll need a weighted bait to reach them [III]. Hike up- or downstream until you see some suckers, then drift a worm or small chunk of fish along the bottom. Suckers don't put up a big scrap, but they're fun on light tackle.

You have no doubt noticed that nothing has been said about edibility. Fishing for these four species is usually for the fun of it and not for the table. They provide action when other species are simply not hitting.

When to Fish

Most fishermen try to arrive at a lake shortly before dawn. If you want to get first crack at the best spots and hit the end of the night's feeding frenzy, get out on the water one to two hours earlier than that—at 4 or 5 AM. You'll get an nour or two of prime nightfishing and the best early morning action before the crowds start to gather.

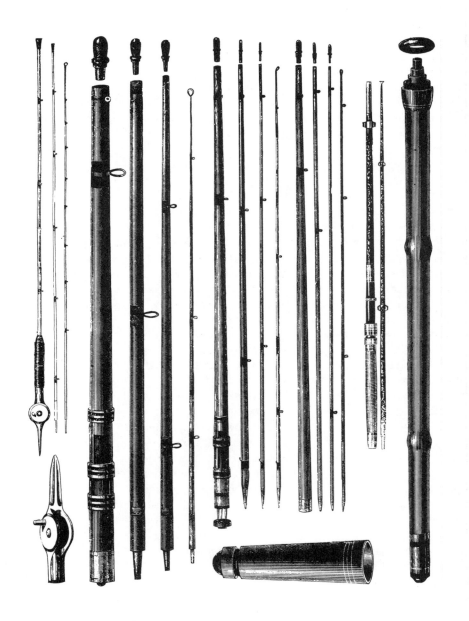

CHAPTER III
GEAR

It's little wonder that so many would-be fishermen get scared away from the sport before they even wet a line. Look through any catalog published by a contemporary outdoor sporting goods retailer, and you'll see page after page of fishing lures, rods, reels, and line. There are all types of fish hooks, bait, knives, and scents. One page advertises stuff guaranteed to make trout flies float on the water; the next page touts stuff guaranteed to make trout flies sink. There's even a selection of special clothes for the fashion-minded angler.

Confusing? You bet. One recent catalog contains nearly 400 color pages of fishing or fishing-related tackle and gear. A total of 96 pages is devoted to lures alone, and by no means is it a comprehensive listing—most of those listed are designed for catching bass!

But for a lure—or rod, reel, or any other type of tackle—to be successful, it must catch the fisherman before it catches the fish. An angler who has a few seasons of experience flipping through fishing catalogs and wandering the aisles of tackleshops soon learns how to discern what's good and what isn't. The "Biotechnic ZX 1000 Super Spectro Daddy Crawler" turns out to be nothing more than a plastic worm shaped and colored a little differently from other plastic worms on the market. Sure, it'll catch fish, but not neces-

sarily any more than that plain old purple plastic worm he used to catch three nice largemouths last Saturday.

This is not to say that the fisherman should forget about modern fishing tackle and revert back to a willow branch, some kite string, a bent pin, and a couple of red worms from the nearest manure pile. Fishing tackle has seen tremendous improvements and innovations over the past few decades, and practically all gear sold now will do a much better job of catching fish than what was around during Grandpa's—or even Pa's—days.

It's well worth the effort to educate yourself about the fishing tackle now available. Don't be put off by the outrageous selection or the cost. Read this chapter first to find out just what type of gear you need for the fishing you'll be doing. That'll narrow the field considerably. For example, if you're planning on fishing mostly for pond bass, with maybe a little bit of stream trout fishing thrown in, you'll do fine with a light- to medium-action spinning rod, a reel with two spools (one to hold light monofilament for trout, the other heavier bass mono), and some line. A small selection of bait, hooks, and lures for each species will round out your gear. You'll be ready to catch fish, and you won't spend a lot of money—or have to take a college course—to do it.

RODS

If you really want a rod that will make you the best caster you can be, go for two: one that casts best with lighter lures and another for heavier lures. It's really simple. Buy two practice casting plugs, 1/4 and 3/8 ounce. Take along your favorite reel filled with 10-pound line and have a snap swivel in your pocket. Look over the rod rack and select at least three rods in each popular action, such as extra-light, light, and medium. Ask the salesperson's permission to take them outside for a bit of testing. By feel—that is, by flexing the tips—line them up from lightest to stiffest. Rig your reel on the lightest and attach the 1/4-ounce practice plug to the snap swivel.

Pick out an imaginary target about 35' away and make at least a dozen casts to it, paying particular attention to smoothness and accuracy. Run the gamut of rod actions and notice how much better the lighter rods feel with the 1/4-ounce plug. Do likewise with the 3/8-ounce plug. You'll note how it tends to overload the lightest-action rod and deliver much better on a stiffer rod. If you find one rod that casts both plug weights quite satis-factorily, buy it for your "one rod." However, if it takes two rods to do your smoothest, most accurate casting, buy both of them.

Timing is the secret of why one rod feels better than another when you cast it with your particular delivery. A rod's timing is determined by the way it is tapered from butt to tip and how that taper delivers a smooth punch to your cast the instant you release the plug. Logic says if you're well muscled and enjoy pounding out fast casts, you probably wouldn't like a lighter-action rod because its timing would be too slow. A firmer tip action would perform better for you. Conversely, if you're of aver-age build and prefer a soft delivery, you wouldn't enjoy a firmer tip at all because you'd have difficulty feeling the lures. A light-action rod with a more responsive tip should fill your needs.

It takes time and patience to ferret out the special rods that bring out the best in your plug-casting accuracy. Once your accuracy picks up, so will your catching, because there are times when a lure drop-ping smack-dab against the target will catch fish while one a foot away will not.

BAITCASTERS

The most versatile, the most reliable, the best rod for general fishing is without question a baitcasting rod. This has never been truer than it is today. In our high-tech world, baitcasting rods have not been bypassed. On the contrary, they've become more refined and efficient. They're stronger than ever, lighter, and more sensitive. More expensive, too, but still reasonable.

With one exception, the best baitcasting rods are made from graphite—really graphite-fiberglass composites. Graphite rods are stiffer and stronger for their weights (compared with fiberglass) and offer a far more delicate sense of feel when you're working a plastic worm or bait. The stronger rods also let you cast farther with less effort and have undeniable advantages when you need hard hook-setting and fish-fighting brawn. Nearly all the best modern graphite rods

have "blank-thru" construction, which means the rod extends into (or in some cases, actually forms) the handle. This makes it easy to feel a lure's action and helps you detect light takes.

The Generalist Rod

Probably the most common casting rod used by experts and pros is a 6' medium-strength, fast-action rod. The 6' length is short enough to be manageable in most boat situations, yet it provides enough whip to make long casts in open water—especially when used with an extended "trigger stick" handle, which allows two-handed casting for extra distance.

Tight conditions where sidearm and underhand casts are necessary may mean scaling down to a 5 1/2' rod. Conversely, long casts in comparatively open water are better served with a longer rod. When pulling crankbaits in deep water, it's wise to move

Rod Action

Strength refers to a rod's power or stiffness; action refers to the way the rod bends. A fast-action rod is one that, when flexed tip-down against a floor—or when held horizontally by the grip, with an assistant pulling down on the tip—bends primarily in the upper third of the rod. An extra-fast tip bends mainly in the upper quarter; a medium action in the upper half; and a slow action bends more or less uniformly from butt to tip. Such a rod will serve well as a general fishing rod. It's strong and stiff enough for sensitive fishing, such as working a worm or jig in heavy cover, yet it has enough flex to cast spinnerbaits, surface plugs, and open-water worm rigs.

Baitcasting Rod Selection Chart

Rod Action	Lure Weight (oz.)	Line Test (lb.)
Extra-light	1/4	8
Light	1/4 to 3/8	10
Medium	3/8 to 5/8	12
Heavy	7/8 and up	14

Balanced Outfits for Baitcasting or Spincasting

Lure Weight (oz.)	Rod Length (ft.)	Rod Action	Line Test (lb.)
1/4	5 1/2 to 6	Extra light	6 to 8
3/8	5 1/2 to 6	Extra light to light	8 to 12
1/2	5 to 6	Light	12 to 15
5/8	5 to 6 1/2	Light to medium	12 to 18
7/8	5 1/2 to 7	Medium to heavy	15 to 30

Flipping and Pitching Rods

Flipping rods are another kind of "casting" rod and are very effective for working heavy cover. Flip casts are generally short—no more than 12' or 15'—and the long 7' to 8' rods allow precise placement at this range. "Pitching" rods are shorter—usually 6 1/2'. These are used much the same as flipping rods, only for longer casts.

to a softer rod with a slower action. Indeed, many pros keep one or two fiberglass rods around just for this purpose. The naturally soft action of glass (compared with graphite) prevents pulling a crankbait away so quickly on the strike that a fish misses it—something that can happen if you rely solely on the stiffer, stronger graphite rods.

Buy with Care

All this can sound complicated to the beginning baitcaster, but the best way to avoid confusion is to buy rods (or rod/reel combos) one at a time, knowing beforehand exactly what kind of fishing you intend to do, then tailoring the rod or outfit precisely to that. As you learn more on the water, you'll know which kind of new rod adaptation to make.

Line Guides

A good working baitcasting rod should have top-quality line guides. Silicon carbide is perhaps the best material—"best" meaning the hardest and smoothest, the least likely to nick or groove, a condition that can lead to line fraying and breakage. Aluminum oxide and Hardloy materials also make excellent, durable guides and are found on many of the better rods.

Rod Handles

The stretch is on in baitcasting rod handles. Squatty pistol grips are giving way to more efficient and more versatile stretch-handle designs. Pistol grips are strictly for one-handed casting. Thus their distance and accuracy are limited, and they don't provide the leverage needed to muscle big fish from heavy cover. They're also more tiring over a long day.

Several features make stretch handles more practical. Instead of the stubby 4" rear pistol-handle grip that was too small for some hands and too big for others, stretch handles have 6" to 10" rear grips with round, tapered contours that fit hands of all sizes. Also, pistol-grip handles have offset reel seats with small foregrips, whereas stretch handles have semi-offset reel seats with ample foregrips to increase leverage.

But the biggest advantage stretch handles offer is two-handed casting. This enables the angler to give more speed to the rod tip with a shorter arc of travel, making it easier to place a lure on target.

Take along a reel and practice plug, rig up a number of rods, and see which feels best when you're casting outside the tackleshop.

What to Look for

When choosing a stretch-handle rod, keep in mind the following criteria:

Cork. If you prefer cork to composition in your rod handle, carefully examine the material: High-tech plastic blends are difficult to distinguish from the real thing. Look for the traditional ring segments and minute blemishes that denote cork.

Graphite. If you prefer graphite, read the literature to determine the percentage being used. It varies from 100 percent in high-quality rods to much less in low-priced rods.

Guide Placement. Check the distance between guides on the tip section above the first, large gathering guide. These should be no more than 6" apart to ensure a proper flow of line during hard casts.

Reel Seats. Beware faulty reel seats. Loose fits can occur if tolerances are allowed to wander. Take your pet reels with you and try them on the rod being considered. Tighten the reel clamp, and if you can still move the reel or pop it off the seat, opt for a positive-locking reel seat.

Action. Rod actions vary with the manufacturer. The best way to determine which is best for your needs is to try each with your own reel and a practice casting plug outside the tackleshop.

SPINNING RODS

Spinning rods come in a variety of lengths, pieces, and actions to fit most any angling situation.

The spinning rod is characterized by a straight handle, or butt, and line guides that decrease in diameter from butt to tip. The design of the spinning rod is dictated by the function of the spinning reel,

Worn Ferrule Remedy

When the ferrules of your favorite two-piece fishing rod become worn and the two sections are always parting company, don't cast the rod aside. Here is an easy and inexpensive solution that will add years of service to the rod: Take a 3" or 4" length of Teflon tape (get it from a hardware store), and place it over the end of the male ferrule. While pulling it taut, mate the two rod sections. Then, using a razor blade, cut off the excess tape where the ferrules interface.

which is attached to the bottom of the spinning rod and releases line in coils when cast. The first guide on the spinning rod must be of large diameter to "catch" the coils as they're shooting off the reel and begin to straighten them, thereby eliminating line-slowing friction. As the line flows up the rod, the graduated guides eventually eliminate the coils completely. When the line reaches the last guide on the rod—the "tip-top"—it flows smooth and perfectly straight toward the target.

A fast-action spinning rod is comparatively stiff, in that only the uppermost section of the rod bends easily when the rod is given a quick shake. Medium-action rods bend a bit farther down the rod, and slow-action rods exhibit a parabolic shape when shaken. Generally, fast-action rods are best used for casting heavy lures; slow actions for light ones.

One-piece spinning rods typically have the smoothest action and delicate feel. Two- and three-piece rods generally sacrifice a bit of this smoothness, but are easier to transport and store.

Ultralight Spinning Rods

Fun is the main appeal of ultralight tackle. There's no question that a 10-ounce crappie, a 2-pound bass, or a 6-pound northern are all at their best when you catch them on ultra-

light tackle [II]. It's also true that there are places and times when featherweight gear will be the most effective spin tackle you can use—for example, in low, clear trout streams, where delicate presentations are essential, and in deep, clear lakes, where a thin line not only proves invisible to the fish but also helps a lure sink quickly to the depths where fish are holding.

Technically, an outfit is "ultralight" if it's capable of casting lures in the 1/20- or 1/16- to 1/4-ounce range, but this definition may be too vague to be helpful. It's easier to break the general notion of ultralight into three specific categories.

The first may be called "heavy" ultralight. This will be a 5' to 5 1/2' graphite rod weighing around 1 1/2 to 1 3/4 ounces, matched with a light reel suited to 4-pound line but able to handle 6-pound test on a replacement spool. Whenever you need enough power to overcome strong currents, large fish, or snags, the heavy ultralight rig is the one to choose.

Next comes "medium" ultralight, and as one might expect, the rod here is ligher, usually around an ounce or slightly less. The matching reel is palm-sized, loaded with 4-pound test.

Most delicate of all is what is called "ultra" ultralight. This category includes the lightest caliber of spinning rods and

Balanced Spinning Outfits

Lure Weight (oz.)	Rod Length (ft.)	Rod Action	Line Test (lb.)
1/16 to 1/4	5 1/2 to 6	Ultralight	4 to 6
1/4 to 3/8	6 to 7	Light	8 to 10
3/8 to 1/2	6 1/2 to 7 1/2	Medium light	12 to 14
1/2 and over	7 to 8	Medium to heavy	14 to 20

the smallest reels available. It is perfect for panfishing in ponds and relatively unobstructed lakes and for trout fishing on small streams and brooks. All such outfits require a bit of finesse to use properly. The delicate rods and lines make technique more important than muscle. Ultralight fishing is not merely a gimmick, as some anglers seem to believe; rather, by its very nature, it offers little margin for error. Lures and fish are easily lost if the rod is mishandled.

Fine lines are delicate and easily frayed, so the ultralight angler must frequently check for nicks and scars in the leading yard or so of line. It also pays to retie knots after hairpinning a few snags or catching a number of fish. It makes sense to tie the strongest knots possible. Use only fresh lines, too, and change the entire spool at least once a season.

What's important are skill and finesse rather than muscle. If you hook a good fish on

ultralight, you need the patience to play it carefully and the skill to give line when necessary. A good drag is helpful here, but on really large fish—those that can easily snap the line with a headshake—it's best to ignore the drag completely and play the fish by backreeling with the antireverse mechanism turned off. This way the fish fights the rod rather than the reel, and the line is never in danger of being stressed past its breaking point.

FLYRODS

How to choose a good flyrod from the many hundreds being designed, advertised, and sold? Let's first define some parameters and a key term or two. Here we're dealing exclusively with graphite rods, because they're really the serious angler's best bet and the beginning angler's best friend. Bamboo rods can be excellent—and beautiful—fishing

Flyrod without Flies

Many fishermen shy away from owning a flyrod because they feel it is a tool for expert fishermen—a delicate wand for placing dry flies on the surface of crystal clear trout streams. Yet you can catch any freshwater fish on a flyrod without flies or flycasting. Its longer length gives a flyrod the edge when it comes to baitfishing for trout in small streams. Trolling, drifting, and still fishing with a flyrod for walleyes is a great way to take these tasty fish. Carp, catfish, suckers, and a variety of other bottom-feeding river roughnecks can also provide many hours of fun for the flyrodder.

Pack Rods

If you travel a great deal, you may prefer a multi-piece rod over a longer and bulkier two-piece model. Advances in construction techniques have made the three- and four-piece rods nearly indistinguishable from the two-piece designs in terms of casting smoothness and efficiency. The smaller rod tubes can be packed in a duffel or carry-on airplane bag, in which they are much less likely to be damaged or lost.

instruments, but they are neither as versatile nor as affordable as their graphite counterparts. On the other end of the scale is fiberglass—that old workhorse material. Because of the great advances in graphite construction, glass is rarely a good choice in a beginner's rod—even for those with limited pocketbooks.

Now about terminology: Perhaps the most frequently used term is "modulus," which is short for "modulus of elasticity," basically a description of a rod's stiffness, its ability to recover from a load (bending). Moduli are measured in pounds of pressure per square inch (psi). For example, Orvis rods have a modulus of elasticity of 32 to 34 million psi, while the stiffer Sage rods rate 40 to 42 million psi. This does not mean that the Sage rods are better; it only shows they are stiffer. Higher-modulus (also known as high-mod) rods can be built thinner and lighter for the same strength values, which translates into quicker loading and unloading—something you can feel in the cast. Higher-modulus rods lack the "soft" or "creamy" feel of the lower-modulus designs, the nice near-bamboo smoothness that some find enjoyable. On the other hand, high-mod rods make it easy to throw fast, tight loops and achieve maximum power and distance. Ultimately the choice becomes one of personal

taste—of finding a rod design that matches your esthetic preference and personal casting stroke and fits the type of fishing you like to do most.

Since a flyrod is the most important component of your equipment, it pays to buy the best rod you can afford. From a quality standpoint, it's hard to go wrong if you stay with such known and trusted names as Sage, Orvis, Scott, Powell, Winston, and Loomis, as well as rods made by smaller, but equally serious, builders—for example, Deerfield. While it's true that rods from these companies are not inexpensive, on the other hand, the prices on some of the no-frills models may not be out of reach.

Now for the rod itself. What size to choose? Traditional wisdom has it that the best all-round piece is an 8 1/2' to 9' matched to a 6-weight line. This is not bad advice, particularly if you fish mid- to large-sized streams and rivers and like to throw weighted nymphs and large flies such as Woolly Buggers and Muddlers or if you fish the big caddis and stonefly hatches of the West. If your fishing preferences run to lighter presentations, the same-length rod in a 5 weight will allow you more delicate deliveries of smaller flies.

If you fish smaller streams exclusively, you might want to lighten the outfit to an 8', 4-weight, for example. Creek fishermen may even choose to go to a tiny 6' rod with 3- or 4-weight line, on which even the smallest brookie or cutthroat is a delight to catch. For those who like all kinds of fishing but do not prefer a single, general rod, another possibility is a conversion model. These rods are made so that separate rod sections are alternately interconnected to make two or three different-weight rods—for instance, an 8 1/2-footer that converts to handle either 3- to 4-weight or 5- to 6-weight lines. This is an excellent combination for small- to mid-sized creeks and streams, made better by fitting into one pack-sized rod case.

Last, always cast a rod before you buy it. It may be the best name, the best construction, the highest modulus, but it may not be for you. Take the rod outside and put some flyline into the air. Listen to your body and the little voice inside your head—not to what your best friend says. Only then do you have the ultimate criterion: If it feels good, buy it!

Featherweight Rods

Featherweight flyrods are not toys. They're practical equipment that can catch fish in the 8" to 16" range. Even the occasional 20" fish can be handled with 1 and 2 weights.

Advantages. The pluses of these rods are easy to see. Their lightness makes arm fatigue a thing of the past. The light, thin lines slice through the air with little resistance and land on the water delicately. With today's heavily pressured trout, such a light presentation can mean the difference between a great and a mediocre day on the water.

Disadvantages. The disadvantages of 1 and 2 weights become clear when anglers try to make them do what they aren't meant to do. These rods aren't designed to double-haul 80' casts across vast, windswept rivers. Most of us, though, would catch more trout if we concentrated on cautiously cutting that distance in half and then casting—no matter what weight rod we're using.

The 1 and 2 weights aren't made to cast heavily weighted nymphs or huge streamers. They will deliver cumbersome offerings at short ranges, but awkwardly and inefficiently. Better to stick with Size 10 or smaller dries, light nymphs, and wets for 2 weights, 14 and smaller for the 1 weight.

Wind can be a problem. The best recourse with 1 and 2 weights is to pick days with light wind.

An alleged disadvantage of 1 and 2 weights is that they can kill fish because they lack the power to let you land them quickly. Anyone who has fished with these rods knows this is not true. They have plenty of power to land fish rapidly.

Travel Tip

Before inserting your rods in a travel case, lay them out on the floor with butts and tips going in opposite directions. Make sure the butts extend beyond the tips and tape all the rods together in this position. You'll eliminate broken tips.

Reels

BAITCASTING REELS

The "conventional," or baitcasting, reel has been
around since the early 1880s,
and it's still in use today. This
longevity alone attests to the
baitcasting reel's reliability and
service to anglers.

As its name implies, the
baitcasting reel's original function was to cast live bait such
as shiners. The baitcasting outfit today still serves this function, although most freshwater
anglers use a baitcaster for
lures such as crankbaits and
spinnerbaits. Although baitcasting reels are available in a
variety of sizes, they're used
mostly by fishermen who are
after the larger gamefish
species: largemouth bass,
northern pike, and muskies.

The main advantage bait-
casting reels have over spinning reels in freshwater fishing
is sensitivity to the movement
of what's at the end of the
line, whether it's a lure, a bait,
or a fish. Other pluses include
strength and casting accuracy.
The baitcasting reel rests on
top of and right against the

rod—not a few inches away
on the bottom of the rod, like
a spinning reel. In addition, the
line goes directly to the spool
on a baitcaster, not around a
ball as on a spinning reel. All
this gives the angler a much
keener sense of what's happening down under, as vibrations are transmitted directly
up the line to his or her hand.

The main feature differenti-
ating baitcasting reels from
spinning reels is the spool. On
a baitcaster, the spool revolves
when the line is cast out or
retrieved, the way a spool of
sewing thread revolves when
line is pulled out of a bobbin.
The experienced baitcasting
angler can place a lure or bait
with the utmost accuracy by
feathering the spool with his
thumb as the lure is on its way
to its intended target. A little
pressure will allow the lure to
continue on its path; a lot will
cause the lure to slow down
quickly.

Knowing exactly when and
how much pressure to apply to
the spool during a cast isn't ter-
ribly easy to master. If you
undercompensate or slow the
cast too late, you'll wind up with
a backlash at the reel, because
the spool is spinning faster than
the speed of the line.

However, almost all current
baitcasting reels incorporate
some type of antibacklash
mechanism. But antibacklash

mechanisms do simplify the use of baitcasting reels and make learning how to cast one much easier than before [IV].

One relatively recent innovation on baitcasting reels is the addition of a "levelwind." This tiny device is mounted on the front of the spool and distributes line evenly along the spool as the handle is cranked. Before this invention, anglers were forced to layer the line evenly onto the spool with a finger or thumb during the retrieve.

The advantages of baitcasting reels are too great to dismiss. A bit of coordination and some time spent practicing casting techniques are all that's necessary to become proficient with them.

SPINNING REELS

Although it's a relative newcomer to the world of sportfishing, the spinning reel is by far the most ubiquitous reel in use on fresh water today by knowledgeable freshwater anglers. From budding fisherman to angling expert, though, the spinning reel does the job and does it well.

Fishermen find that spinning reels enable them to use lures much smaller and lighter than those that could be cast on a conventional outfit. Although a conventional reel is a better choice in many fishing situations (especially where heavy lines and lures are necessary), the spinning reel can't be beat for practicality and versatility.

Casting with a spinning reel is easy to learn and master. The line is wound on a spool, and the weight of the lure cast out spirals the line off the spool. Unlike the spool on a conventional reel, a spinning reel's spool is fixed. The revolving spool of the conventional baitcaster will continue to revolve after the lure has reached the angler's target, and it's necessary to thumb the spool to stop the line from coming off. But on a spinning reel, once the lure stops traveling (hitting the water at the end of the cast's arc, or hitting bottom after sinking), the line stops paying out.

The line is held in place by the bail, a C-shaped mechanism on the outside of the reel. When the reel's crank is turned, the bail revolves around the spool, placing line on the spool. At the same time, gears within the reel move the spool in and out of the spool housing, so the line fills the spool in neat layers.

To make a cast, the angler flips the bail to one side of the reel and holds the free line in the first crook of the index

---

Fill It Up!

Much has been said about the retrieve ratios of high-speed reels. Unfortunately some anglers aren't taking advantage of their speed capability. They aren't filling spinning and casting reels to the recommended line capacity. This means that the spool's diameter is smaller, with smaller revolutions that do not pick up as much line as does a filled spool. Besides hindering the retrieve, a half-filled spool can be less than desirable for long casts. For the openfaced spinning reel, the filled spool is highly recommended. When a spinning reel is only half filled, the cast line hits more of the spool. This slight amount of friction decreases casting distance.

finger on his rod hand. After casting out, the angler can shorten the length of the cast by slowing down the line spiraling off the spool with that same index finger. When the lure reaches the desired area, the angler turns the crank. On most spinning reels, this automatically closes the bail back over the spool, engaging the line. The angler is now ready to begin the retrieve.

SPINCASTING REELS

The successful spincasting outfit, as its name suggests, is a fairly successful attempt at combining the best of spinning and baitcasting tackle. Compared with a baitcasting rig, a spincaster is simple to cast and easy to master. The inherent sturdiness of a spincasting reel also allows the use of heavy line—and therefore heavy tackle—which isn't always possible with a spinning outfit.

Spincasting reels rest on the top of a rod and generally have right-hand cranks, which makes them easy to operate for most people. Line is kept on a spool, enclosed by a cap or cone, and comes through a hole in the top of the cap. Most styles incorporate a but-

ton, located on the top rear of the reel, which the angler depresses with the rod-hand thumb prior to casting. Just before completing the forward arc of the cast, the angler releases the button, which puts the reel into freespool. The lure's inertia then pulls the line along after it.

When the lure reaches the destination, the angler simply turns the reel crank to engage the reel. However, the angler can shorten a cast by depressing the thumb button when the lure reaches a desired area. This also engages the reel and stops the line from flowing.

Such a simple operation makes the spincaster an ideal outfit for children, as well as for adults who have no prior rod-handling experience. However, spincasters do have limitations—deadened feel of line and lure action, difficulty in casting accuracy, poor fish control. Those who become involved in fishing typically graduate to spinning or baitcasting outfits.

FLYREELS

Two schools of thought predominate when it comes to flyreels. One regards the reel as nothing more than a storage device for flyline, since most fish are hooked close to the rod and can be "played" by hand, the fingers gathering and releasing line when needed. The flip side of this logic is that no human can effectively control the vicissitudes of a fighting fish—the runs, surges, and soundings—as optimally as can a quality reel, built to exacting tolerances, with a built-in drag system.

So does the angler spend $20 or $200 on a flyreel? The fly angler will often be in situations where a cheap reel can and will cause him to lose fish. So the answer is somewhere between the two extremes, with the final decision depending on the species sought and conditions encountered.

Most flyreels today are of the exposed-spool type, resembling a squat pepper mill. Some are single-action, meaning that one complete turn of the reel handle will revolve the spool one time. Multipliers will turn the spool twice ("double action") or even three times for every complete turn of the handle. This type of reel is handy for retrieving long lengths of line in a hurry.

Drags on exposed-spool rims come pre-set or adjustable. A major advantage of the exposed spool is the ability to place additional drag on the reel with finger or palm pressure (called "palming" the reel). Such a reel also allows the angler to quickly change lines—from floating to sinking, for example, or from double taper to weight-forward—by buying an extra spool and loading it with another type of line. Spools are removed easily and can be changed in seconds.

"Automatic" reels retrieve line via a spring-loaded mechanism, which the angler engages simply by depressing a lever protruding from the reel. Although they're easy to operate, they're comparitively heavy, have inconsistent drag (no palming is possible on an automatic), and don't offer the ability to play fish directly from the reel.

Fly anglers after panfish and typical stream-sized trout would do fine with a single-action reel with a basic drag system: Casts are usually kept short, and there's small chance that these fish will empty the reel of line. Largemouth, big-river trout, and salmon/steelhead anglers may very well hook a fish that could put their tackle to the ultimate test, so a double-action reel with an adjustable drag suits them.

If in doubt about reel selection, always err on the side of quality. A smooth-running, well-built flyreel will bring you more years of service and, probably, a few more fish, than will a poor one.

Reel Size

It's important to match the size of the flyreel to the size of the rod and line. An oversized reel adds unnecessary weight to the entire outfit and can make casting awkward, even difficult. An undersized flyreel won't hold all the line and backing.

Carrying Cases

The new soft-sided thermal lunch or beverage bags make great flyreel-carrying cases. Desiged to hold a six-pack, these bags are just the right size to stow a combination of reels and spare spools. The padded sides protect the reels, and the pliable material allows easy storage in a gear bag. They are inexpensive (less than $10) and available at most variety stores and can be flattened and stuffed away when not in use.

Line

FISHING LINES: WRONG VS. RIGHT

Line is the vital link between fish and fisherman. It's surprising how many anglers judge a line by asking: "Is it strong enough?" Well, adequate strength is important, but many other factors are of more importance to the overall scheme of fishing.

Balance Line to Lure Weight and Rod Action

Balancing line, lure, and rod is the key to efficiency, accuracy, and pleasurable casting. There is a correlation that, when followed, virtually assures more fish per trip. For instance, suppose most of your pet lures weigh around 1/4 ounce. The heaviest line you normally need is 12-pound test. Anything heavier will retard your casting on a spinning or spincasting reel and have you cussing overruns on a levelwind reel. Further, a heavy line can act as a damper to the action of a lightweight lure and reduce its enticement to fish.

Although we're talking here about line intended for spinning, spincasting, and baitcasting [IV], the assembly of a properly balanced flyrod outfit will illustrate the importance of matching line to rod. There are some situations where you

need to cast a heavier lure an extremely long distance to reach fish of normal size. Here you use a light line—say, 12-pound test—with a 6' shock leader at the end. A 20-pound shock leader will take the pounding of long casts, and the 12-pound running line will attain the distance.

Avoid Bedspring Coils

Beware the line that comes off your reel in coils that look like old-fashioned bedsprings. These have to fight to get through the levelwind on a casting reel, as well as the gathering guide on your rod.

An inferior line, even when new, can have this deficiency. You can check in advance by pulling about 5' from the spool. If it lies in loose coils, it's normal and okay to use. If it lies in tight coils and acts springy when you jiggle it, shun it. However, if your line coils up while fishing and you don't have spare line along, do this: Tie the line to a tree and stretch the heck out of it. This usually tames the coils into submission.

Braided or Monofilament Line?

Monofilament is the most widely used for all-around fishing and is hard to fault. Yet there are those who are con-

Mono Line Care

Monofilament fishing line is not affected by gasoline, oil, insect repellant, suntan lotion, and similar substances that anglers are likely to have onboard. However, two things can cause mono lines to begin deteriorating: prolonged exposure to heat and direct ultraviolet rays from the sun. So never leave rods and reels lying in the bottom of a boat when it is parked in your driveway or moored at a dock. Don't leave them standing on the back porch, sitting on the rear window ledge of your auto, or stored in the trunk of a car—the inside of a car trunk can reach 120°F in summer. The best place to store rods and reels and unused spools of mono line is a cool, dark, dry corner of your basement, in a closet, or in a rod-locker in your boat.

Proper Line Test

Lure Weight (oz.)	Rod Action	Line Test (lb.)
1/4	Light	10-12
3/8	Medium light	12-14
1/2	Medium	14-17
5/8	Medium heavy	17-20
7/8 and up	Heavy	20-30

vinced that braided monofilament or braided Dacron is far superior. Try each, then judge which best suits your needs.

What Color Line?

You've got a bunch to choose from: brown, gray, green, blue, white, clear, yellow, red, and variegations. And if you're a thinking fisherman, you've probably wondered about those bright colors like yellow, gold, and red. Because the colors are fluorescent, they are highly visible above water. Yet the manufacturers assure us that down where the fish are, the lines are invisible.

Stretch or No Stretch?

Fishing line needs some elasticity. For instance, when a big fish wraps around a snag, that fish would pop your line more often if it weren't for the elasticity of the line. When you set the hook forcefully on a big fish close to you, it's easy to snap a 20-pound line if you

overdo it. It would be doubly so if the line had no stretch.

For best results, go for the line with no more than 20 percent elongation, or 4" of stretch in 20" of line.

Trolling Needs

Trolling calls for different line requirements. Because bigger fish hang close to the bottom, you want your lure to get down there. It can't if the line is too heavy. It's a retardant. It puts so much drag on a light lure that the plug can't swim freely or dive properly.

So use the lightest possible line for the fish you're after. The light line cuts through water more efficiently and reduces drag, and the lure gets down where the fish are. If the fish you are fishing for have teeth, use a short wire leader.

Proper Storage

To be strong and effective, monofilament line must be fresh and pliable. Mono's

Line Tips
• *Match the line weight to the lure for optimum action.*
• *For big fish, combine colored line with a clear-blue leader.*
• *Tightly coiled monofilament can be stretched into submission.*
• *A bit of "give" in line acts as a cushion against breakage.*
• *Small-diameter line offers the least resistance in the water.*
• *When fishing worms or jigs, choose line that telegraphs even the slightest touch of a fish.*

Avoid Tangling

When a loop of line forms several layers down on a spinning reel spoon, it must be removed carefully to avoid tangling. Put the forefinger of your rod hand on the lip of the spool and then pull the single strand of monofilament with the other hand. Your forefinger will keep the loop and associated double line from wrapping around the single strand. When the loop has been cleared, let the line run through the fingers of one hand as you crank the reel handle with the other.

Keep Line in Line

Somehow a rubber band is never where you need it when monofilament line, whether on a bulk spool or a reel, starts to do its unwinding trick. Some reels have clips where you can stick the end of the line, but most don't, and bulk spools don't. An easy solution is to drill a 1/8" hole on the lip of the reel or bulk spool. Just run the end of the line through the hole a couple of times and you're free of the unwinding blues.

greatest enemy is solar ultraviolet rays, which eventually make it hard, brittle, and prone to breakage. Never keep your reel in the sun any longer than necessary.

It's a good practice to use a spool of line for one active season and no longer, stripping it off and replacing it with fresh line at the beginning of each new season. Another important note: Old line should never be left in the water or at bankside where it can ensnare geese, shorebirds, and mammals. Do wildlife a flavor: Pick up discarded line and make sure it's disposed of in a proper trash facility or sent to a manufacturer's recycling program such as Berkeley's. (Berkeley Recycling Center, P.O. Box 456, Spirit Lake, IA 51360-0456.)

Solving Line Problems

Line twist, a major bugaboo for beginning anglers, usually results from improper use of tackle. Badly twisted line casts poorly, breaks easily, and is prone to loops and tangles. To avoid twisting the line, fight fish (and snags) with your rod instead of the reel; that is, don't crank against stationary or moving resistance. Instead, pump with the rod to gain slack, then reel it tight and pump again. Line twist also occurs when a revolving lure (especially a spoon) is tied directly to the end of the line, or when a stabler lure is tumbled in swirling

currents. Both problems are easily solved by using a swivel. You can straighten twisted line by removing the lure and trolling the free line behind the boat, or by paying it out downstream and then tightening up, letting the current work out the twists.

Another problem is damaged line—line nicked or frayed from contact with rocks, snags, coarse bottoms, or fish anatomy. It takes only a moment to inspect the line visually and to run your fingers over the surface, feeling for nicks and abrasions. When in doubt, cut back the line and retie your lure. It also pays to inspect your rod's tip-top guide periodically to be sure it is not worn or burred in a way that will damage the line.

Finally, if your spinning reel tends to throw off tangling loops instead of a steady stream of line, chances are you've either overloaded the reel or reeled in line while it was extremely slack. Spinning reels should be filled to within a 1/4" of the rim, no more. When retrieving line, especially line that is slack because of a break-off or heavy wind, keep it taut by feeding it through your thumb and forefinger. This allows the line to layer on the spool evenly and tightly.

FLYLINES

While the quality of flylines has increased dramatically, so

Double Taper (DT)

Level Line (L)

Weight Forward (WF)

Shooting Taper (ST)

has the variety available and, therefore, the complexity of selecting a line for a specific type of fishing.

Do you really need two dozen different tapers, sizes, and sink rates? Complex setups of interchangeable heads and shooting lines? For the average angler, the answer is a definite no. Such a fisherman can usually get by with three or four lines.

Whether you choose to buy two lines or twenty, it's important to select them carefully, in the sizes, shapes, tapers, and floating levels appropriate for the fishing you plan to do.

Tapers

Anglers must understand the basic difference between fly-lines and spinning or baitcasting lines. In flyfishing, the weight of the line itself is cast [IV]; the fly is simply pulled along by the line. This is the opposite of spinning or bait-casting, in which the weight of the lure pulls out the line, and the lighter the line, the farther the lure can go. That's why fly-lines are thick and heavy, while spincast and baitcast lines are

thin and light in comparison.

The flyrod is flexed, or loaded, by the pull of the line's weight during falsecasting. When that energy is released on the final forward power stroke of the cast, the rod sends the line out over the water, carrying the fly behind. Depending on the fly's size and the distance you're casting, different tapers are used. These are designated by letters on the flyline box: L stands for level, DT for double taper, WF for weight forward, ST for shooting taper.

A tapered line provides more efficient energy transmission; the narrowing diameter eases energy out of the line and into the leader at the end of the casting cycle. This allows much more delicate and efficient fly deliveries.

The double-taper line is even and fairly thick in the middle, but tapers down gradually to a finer point on each end.

Weight-forward lines are also known as rocker or torpedo tapers. In most modern lines, weight forwards are identical to double tapers for the 30' closest to the fly. But

Flyline Color

Flylines come in virtually every hue in the rainbow. In most cases, a bright line is not likely to hinder your chances for success. This is particularly true when you're surface fishing and using long leaders. Your line is rarely over the fish; just the leader and fly are. There are also some advantages to using highly visible lines. During periods of low light or when fishing a nymph, bright lines help you control your fly drift better and detect strikes more readily. With sinking-tip lines, you can get the best of both worlds: a light-colored floating section, which helps in line control and detecting strikes, and a dark sinking portion, which is closest to the fish.

Matching Flylines

Today manufacturers mark flyrods with a number designating the exact line weight the rod was designed to cast. Buy a line with the number indicated on the rod, and you should have a well-balanced outfit.

If you don't feel you're getting the potential from your rod, try experimenting with a lighter or heavier line. Generally, for casting small, featherweight flies, a line one weight lower in number might be more effective. For fishing heavy nymphs and streamers, you may do better with a line one step heavier.

Reeling In

Flylines exhibit a frustrating tendency to coil around the tip-top of the rod when being reeled in. You can eliminate this problem by pushing the rod tip underwater as you reel.

they quickly taper down to a thinner running line for the remainder of their length.

For casting heavy, bulky bass bugs, poppers, and saltwater flies, the concept of the weight-forward design is carried even further. These lines—called saltwater, bass bug, or blunt-tip tapers—have heavier front sections and shorter tapers, to further concentrate the weight of the line and help carry the flies to the target.

Shooting tapers are the final major flyline type available. These are specialty lines useful where extreme long-distance casting is required. This flyline setup consists of two parts. The head is designed much like the end of a normal weight-forward line. This is connected to a second thinner segment called the shooting line. The shooting line's extremely fine diameter enhances the angler's ability to make very long casts.

Floating and Sinking Lines

When you're shopping for a flyline, check the letter code on the box to determine if the line is designed to float or sink. The letter F stands for floating; S for sinking; F/S means that the forward or tip section of the line sinks and the remainder floats; and I stands for intermediate- or neutral-density line—one that stays near

the surface or sinks very slowly.

A line designated WF-6-F, for example, means a weight-forward Size 6 line that floats. A WF-6-S is a weight-forward Size 6 line that sinks. A WF-6-F/S is a weight-forward 6 line that has a sinking forward section and a floating mid- and rear section. A WF-6-I designates a weight-forward 6 line with neutral density.

Full-sinking lines are useful for fishing deep in lakes or large rivers, particularly when drifting, trolling, or fishing from an anchored boat where flies are left suspended in the current.

Use sinking tips when you want to get your fly down deep but have most of the line floating where you can detect strikes. These lines are less tiring and troublesome to use when you have lots of casting to do. The floating part lets you keep better track of the drift of the fly, control the line more effectively, and lift the line out of the water more easily for the next cast.

In addition to different lengths of sinking tips, these lines come in sink rates ranging from slow sinking (around 1.25" to 2" per second) to fast, extrafast, and superfast sinking. These latter lines descend at speeds of 3" to 6" per second and are particularly useful for nicking a streamer along a riverbottom for trout and smallmouths or probing a largemouth lake for deep-hanging summer fish.

Flyline Sizes

Type of Angling	Weight
Small-stream trout	1-5
Medium trout streams and rivers	3-6
Large trout waters and steelhead rivers	5-8
Panfish in ponds, lakes, streams	4-7
Pickerel in ponds and rivers	7-9
Smallmouth bass and shad rivers	6-8
Largemouth bass lakes and large rivers	7-10
Northern pike lakes and large rivers	7-10
Salmon rivers	7-9

Line Sizes

Line sizes and tapers were once categorized by a complicated lettering system. Now letters are used to designate the line's taper and whether it sinks or floats. Numbers indicate the weight of a line. The smallest or lightest line is a No. 1; the largest is a No. 15. Lines are given their number rating based on weight, because the weight of the line determines its ability to flex a particular rod.

Here are some guidelines for the proper line weight for various kinds of angling. Depending on the size of fish present, wind, the length of casts required, and the size of flies being used, you may want a line in the upper or lower end of the ranges given.

Which Taper to Use?

Double Taper. Good for fishing small trout streams where casts longer than 30' or 40'

are seldom required [V].

Weight Forward. This is the best bet for virtually all trout, steelhead, salmon, shad, panfish, pickerel, and smallmouth bass fishing unless large poppers are being used.

Bass Bug and Saltwater Tapers. The heavy, short tapers on these weight-forward lines make them ideal for casting large, air-resistant poppers and hair bugs.

Shooting Taper. These lines can be used in a variety of situations, but their fine-diameter shooting line makes them especially useful for casting extremely long distances. Steelhead and salmon fishermen favor them for probing deep, broad rivers.

Care and Storage of Flylines

Modern flylines don't need much care, but they do require occasional attention to prolong the life of your line. For example, avoid casting

Quick-Change Flyline
If you need to store your flyline off the reel, don't cut the backing off too close—leave about 2' attached. Then when you need that line, instead of installing another nail knot to attach the backing to that line,
you need only tie on a blood knot, which is quicker and easier to tie than a nail knot.

without a leader, stepping on the line, pinching it between the frame and spool of your reel, snapping it in the air behind you by starting your forward cast too quickly, and allowing it to make contact with insect repellent, gasoline, and suntan lotions.

The only care necessary to keep your line in top condition is occasional cleaning. You may see a dirty film developing; the flyline may stick in the rod guides and not shoot as well as it should; or if it's a floating line, it may begin to sink. In all these cases a cleaning is in order since algae and microscopic particles of dirt have likely built up on the line. These attract and hold water, reducing the line's buoyancy and shootability.

Flylines require no special care during the off-season. You can remove the line from the reel if you like and store it in larger loops around a wooden peg, but the easiest storage method is simply to leave it on the spool. Be sure not to put the spool in an airtight container while it's still wet, or mildew may develop.

Hooks

POINTS ABOUT HOOKS

Fishhooks are one of the most critical aspects of the tackle system regardless of the species one seeks.

The most important criterion for any hook is its ability to penetrate easily. The lighter the wire, the easier it will push through the skin of the fish and into the jaw.

Some fishermen believe that a huskier sized hook will hold better or that it's not important to match hook size to the task.

If a species has a soft mouth, a larger wire hook will generally open a bigger hole and make it easier for the barb to back out. On the other hand, if you are using heavy gear for heavy fish and want to apply pressure, you must resort to a stouter hook so that it won't straighten. In artificial lures, hook sizes are an important part of the balance.

Hook size and wire diameter are also important considerations for the flyfisherman. Combined with the type and amount of dressing, the hook helps to determine the sink rate of the fly.

Selecting the right hook can be critical when fishing natural bait. In some instances the hook should be buried inside the bait. Several patterns are made for this task, including the tiny, short-shanked hooks tailored for salmon eggs. When live bait is used, wire

Parts of the Hook

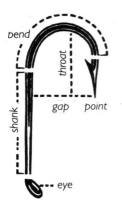

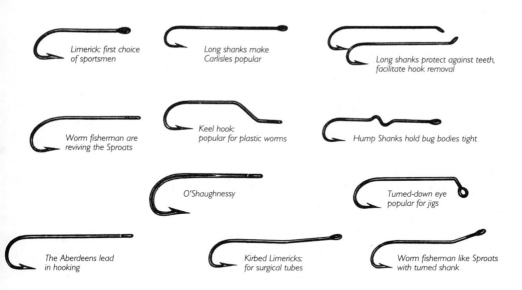

Limerick: first choice of sportsmen

Long shanks make Carlisles popular

Long shanks protect against teeth, facilitate hook removal

Worm fisherman are reviving the Sproats

Keel hook: popular for plastic worms

Hump Shanks hold bug bodies tight

O'Shaughnessy

Turned-down eye popular for jigs

The Aberdeens lead in hooking

Kirbed Limericks: for surgical tubes

Worm fisherman like Sproats with turned shank

diameter and size become critical. Too large a hook deprives a baitfish of its ability to swim effectively. Pick a hook that will present the bait in the most natural manner.

A number system serves as a guide so you can compare hooks within a given pattern. The higher the number, the smaller the hook: Size 16 is smaller than Size 4, for example. When the size reaches 1, the process is reversed and a 0 is added. Thus, a No. 4/0 hook is larger than a No. 1/0, and so on.

Hooks have a normal shank length and wire size. If a hook is designated as long or short, that means it has the shank length of the next hook size larger or smaller. An X following the number indicates it is the same as a hook two sizes away, and 2X shows that there

is a difference of three sizes. Wire size variations are listed as heavy, stout, or strong if the wire is thick, and light, fine, or thin if it is not as heavy.

Draw an imaginary line from the point of the hook to the shank—this is the gap. A perpendicular dropped to the bend of the hook measures the bite, or throat. If a fish has a mouthful of sharp teeth, use a hook with a wider gap that can get around those projections.

Hooks with a deeper bite seem to have more holding power on big fish.

For species such as trout, which many anglers prefer to release, barbless hooks are also helpful. They hook more bass, pike, and other species, too.

Before you buy hooks again, take the time to analyze your needs and then ask for specific patterns and sizes.

Double Hook

Treble Hook

Leaders

Leader Logic

The leader can be a critical factor in catching fish. Yet anglers concern themselves with the rod, reel, and breaking strength of the line—and use a completely inappropriate leader.

Not every situation demands a leader; you can often tie your hook or lure directly to the line. For those who use braided line on casting reels, a monofilament leader should be incorporated at the terminal end.

A leader serves a specific purpose. It may be to protect the line against the teeth or gill plates of a fish. Or you may need an extra length to prevent abrasion. If you are using a sinker, it's a good idea to attach it with mono that has a finer diameter than your line. That way the sinker will break off and you won't lose the whole rig if it gets snagged.

Nylon-coated twisted wire is more flexible than other types, but short lengths of single-strand stainless seem to be less offensive to fish.

When used for protection against sharp teeth or abrasion, a leader should be as short as practical. Shock leaders for casting should be as long as the rod plus enough for the terminal gear to hang

past the tip-top with three to five turns on the reel.

Flyfishermen often let tradition saddle them with handicaps. Gossamer threads help make the presentation look more natural than larger strands, of course. The primary purpose of a leader, however, is to create a separation between flyline and fly.

Remember a leader should be adjusted to conditions. A long leader is much more difficult to cast and handle than a shorter one. When you're fishing a sinking flyline and want your offering to be swept right over the bottom, long leaders will defeat your purpose. The weighted line will hug the gravel, but the leader will float the fly well above it. A short leader of a few feet should keep the fly in the payoff zone. You need to ask whether it is more important to be able to cast a shorter leader on the mark or stray with a longer one.

A fallacy in dry-fly fishing lore is that the leader must turn over and the fly must land at the end of a taut tether. What you really want is the fly to alight on the water with serpentine curves in the leader behind it. This prevents drag and spells trout on a dry fly.

Erasing Leaders

Nothing can ruin the presentation of a perfectly drifting dry fly as quickly as a floating leader. One easy answer to this comes in the form of a double-ended eraser. First, drill a hole in the pencil-erasing end and attach a lanyard to secure it to your vest. Next, with a razor blade, slice a thin notch in the end designed for ink removal. Then simply draw the leader through the notch. This removes both the accumulated scum and the shine. Since it abrades only the finish, there is no noticeable loss in strength. Once you have erased your leader from the trout's vision, it will only have your fly on which to concentrate.

Knots

Knots to Know

First, let's examine the world's worst, weakest knot. It's a simple overhand knot tied in a line—the first part of the bow knot you use to tie shoelaces. This knot will cause line to break at about 50 percent of its given test. Ten-pound test will break at 5 pounds of pull. So never tie a fishing knot with an overhand knot in the main line, especially if the line tests 25 pounds or under. The lighter the line, the more potentially damaging an overhand knot is.

Before looking at specific knots, let's examine some properties of lines from early fishing days until the present. Here are the "breaking loads," measured in pounds per square inch (psi) of line diameter:

The earliest material was braided horsehair, which yielded 20 to 40 psi; later came braided silk at 40 to 60 psi. Nylon emerged in the mid-

1930s at psi levels slightly higher than those of silk, but modern nylons rate 60 to 100 psi. Incidentally, our most advanced lines today pale when compared with a spider's monofilament, which checks out at 200,000-plus psi.

Here are the keys to tying a strong knot of any variety: (1) Tie it slowly, and carefully watch each wrap as you lay it on; (2) tighten it gradually, paying close attention to make certain the strands remain parallel; (3) draw it down tightly so that no slippage can take place when the final knot is stressed.

Today's miraculous nylon monofilament lines are twice as strong as yesteryear's silk and linen lines. Even poorly tied knots will hold ordinary fish. But let's talk about knots that will hold that behemoth you hope to catch. And let's begin with old-time, dependable favorites.

Draw a Knot Tight
If you could look through a microscope as pressure is applied to any knot tied in monofilament line, you would see the knot slip just before it breaks. That's why it is so important to draw a knot tight after you tie it. If it is going to break, it's better that it does so in your hands than with a fish on it.

EYE KNOTS

Eye knots are used for tying line to the eye of the hook, swivel, snap swivel, or a lure. Those below are specially selected from dozens of known eye knots because they can be tied in under 30 seconds and they are strong.

Improved Clinch Knot

The improved clinch knot may well be the knot most favored by American anglers—probably because it is easily tied, even with cold fingers, and consistently holds to about 90 percent of the line test. Here are the steps for tying it.

Step 1. Run line through eye of swivel or hook. Make five turns (some anglers use six) around main line with tag end. Thread standing end through eye loop, then through main loop. Tighten slowly by pulling on main line and swivel.

Step 2. This is how the finished knot should look, with strands lying parallel, not overlapping.

Palomar Knot

Chet Palomar noodled out a durable, facile knot here. Remember to avoid twisting or overlapping the strands as you proceed, making certain they lie parallel.

Step 1. Double about 4" of line and run doubled section through eye of swivel or hook. Use 6" when tying to a lure.

Step 2. Let hook hang free; tie overhand knot in doubled line. Try to keep lines parallel, with no crossovers.

Step 3. Extend loop of doubled line far enough to pass it over hook, swivel, or lure.

Step 4. To tighten, pull in opposite directions on hook and doubled line. Snug tightly.

Duncan Loop

The Duncan loop has been around many years and is similar to the clinch knot except for the doubling of the tag end and main line before making the wraps. It's a strong knot, attaining about 95 percent of the line test, and is easy to tie even when you forget your glasses.

Step 1. Insert line through eye of hook or lure, leaving about 6" of tag end. Parallel the lines for about 3" and make loop with tag end.

Step 2. Wrap tag end 6 times around parallel lines, inside loop. Pull on tag end to tighten turns.

Step 3. Pull main line and hook/swivel/lure in opposite directions, and tighten knot securely.

A PAIR OF PARAGONS

The next two knots are paragons because they are excellent performers. Neither is difficult to tie, but each takes a bit of getting used to before you find the moves easy. Both knots originated with *Sports Afield* magazine through its ongoing efforts to promote the latest in angling how-to.

Brinson Knots

Not only does the Brinson knot prove stronger than the line at least three-quarters of the time, but it is the only knot that remains true to itself. Often it's difficult to tell if other knots have drawn down properly; they may have a concealed crossover to weaken them. Not the Brinson. When this one is tightened, it will break quite easily to let you know it's misbehaving. When it draws down properly, you can both see and feel it pop through itself and lay a neat row of parallel strands. Just try tying it a few times.

Step 1. Pull about 6" of line through eye. Lay about a 3" length of tag end against main line.

Step 2. Make five wraps with tag end around doubled line, wrapping toward eye. Hold wraps with thumb and forefinger while inserting tag end through loop.

Step 3. Pull lightly on tag end to slightly tighten turns. Release tag end, and pull main line and eye in opposite directions. When knot elongates suddenly, you'll know it's a virtually 100 percent knot. If it misfolds, this honest little cuss will break easily to warn you to do it over again, correctly.

Sports Afield Knot

This knot is slightly more involved than the others, but easy once you get the motions worked out. In force-gauge tests, it checks out at 100 percent—meaning the line will break before the knot fails most of the time. Try the Sports Afield knot—it could become your favorite.

Step 1. Feed about 6" of line through eye. Tie half hitch in tag end around main line and snug it tightly, but leave opening between it and eye.

Step 2. Wrap end around main line 6 times and thread it through opening just ahead of eye.

Step 3. Draw down knot by slowly pulling in opposite directions on tag end and main line. Check to see that wraps lie parallel before final tightening.

KNOTS FOR JOINING TWO LINES

Often it's necessary to join line to line, or leader to line. The knot for this purpose needs to be minimal in size, tapered at both ends to flow through rod guides, and passably strong. Here are some good ones.

Joiner Knot

The joiner knot, recommended for lines below 30 pounds, is so versatile it meets a variety of needs. It was originally used by commercial fishermen for suspending dropper lines at right angles to the main line, to reduce tangling.

Step 1. Join ends by tying an overhand knot.

Step 2. Form a loop that stands above knotted ends.

Step 3. Make six foldovers with lapped lines, keeping center loop open.

Step 4. Pull knot through center loop. Pull on each section of main line, and draw knot tight until ends taper.

Step 5. Clip ends close to knot. They will not slip, as a blood knot sometimes does.

Dropper Loop

The dropper loop is superior to the usual figure eight knot because it suspends dropper lines at right angles to the main line to minimize tangling when trying for school fish like yellow perch, crappies, bluegills, smelt, white bass, and catfish.

Step 1. Use same procedure for making six foldovers as in joiner knot. Pull loop through to desired length of dropper.

Step 2. Snug tightly, and loop will stand at right angle to main line, reducing tendency of dropper line to tangle.

Blood Knot

The blood knot is an old favorite of flyfishermen for tying tapered leaders and for joining lines of equal diameter, such as when your fishing line breaks for some reason after you have out 20' or 30' of it. The blood knot is also suitable for joining fresh line to spool backing.

Step 1. Lap ends of both lines about 6". Make five turns with each end, holding open middle loop with thumb and forefinger. Insert tag ends in opposite directions through middle loop.

Step 2. Draw down by pulling alternately on tag ends and main lines, until tightly snugged. Cut off tag ends close to knot.

Surgeon's Knot

The surgeon's knot is better for connecting lines of unequal diameter, like adding a 30-pound shock leader to a 10-pound fishing line when seeking toothy fish or working abrasive cover.

Step 1. Lap leader and line about 6", and tie an overhand knot.

Step 2. Tie a double overhand knot by making another turn through overhand knot.

Step 3. Hold both strands on each side of double overhand, and pull in opposite directions to tighten.

TYING BACKING LINE TO FLYREEL

Slip Knot

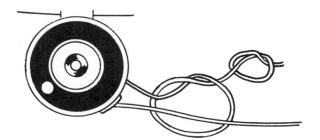

Loop the backing line around the reel arbor, as shown. Tie a simple overhand knot around the lower strand and then tie another overhand knot at the end of the line. Pull on the line, and the knot will slide right up against the arbor. The knot at the end of the line will prevent slippage.

TYING FLYLINE TO BACKING

Nail Knot

This knot was originally tied with a nail, but a simpler method is to use a small tube, such as a basketball air valve needle.

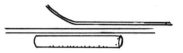

Step 1. Arrange flyline, tube, and backing line, as shown. Allow ample backing line extended for wrapping.

Step 2. Holding three parts firmly, wind backing line around itself, flyline, and tube.

Step 3. Holding turns in place, push end of the backing line through tube.

Step 4. Continue to hold turns as you carefully slide tube out. Slowly draw knot tight. Trim ends close.

TYING LEADER TO FLYLINE

Perfection Loop

Most commercial leaders come with a loop already attached to the butt. If not, or if you decide to make your own, here's how to tie one.

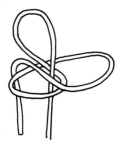

Step 1. Take one turn around monofilament forming upper loop, as shown. Hold at crossing point with thumb and forefinger.

Step 2. Take second turn around crossing point and bring end around once more between turns, forming lower loop.

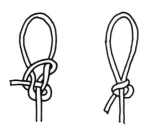

Step 3. Then pass lower loop through upper loop.

Step 4. Pull slowly on lower loop and leader until knot jams.

Jam Knot

The jam knot is a simple and efficient way to tie the leader to your line and can be used for all ordinary fishing conditions with perfect safety. However, if you expect to encounter really big fish, it is best to employ the following method: Tie a heavy mono butt to the flyline with a nail knot. Tie the other end of the butt to the leader with a blood knot and coat with Pliobond.

Step 1. Tie an ordinary overhand knot at the end of the flyline. Thread this under the leader loop, over one strand and across and under both strands, over the other strand, across the line and under the loop.

Step 2. Draw the knot up tight until the overhand knot at the end of the line is jammed against the loop.

TYING THE FLY TO THE LEADER

Double Turle Knot

Although this knot has about 8 percent less breaking strength than the improved clinch knot, it is preferable for attaching a trout fly because it holds the fly straight, makes it ride more naturally, and improves hooking.

Step 1. Thread the leader tippet through the hook eye, as shown, and slide the fly up the leader.

Step 2. Turn back the end of the tippet and make an ordinary slip knot, but bring the end around twice instead of once before sticking the end through both turns.

Step 3. Draw the knot tight and push the fly through the resulting loop. Tighten the knot again until it slips up snug behind the eye, and the loop will slip up securely over the head of the fly.

HOW TO FISH TWO OR MORE FLYS

Old-time wet-fly anglers often fished two or three flies at once, but then this practice fell out of favor. Now, however, multiple wet-fly fishing seems to be undergoing a slight revival; you might want to try it. The way to attach additional flies is by tying one or two lengths of monofilament (known as droppers) to the leader with a dropper loop knot (see page 101).

To attach the droppers, tie a perfection loop (see pages 103–104) at the end of a length of monofilament. Pass this loop through the dropper loop, thread the end of the monofilament through the perfection loop, and pull tight. Tie a fly to the end of the monofilament.

Blood Knot Extension

This is an even better way to tie a dropper to a leader. It is tied the same way as a blood knot (see page 102).

When making your own leader, you can form the dropper by allowing an overlap of about 8" when you start to tie the knot. When the knot is tightened, you will have an extension to which you can tie an additional fly.

ATTACHING A SHOCK TIPPET TO THE LEADER

When flycasting for fish with sharp teeth or razor-edged gill covers, tie 6" to 12" of heavy monofilament (30-pound test or more) to the end of the leader. The approved method of attaching a shock tippet is with the Albright special knot. It is also an excellent and easily tied knot for joining flyline to backing.

Albright Special Knot

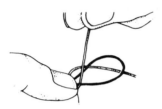

Step 1. Make a U-loop in the heavy monofilament and lay the end of the leader alongside. Allow enough leader to extend for wrapping.

Step 2. Hold in place with the thumb and forefinger of your left hand. Wrap about a dozen turns of the leader around itself and the loop. Hold the turns in place and push the end of the leader through the loop.

Step 3. Tighten the knot slowly by pulling the shock tippet and leader. Trim the ends.

TIPS FOR KNOT TYING

A generations-old knot-tying practice of fishermen: spitting on the knot before drawing it down. They say it makes the knot stronger. Does it?

No, it actually weakens the tie by about 5 percent. But doesn't the spit lubricate a knot, enabling it to be drawn down tighter, thus minimizing slipping? No, this is also a misconception. Just remember the most important factors when knot tying are the skill and care you exercise. Take the time to practice tying the knots of your choice, the ones you trust to bring back that catch of a lifetime. Practice until you know the look of a knot that has the strands in order. Then, when a knot does break, you'll know it was an internal foldover impossible to detect—or a faulty piece of line.

FISHING LURES

SOUND PATTERNS

The sound patterns of lures can be measured in two ways, with a few exceptions. One is beats per second. You can feel these all the way to your rod handle, though it's stronger with some lures than with others. And you can increase or decrease the beat by varying the speed of your retrieve.

The other measurement is the vibration frequency per second. Varying the speed of retrieve will not change this; it remains constant once the lure begins its normal action.

An example of this would be striking a key on a piano. The key of C vibrates at a set frequency. If you strike it 1 or 10 times a second, it vibrates at the same frequency.

Thus a small version of a large lure may appear to be swimming with a much faster wiggle than its larger counterpart. While the frequency rate is identical, the smaller lure has a greater repetition rate (more beats) than the larger lure. Both can have identical frequencies and still appear to move quite differently through the water.

Special Lures
No one can explain it, but certain lures contain some kind of releaser that triggers a response from fish. Even though a duplicate fly or lure looks identical to your eye, it may not have the same effect on fish. When you discover an artificial that produces, treasure it and guard it carefully.

Plugs

"Plug" is actually a general term for fishing lure that imitates a baitfish, crustacean, amphibian, reptile, or small mammal that fish eat. Originally fashioned from wood, plugs now are made of hard or soft plastics and are shaped and colored to resemble a particular forage type. Most all plugs are designed to wiggle, dart, dive, gurgle, or vibrate to attract fish, and each type of plug is made to fish a specific section or column of water. The various names for plugs—floater-divers, crankbaits, poppers, jerkbaits—imply their respective functions.

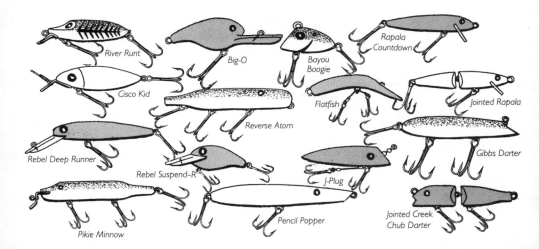

River Runt
Big-O
Bayou Boogie
Rapala Countdown
Cisco Kid
Flatfish
Jointed Rapala
Reverse Atom
Rebel Deep Runner
Rebel Suspend-R
J-Plug
Gibbs Darter
Pencil Popper
Jointed Creek Chub Darter
Pikie Minnow

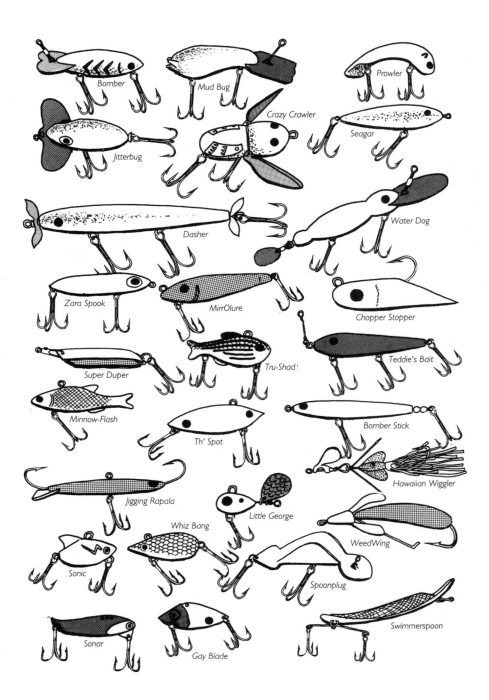

Bomber

Mud Bug

Prowler

Crazy Crawler

Jitterbug

Seagar

Dasher

Water Dog

Zara Spook

MirrOlure

Chopper Stopper

Super Duper

Tru-Shad

Teddie's Bait

Minnow-Flash

Th' Spot

Bomber Stick

Jigging Rapala

Little George

Hawaiian Wiggler

Whiz Bang

WeedWing

Sonic

Spoonplug

Sonar

Gay Blade

Swimmerspoon

Spoons and Jigs

Both spoons and jigs are made of metal and are made to imitate baitfish, but their similarities end there. Spoons look just like their eating-implement namesakes, though there are variations, and their shape imparts an enticing wiggling or spiraling action when retrieved. Spoons can be be fished at any depth, although their weight allows them to be fished at or near the bottom. Jigs, or leadheads, are also made to be fished deeply, often straight down from the side of a boat or bounced along the bottom. Unlike most other lures, jigs have no inherent action when retrieved. The angler must impart motion by jerking the rod tip up and letting the jig fall (called "jiggling"). Unadorned jigs will catch fish, although many anglers dress them up with skirts, rinds, or bait for added attraction.

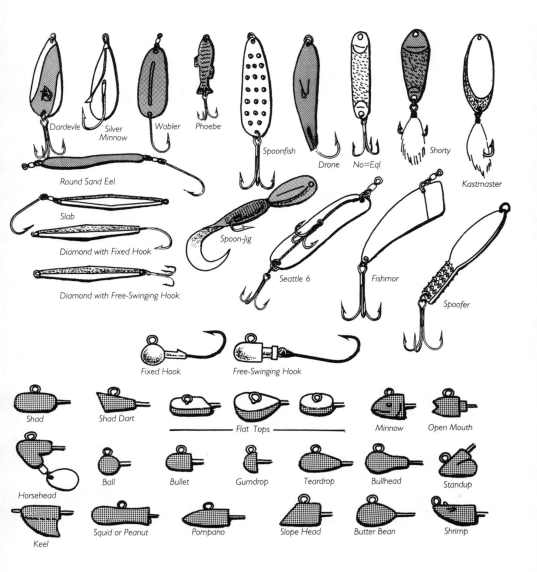

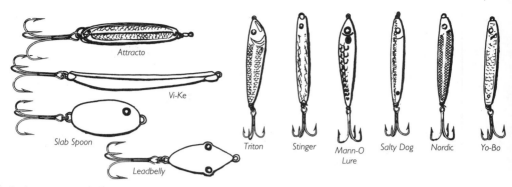

Spinners and Spinnerbaits

The spinner lure consists of a metal blade, shaped as anything from a teardrop to a willow leaf, that revolves around a wire or lead-bodied shaft when retrieved. The resulting flash and vibration simulate the motions of an alarmed or fleeing baitfish. Different shapes of blades spin at various speeds and positions. The spinnerbait, which resembles an opened hairpin, also employs a spinning blade, usually on the top arm of its Y-shape. The bottom arm has a leadhead jig or some other weighted attractor attached to it. This combination results in much flash and commotion when retrieved.

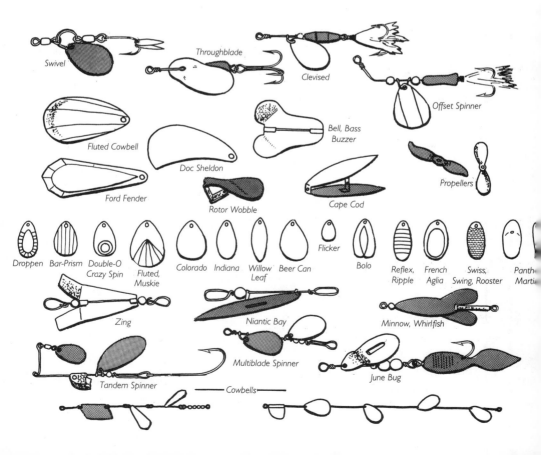

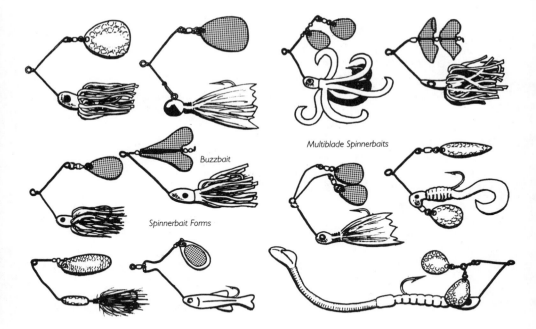

Multiblade Spinnerbaits

Buzzbait

Spinnerbait Forms

Plastic Baits

This family of lures imitates dozens of creatures, but the most popular and successful member is the plastic worm. Many anglers believe it to be the best overall lure for large-mouth bass, when slithered across the bottom and through the weeds. Varieties abound, from small red-worm imitations to foot-long paddle-tailed worms that look like snakes. Another popular plastic lure is the twist-tailed grub, which is usually attached to a jig and either bounced across the bottom or retrieved steadily. Other varieties include replicas of frogs, lizards, baitfish, crayfish, hellgrammites, and many more fish-forage favorites.

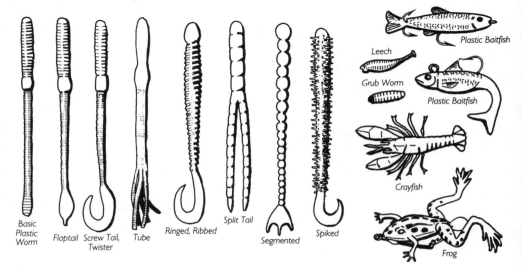

Basic Plastic Worm

Flaptail

Screw Tail, Twister

Tube

Ringed, Ribbed

Split Tail

Segmented

Spiked

Leech

Grub Worm

Plastic Baitfish

Plastic Baitfish

Crayfish

Frog

PLASTIC WORMS

There are many ways to fish the best-of-all bass lures— the plastic worm. Methods range from canny to crazy, but each can be the key to a bonanza day. The best way to turn that key is to try each tactic for at least a half hour, or use the one that best fits the type of cover you are probing.

The choices and variations of worm colors are endless, but a logical assortment would emphasize the six best-sellers among worm-wise bass anglers across America. Those colors are, in order of usage: purple, blue, black, brown, motor oil, and (a recent addition) pumpkinseed.

As far as sizes are concerned, 4", 6", and 12" are best. Always begin with the 6", and if the bass don't respond, switch to the 4". When the bass are really turned on and the strikes come often, think "big bass" and use the 12" monster worm.

Hook sizes should conform to worm lengths—2/0 for the 4", 3/0 for the 6", 5/0 for the 12". In slide sinkers, take along weights of 1/8, 1/4, 3/8, 1/2, and 1 ounce. Use the one that casts well but makes the worm sink as slowly as possible—unless you are fishing in really deep water, which calls for a 1-ounce sinker.

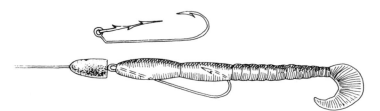

Slinky Lures
Topwater lures such as the Jitterbug offer the most exciting night fishing for bass. But when these noisy surface plugs don't produce, try a plastic worm fished across points and near logjams and docks along shore. Bass can pick up the movement of these slinky lures even on the blackest nights.

Top 10 Worm Rigs

Common sense has it that offering bass a variety of worm riggings is a good approach. Here are 10 ways to rig plastic worms that you can try when your usual rig fails.

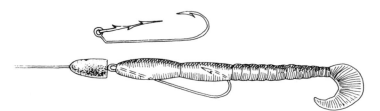

Texas Rig. The most popular in the nation, it can be fished in all types of cover and gets snagged the least. Two styles of hooks have their merits. Use a 1/8-ounce sinker with 3" worms and a 3/8-ounce sinker with 6" worms. Be sure that the body hangs in a straight line, or it will twist your line and foul up casting.

When fishing in timber or heavy brush, you should peg the sliding sinker against the hook eye with the top of a wooden toothpick. This minimizes hangups and allows you to feel gentle pickups.

Carolina Rig. When you're fishing on weedy bottoms, the Texas rig buries the worm in cover out of a bass's sight. The Carolina rig suspends a floating worm above weedy cover, while the sinker kicks up debris to get bass's attention.

Some pros use an extra-heavy, 1-ounce sinker to reach bottom faster when bass are in deep water. How do you set the hook against such sinker weight? You don't. Just begin reeling rapidly, and some, but not all, bass will hook themselves against the line tension.

Jig Rig. One of the oldest rigs, this one is especially effective when bass are holding close to shore cover over clear or rocky bottoms. It's also ideal for vertical jigging or bottom bumping while trolling with the wind. Use a 1/8-ounce jig head on 3" worms and a 1/4-ounce jig head on 6" worms.

Leaded Weedless Rig. This one has several merits. Bass see mostly worm because the lead is on the shank of the hook and buried inside the worm's body. This internal weight makes it easier to cast, especially into a breeze. The weedguard fends off snaggy cover, and the rig's compactness makes it easier for a bass to suck in.

Tandem Hook Rig. There are frustrating moments in worm fishing when you miss one bass after another. Usually these are smaller bass that strike fast and short, missing the hook. The tandem hook outsmarts these fish with its rear-end positioning. Should the barb be extra high on the forward hook, use pliers to bend it slightly until it pops through the eye of the tandem hook.

Weedless Surface Rig. If you know where a cagey whopper bass lives, try this. Rig a 12" plastic worm on a 5/0 long-shank hook. No sinker is needed, because a worm this size has enough weight for casting. Just crawl it over all types of shore cover. Don't be in a hurry to set the hook. Wait three seconds longer than usual to give bass time to swallow the entire worm. And just for the heck of it, set the hook twice against a taut line.

Gyrating Rig. This one takes some patience. Attach a barrel swivel about 1' above the hook and mount the sliding sinker above the swivel. Affix the worm, with a sharp bend in the body, which makes it gyrate, or whirl. No tricky stuff needed; just cast out, give it time to sink, then reel it in very slowly. You can vary the bend to get wide or narrow gyrations.

Slider Rig. This one can be deadly. Pioneered by master angler Charley Brewer, these flat jig heads make the worm descend slowly and slide off to one side or the other, planning its way downward. Charley says that the less you do with it, the more bass it will catch. Just keep casting it out, let it settle slowly, then creep it back to your rod tip.

Spinner Rig. Any thinking fisherman has several Mepps spinners in his tacklebox. Replace the treble hook with a 3/0 single and rig weedless. Use a No. 3 spinner for deeper fishing or a No. 5 and hurry it just under the surface.

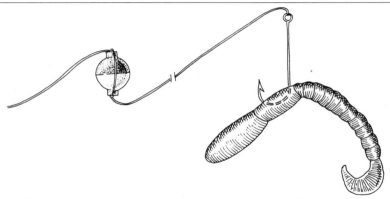

Droopy Rig. This one may look funny, but just try it now and then when nothing else works. Hook the worm through the egg sac once—no weight needed—and add a 1" bobber a couple of feet above the worm. Lob it into pockets and weed rifts, adjusting the bobber for various depths. Let the droopy worm settle, then minutely twitch it at 30-second intervals. It takes patience—and occasionally a big bass.

Choosing Worm Colors

One of the challenges of bass fishing is to find the lure color that works best in a particular situation. This question is especially thorny when using the plastic worm, because there are so many combinations. Here's how to find the right color.

First, it helps to get a feel for the visibility of the water you plan to fish. Tie on a white or bright-colored worm and reel it tightly against your rod tip. Push the worm downward and note at what point it fades from sight. Take two readings, one in sunlit water and the other in shaded water.

Suppose the worm disappears at 2' in shaded water and 6' in sunlit water. (It pays to recheck visibility as the sun's brightness changes.) In 2' visibility water, use brighter, more light-reflective combinations such as a white or blond body with a fluorescent red tail or light blue with metallic flecks. In water with 6' visibility, try quieter colors such as motor oil, pumpkinseed, brown, black, or green.

In dingier waters, it pays to offer a larger worm—9" to 12"—because of its greater visibility. In very clear water, 3" and 6" sizes usually produce much better.

Remember that in shaded or low-visibility water, bass rely on sonar sense rather than sight to first detect the presence of a plastic worm. So the slower the worm sinks, the more time a bass has to home in on it.

Rigging a slow-sinking worm requires slip-sinkers in the 1/8- to 1/16-ounce range and line in the 10- to 15-pound-test range.

Rejuvenating
Plastic Worms
Tom Mann, nationally known lure maker, advised a fisherman who inquired about what to do with faded plastic worms: "Set them where the sunlight can reach each one and the color usually returns." The fisherman wrote back: "We don't have much sunlight in the winter so I put them near the heat duct and at least three-fourths of them look as good as new."

Speed Retrieve for Worms

There is little doubt that slow is the best way to fish the plastic worm— most of the time. But at certain times fast is better. In the hot summer months, when bass appetites rise, they're through with spring roaming rituals and in predictable hangouts. Try retrieving a plastic worm as most fishermen do a crankbait, at about three turns of the reel handle per second. It may sound crazy, but it works.

Another time to try quick retrieval is when you run into overly clear water and visibility is 10' or more. In this situation, bass can see all too clearly the usual slow retrieval of a plastic worm. But when a worm alights and moves quickly away, it can trigger impulse strikes.

There are two ways to "hot-rod" a worm. One is to use a 1/2-ounce slip-sinker to keep the worm down as you hurry it along over the bottom. The other is to use a 12" curly-tail worm with no weight and retrieve it fast enough to make the tail churn the surface like a buzzbait. Either way, don't stop cranking once you begin the retrieve.

Nailing Worms

Here's an entirely different approach for finessing a plastic worm. It may take a while to develop the timing and feel

this technique demands.

First, acquire about a half-dozen each of three sizes of nails, say, from 5- to 20-pennyweight. Cut off the heads and size the pieces from 1" to 2". Rig a plastic worm weedless but without the usual slide-sinker or jig head—the nail pieces will provide casting weight. (The size/weight needed depends on the worm you're using.)

Insert a nail into the fat segment behind the worm head. Use only enough nail to cause the worm to sink slowly and naturally, just a shade over neutral buoyancy. This rig eliminates the disjointed feel and fast plunge of the slip-sinker rig or the heavy-headed feel of a jig head.

Cast next to cover bordering deepening water and let the worm settle slowly to the bottom. This slow drift makes it very tempting and easy for a bass to inhale.

PORKRIND

In the early 1930s commercially made pork lures appeared on the scene. They were preserved in salt brine. These early lures were smelly, the lids of the cans they were preserved in rusted shut, and they eventually spoiled. Today's pork lures are packed in various solutions of formaldehyde, making them more pleasant to handle and longer-lasting. They come in a wide variety of

Experiment

It pays to experiment in clear water to see what motions bring out each artificial lure's best action. Try various speeds of retrieve, twitching sharply, pulling with long sweeps of the rod and stop-and-go actions, to see which brings out a lure's most seductive movement. Then incorporate these findings in your fishing technique as you cast to likely cover. Don't just toss your lures out and immediately crank them in.

shapes and sizes for seemingly endless applications by imaginative fishermen.

There are straight strips, ripple strips, and split-tail strips, all with no hog fat on them. The ones with fat attached are eels in various lengths (single or split) and frog bodies in several sizes. The best-selling colors are, in order, black, green frog, and orange-brown.

All these porkrinds are designed to give extra allure to spinners, spoons, plugs, jigs, and metal wobblers made especially for fishing pork. However, to increase your odds of success, you should use the combination and method that are bringing in the most fish nationwide.

First, you need a lead-head jig. These come in a wide variety of weights, shapes, and colors. To give them bulk and a fishy shape, bodies are added. These can be composed of hair, feathers, synthetic yarn, and skirts made of plastic or rubber. Some prefer a black jig and black hair body, with a tuft of black nylon bristles forming a weedguard in front of the hook. Attach a pork-black frog to the hook. You can fish it anywhere, and get it back most of the time.

Use a jig that weighs 3/8 ounce because it casts well, even into a breeze, and has enough resistance to allow you to feel it over bottom cover. The fat in the frog body adds buoyancy and slows

down the lure's descent. It also gives the lure a lifelike softness that possibly makes fish hold on to it longer. This gives a fisherman more time to set the hook than he would have with a hard lure.

How does one fish a porkrind rig? It's weedless, so you can cast it onto any kind of shore or bottom cover and work it through without snagging about 90 percent of the time. Anyone can fish this lure and catch fish on it. Just cast it out, and let it sink until a slack line indicates it is on the bottom.

Reel the slack out of the line and hop the lure off the bottom with a slight upward nudge of the rod tip. Keep it coming at a slow, steady pace, reeling and undulating your rod tip slightly. This gives the lure a natural, unhurried swimming action; it's as simple as that. A pickup is rarely a sharp tug; it's more like a slight heaviness on your line. When that occurs, set the hook—fast and hard. The more hours you devote to "jiggin' and piggin'," the keener your senses become.

Any type of fishing rig will work satisfactorily with porkrind, be it baitcasting, spincasting, or spinfishing [IV]. Even a canepole will do if the line will reach bottom. However, in shallow, clear waters, lighter lines and smaller jig-frog combinations are used.

Top Offering

A top offering for early season walleyes is a 1/16- or 1/4-ounce jig tipped with either a live minnow or ripple porkrind. Work this combination slowly over the bottom, trying both crawling and hopping retrieves. Don't expect savage strikes— just a slightly different feel to the lure or weight on the line.

SCENTS

Adding a fish-attracting scent to your bait or lure will sometimes increase the odds of catching fish. Scented offerings don't work magic for the fisherman—they won't make up for a lack of fishing skill, improper equipment, or a scarcity of fish—but in some cases they will outfish scentless baits.

A variety of scents are sold commercially and come in different forms: pastes, spray mists, liquids, and sponge- or dough-like substances that are fished as bait itself. Some lures, such as plastic worms, are available prescented.

It's important to match the scent with the species of fish you're after, so read the product label before buying.

How to Apply Scent

Some anglers put fish scent on each of their lures just before fishing them. It's much easier to put a handful of lures into a sealable plastic bag, pour in some scent, and close the bag. This ensures even distribution of scent on all the lures and saves time when changing them. This system works best with soft lures such as plastic worms and twist-tail type jig trailers, although crankbaits and spinnerbaits can also be prepared via this method. Porkrinds and similar trailers come in jars, so it's a simple matter to drain the brine and fill with scent.

The tube lure, a popular offering for bass, seems practically custom-made for using fish scent. Simply jam a small wad of cotton into the rigged tube lure and drip scent onto it. When the tube lure is fished, the saturated cotton will slowly disperse scent into the surrounding water, and it'll last cast after cast. Use a piece of foam instead of cotton, and the tube lure, if rigged Carolina style, will rise off the bottom, emitting an attractive odor.

Smaller tube lures, typically used for crappies, can be filled with dough or paste scent and fished on the bottom for catfish.

Types of Scents

Scents based on aroma simply smell like something good to eat (to the fish, not the fisherman). The ingredients may consist of fish, blood, garlic, or even anise. Most aromatic scents are used for catfish or trout.

The key ingredient in other scents is an amino acid. Inosine, exuded by fish, is known to stimulate feeding.

Scents called pheromones are given off by animals and bring about many different reactions, such as sexual impulses. Pheromones are also used in some fish scents.

If nothing else, using scents will reduce or eliminate foreign odors—perspiration, gasoline, undesirable food smells—on the bait or lure, which could inhibit a fish from striking.

Stink Lures

Commercial salmon fishermen on the Oregon coast sometimes use a trick to catch fish that may have application for the sportfisherman. To mask the human scent on artificial baits, and to attract fish, a special scent is applied to lures. Spoons, plugs, and other lures are dipped in the mixture before being placed in the water. The ring of grease which forms on the inside of the container holding the mixture is rubbed into streamer flies. To prepare the scent, pour 3 cups of rock salt into a quart of water and stir thoroughly. Next, mash 8 or 10 herring and mix them in the solution. Add two 13-ounce cans of condensed milk and mix it with the other ingredients. The solution is then ready to use, and it will keep well without refrigeration.

FLIES FOR FLYFISHING

Flyfishermen love hatches. A good angler can pick up the occasional fish throughout the day, but the hatch is when the really hot fishing takes place. Now the large trout finally come to the surface to feed, moving up from the bottom to slurp away at the tidbits floating overhead. Imitate that insect—from proper presentation to drag-free float—and you stand a good chance of catching that fish.

Flyfishing is a scientific art, shared by entomologist and romantic alike. Go astream and spend some of your time concentrating on your mark, gleaning information from the insect hatches that will help you succeed in your quest. The trout is a predator—not just of mayflies, but of caddisflies, terrestrials, stoneflies, and other fish.

The next time you're out fishing, take a few moments to observe one of the objects of the trout's predation—the adult mayfly. This fascinating insect is a prime item on the trout's menu and a beautiful creation, with no two exactly alike.

The adult mayfly actually lives a very short life—often no more than a day or two. Most of its life is spent underwater as a nymph. It all begins when eggs are deposited in the stream. In some species (there are over 600 in North America), the female drops down to the surface and forces the eggs from her body. Other females crawl into the stream and lay their eggs on a rock on the bottom. In most species, the eggs hatch after a month and the newly hatched nymphs disperse to a preferred part of the stream. They go through a succession of molts, throwing off their outside skeletons as they outgrow them. When they near maturity, some species migrate to parts of the stream preferred for emergence.

Emergence differs among species, but in most the nymph either floats or swims to the surface, where it struggles to shuck its husk. After it transforms into the first winged stage—called a *dun*—it flies slowly and steadily to vegetation on the bank. There it rests overnight and readies itself for its transformation into a second winged stage, called the *spinner*. For most species, the next day is the most critical in its life. On this day the females fly into great swarms of males, mate, and lay the eggs soon afterward. Neither the male nor the female of most species feeds as an adult, since that stage of life is totally dedicated to procreation. The males in the swarms soon exhaust themselves and join the egg-laying females in death on the water's surface.

Try Terrestrials
Usually any number of terrestrial fly patterns will catch trout during summer. However, check the shoreline or skim the water with a net to see if any one variety of land insect (ants, beetles, crickets, or grasshoppers) is most abundant. If one is prevalent, tie an imitation of it to your tippet.

Dry Flies

Dry flies imitate a number of insects that, as their name implies, float on the water's surface. Most of these flies simulate two stages of an insect's life: the adult fly, which rises to the surface and dries its wings before mating, and the spent fly, which has completed mating and drops back onto the water, its short life over.

To enhance their floatability, dry flies are tied with buoyant materials on lightweight hooks. Many species of fish, especially trout, feed selectively on the insects hatching at a given moment, and the angler must "match the hatch" by using a fly that duplicates the size, shape, and color of that particular insect. Myriad fly patterns exist to help the angler do just that.

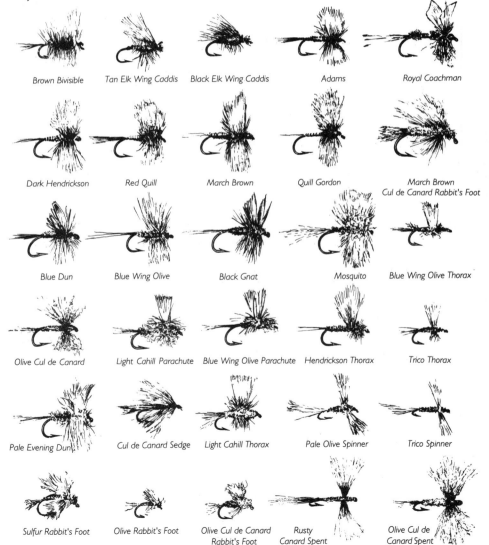

Brown Bivisible   Tan Elk Wing Caddis   Black Elk Wing Caddis   Adams   Royal Coachman

Dark Hendrickson   Red Quill   March Brown   Quill Gordon   March Brown Cul de Canard Rabbit's Foot

Blue Dun   Blue Wing Olive   Black Gnat   Mosquito   Blue Wing Olive Thorax

Olive Cul de Canard   Light Cahill Parachute   Blue Wing Olive Parachute   Hendrickson Thorax   Trico Thorax

Pale Evening Dun   Cul de Canard Sedge   Light Cahill Thorax   Pale Olive Spinner   Trico Spinner

Sulfur Rabbit's Foot   Olive Rabbit's Foot   Olive Cul de Canard Rabbit's Foot   Rusty Canard Spent   Olive Cul de Canard Spent

Wet Flies

The wet fly is more than just a submerged version of the dry fly. Although fish may strike at a wet fly for its resemblance to a drowned insect, the wet may also imitate the larval stage of a fly, an egg-laying female fly, or even a small minnow. Some patterns of wet flies are flexible enough to imitate more than one of these forms during the same cast: drifted, the wet resembles an insect drifting in the current; retrieved, a small minnow darting upstream. Wet flies must sink, so they're tied with materials that absorb water readily. Some anglers fish up to three wet flies at a time, spacing them along the leader on short "dropper" lines.

Some wet-fly patterns exactly resemble certain insect species. Other wets, usually colorful, imitate nothing in particular and are meant to attract fish that aren't actively feeding upon one type of insect.

Hendrickson Wet

Quill Gordon Wet

March Brown Wet

Olive Emergent Caddis Pupa

Tan Emergent Caddis Pupa

Hare's Ear Wet

Royal Coachman Wet

Black Gnat Wet

Zug Bug

Brown Woolly Worm

Streamers

Although technically a "fly," a streamer actually imitates a small fish. The largest of flies, streamers are usually tied on long-shanked hooks to lend the streamlined appearance of a baitfish. A few streamer patterns imitate certain baitfish species, but most of them don't resemble anything at all in nature. These streamers are constructed of brightly colored, even gaudy material, because they serve to attract fish out of curiosity.

Some streamers are constructed of feathers, others of deer hair (or a combination of both). The latter are often called "bucktails" but are streamers nonetheless.

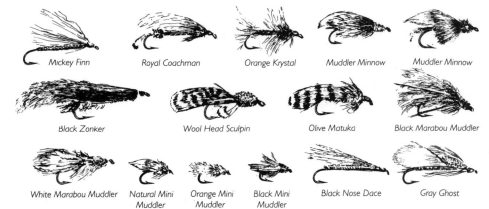

Mickey Finn   Royal Coachman   Orange Krystal   Muddler Minnow   Muddler Minnow

Black Zonker   Wool Head Sculpin   Olive Matuka   Black Marabou Muddler

White Marabou Muddler   Natural Mini Muddler   Orange Mini Muddler   Black Mini Muddler   Black Nose Dace   Gray Ghost

Nymphs

The nymph imitates the larval stage of an insect that lives at the bottom of a stream or lake before emerging as a winged adult. Many fish feed constantly on nymphs, and they make up a large portion of some species' diets, especially trout. This feeding becomes more pronounced when the nymphs become active, such as immediately before hatching into adults.

Nymph patterns must closely resemble the real thing, although exacting, precise imitations aren't always necessary. (Some nymph fishermen swear that a well-worn nymph produces more fish than a brand-new one.)

Because nymphs must sink quickly to the bottom, they're tied on heavy hooks. Extra weight, in the form of lead wire wrapped around the shank of the hook, is occasionally tied on before other materials are added.

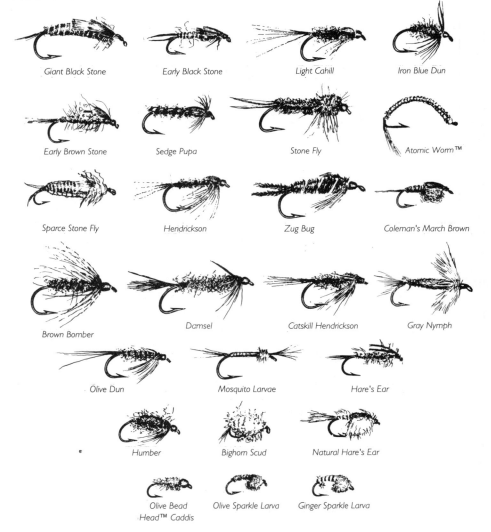

Giant Black Stone   Early Black Stone   Light Cahill   Iron Blue Dun

Early Brown Stone   Sedge Pupa   Stone Fly   Atomic Worm™

Sparce Stone Fly   Hendrickson   Zug Bug   Coleman's March Brown

Brown Bomber   Damsel   Catskill Hendrickson   Gray Nymph

Olive Dun   Mosquito Larvae   Hare's Ear

Humber   Bighorn Scud   Natural Hare's Ear

Olive Bead Head™ Caddis   Olive Sparkle Larva   Ginger Sparkle Larva

Terrestrials

Terrestrials is the name angling great Charlie Fox coined to describe imitation fly patterns more than three decades ago, using the word *Webster's* defines as "living on the land."

Terrestrial insects enter streams and lakes by the thousands over the course of a single day. Some fall in, others are washed in by rain, some get blown in by gusts of wind. Once they fall into the water, these insects are held firmly by the surface tension between air and water. Trout know that insects are helpless in this situation.

By imitating this important food source for trout, you can enjoy some of the most consistent dry-fly sport of the season. For unlike mayflies and caddis, whose hatches occur only during certain time frames of the season, at certain times of day, terrestrials are always on the water, from dawn to dusk, spring through fall.

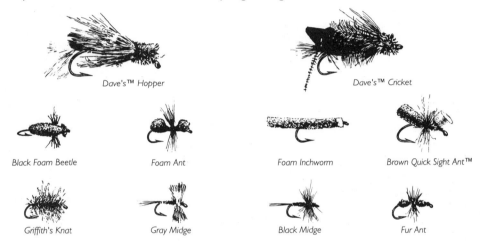

Dave's™ Hopper   Dave's™ Cricket

Black Foam Beetle   Foam Ant   Foam Inchworm   Brown Quick Sight Ant™

Griffith's Knat   Gray Midge   Black Midge   Fur Ant

Bass Bugs

Other popular lures are bass bugs, which resemble their real-life counterparts as closely as possible. While these creatures are most often used for bass fishing, they can also land panfish and other gamefish. Try casting bugs 20' to 30' feet from shoreline among lily pads, weeds, fallen logs, and rocks; adjust your cast so that the lure travels slowly and easily through the air.

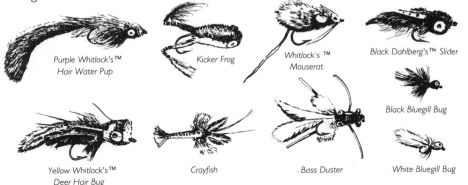

Purple Whitlock's™   Kicker Frog   Whitlock's ™   Black Dahlberg's™ Slider
Hair Water Pup   Mouserat

Black Bluegill Bug

Yellow Whitlock's™   Crayfish   . Bass Duster   White Bluegill Bug
Deer Hair Bug

LIVE BAIT

There are times and situations when live bait will outscore artificials by a wide margin. And bait will often take more jumbo-size fish as well. Large fish can be caught on just about any live offering—from a fingernail-size cricket to a foot-long Florida shiner—but for practical purposes, four baits stand out as the best: nightcrawlers, baitfish, crayfish, and water dogs or salamanders.

Fishing with Worms

Worms are often thought of as a kid's bait—fodder for catfish and sunnies. A soft, slinky, writhing nightcrawler, however, can be every bit as tempting to a hungry bass as it is to a bull bream or heavy-shouldered channel cat. Did you know that the third-largest bass ever landed—a 20-pound, 15-ounce large-mouth—fell for a nightcrawler?

Gathering. Earthworms are so inexpensive and so easily purchased at most fishing destinations that most fishermen don't bother to collect them. You can gather your own, however, simply by scouring lawns after dark with a flashlight covered with a thin piece of red cloth. Walk swiftly and snatch the exposed worms from the ground before they burrow back into their holes. The best time to look is after a lawn has been watered or following a rain.

Rigging and Fishing. Worms can be rigged in countless ways. A very basic setup that works quite well consists of a worm impaled once or twice near its collar on a No. 2 or 4 hook, with a split-shot crimped a foot up the line and a bobber 2' to 5' above that. Cast the rig near cover and wait several minutes. If a strike doesn't come, slowly reel in the offering and flip it out to the next likely piece of structure or stretch of shoreline.

A variation of this technique involves eliminating the float and allowing the worm to settle all the way to the bottom. Wait a few minutes, then slowly reel the offering back in, being alert for a take on the retrieve. If a fish hits, give slack line for a few seconds, then set the hook.

This simple rig is also deadly on river bass. Cast to midstream cover, deep undercut banks, shoreline logjams, back eddies, or deep pools. Let the worm drift naturally with the current, and bass will find such a squirming morsel hard to resist. This is a

---

Worm Farm
Discarded felt (not rubber or plastic) carpet padding can be turned into a worm farm. In an area not illuminated by lights turn over the soil as one would for a garden. Rake fine and smooth. Cover with the rug padding. Keep well watered, but not flooded, with a sprinkler. After several days, when dark, carefully lift off the wet padding. There will be gobs of nightcrawlers and dew worms on the ground. Replace pad and keep wet for your next fishing trip. The padding will prevent weeds from growing.

favorite trout-catching technique, but it also works wonders on bigmouths.

For a more active fishing approach, try rigging a nightcrawler Texas style, just as you would fish a plastic worm. Thread the hook through a quarter inch or so of the tip of the worm, then bury the point in the side of the crawler so it hangs straight on the hook. This rig is fragile compared with Texas-rigged plastic worms, but fish usually strike it so aggressively that it needn't last more than a few casts.

If snags are not a problem, you can simply thread as much of the worm as possible along the hook shank and then allow the point to protrude so that the worm rides straight. A fine way to hook nightcrawlers is with an egg sinker threaded on the line above a swivel or split-shot, with the hook trailing 18" to 36" behind. Drag the offering over cover as you drift with the wind, or use your trolling motor set on low speed.

Baitfish

No other natural offering for larger fish can match the effectiveness of live baitfish. Whether you choose small creek chubs and dace, store-bought minnows, wild golden shiners, or deepwater species such as shad and alewives, a small live fish almost always

proves too tempting for a fish to resist.

The type of baitfish to use depends on the water you're fishing and its indigenous forage fish. A species of baitfish normally preyed upon by the bass in the lake is often more effective than one that isn't. Creek minnows, for instance, are often very effective in rivers. Shad are best in deepwater reservoirs and impoundments where these baitfish are native. Wild Florida shiners are considered the best live bait for the heavily vegetated waters of the Sunshine State.

It's also important to match the size of the baitfish to the anticipated size of your quarry. In general, figure an inch of minnow for every pound of fish you're after. For average bass in the 2- to 4-pound range, for example, a 2" to 4" minnow works well. For 5- to 7-pounders, go with 5" to 7" baitfish. If you're after jumbo bass, shiners from 8" to 12" long are not out of place.

Gathering. "Minnows for Sale" is a common sign at baitshops across the country. If your time is tight, buying baitfish is usually the quickest and certainly the easiest way to get them. However, minnows can be readily caught in a number of ways with simple equipment and little time.

Rigging and Fishing. Spring fishing with baitfish means

Keeping Minnows Fresh

Keeping minnows fresh for several days is sometimes a problem. Professional bait dealers offer these tips:
* *Place about ten ice cubes in your bait bucket when transporting minnows on a long drive. If the ice cubes are made with chlorinated tap water, keep them in a plastic bag—chlorine can kill minnows.*
* *Every time you dip for a minnow, replace the bucket lid immediately. This keeps the water cool and oxygenated. Warm water depletes oxygen.*
* *If the minnows swarm to the surface, the water probably needs changing. Refill only half the bucket each time—a full bucket of fresh water can shock the minnows and shorten the life span. When you add water to the bucket, don't let it increase or decrease the water temperature more than 10°F.*

Favorite Foods

Favorite foods for walleyes include minnows, shad, alewives, as well as young crappies and yellow perch. Locate schools of these species, and you should find walleyes nearby.

two things: shallow water and cover. Look for weedbeds, stump fields, docks, points, blowdowns in shallow coves, stone riprap, flooded timber, and the like [I]. You can hook minnows through the back below the dorsal fin, in the lower body just ahead of the anal fin, or through both lips from the bottom up. The last method is best if you plan to cast and retrieve the minnow, because it will swim more naturally. The bait will also live longest when lip-hooked. The other two hooking methods work better for still-fishing with or without a bobber, because the minnow will struggle, which will attract bass. To make a minnow swim even more erratically, you can clip off one small corner of its tail.

Casting and retrieving is a technique few anglers use with live minnows, but it can be extremely productive. You have the appeal of a live offering but can cover lots of water by retrieving it as a lure. Use several split-shot for weight (or an egg sinker, Bait-Walker, or Lindy Rig in deep water) and cast the minnow as delicately as possible, with little splash. Let it swim to the bottom near the cover. Then begin a slow retrieve, either simply crawling the minnow in steadily along the bottom, or gradually raising the rod to the noon position, then lowering it to the 9 o'clock posi-

tion as the minnow drops back down. Be ready to press free spool or open the bail the minute a fish strikes. Feed line for several seconds, close the bail, allow all slack to be taken up by the fish, then jab the hook home.

A more common minnow-fishing method is to use a float, which can be particularly effective during spring. Adjust the cork anywhere from 2' to 6' above the bait. Lightly lob the rig to the edge of reedy islands or small openings and points in thick mats of vegetation such as hyacinth, bulrush, pepper-grass, milfoil, lily, and hydrilla. Keep slack out of the line, but leave the reel on free spool, so a fish won't feel tension when it takes. Allow the minnow to swim around naturally. If a fish is nearby, it'll likely clobber the minnow in short order.

Crayfish

Bass seem to relish these crustaceans as much as humans do. Though they're particularly effective on smallmouths, the protein-rich, bottom-scuttling creatures are favorites in largemouths' diets as well.

Largemouths will eat hard-shelled crayfish, but they're inordinately fond of soft-shelled or semi-soft-shelled crayfish that have recently molted. Bass also seem to·

favor lighter-colored (usually younger) crayfish over darker ones. Best size is 2" to 3".

Gathering. Some bait dealers sell crayfish, although they're difficult to find in many areas. If you want to fish them, plan on catching your own. There are a number of easy ways to do this, since crayfish are common in lakes, rivers, and streams. Crayfish are largely nocturnal, so night is the best time to catch them, with the aid of a good spotlight.

Setting an umbrella net in the shallows and baiting it with scraps of chopped-up raw meat is one tactic. Place the bait out late in the day and check the trap after dark or just before daybreak. A minnow trap can also be baited the same way and checked later for crayfish. You can also go for crustaceans by lowering a chunk of chicken meat into a lake on a string. Check it periodically, netting any attached crayfish when you slowly pull it off the bottom.

Seining can pay off if you find a shallow area where crayfish are concentrated. Lifting individual stones and catching the crawdads with your hand or a dipnet also works. You'll find crayfish in and near rock-strewn shorelines, bridge pilings, riprap near roads, and boat ramps.

Rigging and Fishing. The most popular way to rig a crayfish is to hook it through the rear of the tail, from the bottom up. Pull the line, and the crayfish will move backward, which is how these crustaceans naturally travel. You can also wrap a pipe cleaner or rubber band around the middle of the crayfish and slip the hook through that, allowing the bait to move in a lifelike manner.

One of the best tactics is to drift in an area where the crustaceans would normally be found, keeping the crayfish on the bottom. You can use several split-shot, a Lindy Rig, Bait-Walker, or egg sinker. Likely spots include points, bars, shoals, areas near bridges and piers, gravel, and mud bottoms near brush, stickups, weedbeds, or rock shelves. The wind should be low to moderate, since you want the bait to just barely move across the bottom. If it's too breezy, drag a bucket over the side of the boat to slow down your drift, or keep your anchor out so it drags lightly across the bottom. (The last technique can actually attract bass by kicking up bottom debris and dislodging forage such as crayfish from the lake floor.)

Another approach for fishing crayfish is to cast out, allow the bait to settle to the bottom, and then crawl it back slowly with frequent pauses. Never wait more than 20 seconds or so between pauses, or the crustacean may crawl under a rock, hiding from

Bridge for Crayfish
You've got to look under aquatic rocks to find crayfish for bait, since this crustacean's defense is to scurry backwards under a rock. However, bait hunters can quickly make a mess of crayfish habitat by overturning all the best hiding spots, leaving survivors prey to smallmouth bass. Simply by placing a flat rock atop two others to form a small bridge, you can form a crayfish retreat. Man-made bridges might even make it easier to find and catch more crayfish the next time you want bait.

Guide to Fishing Live Bait

Bait Type	Use For	Bait Size	Hook Size	How to Rig
Garden worms,	Sunfish	Small	No. 6–10 long-shanked	Cover hook
night crawlers	Trout	Small-medium	No. 4–10 baitholding	Hook once in mid
	Bass	Large	3/0–No.2 baitholding	Hook several tim
	Walleyes	Large	Harness rig	Once each hook
	Catfish	Large	3/0–1/0 baitholding	Hook several tim
Grubs, meal-	Sunfish	Small-medium	No. 8–12 baitholding	Cover hook
worms	Trout	Medium-large	No. 6–10 baitholding	Hook once
Minnows				
(shiners, chubs,	Crappies	Small	No. 2–6 fine wire	Through lips
shad, dace, etc.)	Trout	Small-medium	No.1–6 straightshank	Through lips
	Bass	Medium-large	4/0–No. 1 baitholding	Through back
	Walleyes	Medium-large	3/0–No.1 baitholding	Through back
	Pike/Pickerel	Large	4/0–1/0 baitholding	Through back
	Stripers	Large	4/0–1/0 baitholding	Through back
	Catfish	Large	5/0–1/0 baitholding	Through back
Crayfish	Crappies	Small	No. 2–6 baitholding	Through back
	Yellow Perch	Small	No.2–6 baitholding	Through tail
	Trout	Small-medium	No. 1–4 baitholding	Through tail
	Walleyes	Medium-large	2/0–1/0 baitholding	Through tail
	Bass	Large	4/0–2/0 baitholding	With rubberband
	Catfish	Large	5/0–2/0 baitholding	Through back
Crickets,	Sunfish	Small	No. 6–8 long-shanked	Beneath collar
grasshoppers	Crappies	Small-medium	No. 1–8 long-shanked	Beneath collar
	Trout	Small-medium	No. 1–8 long-shanked	Beneath collar
	Bass	Large	2/0–No. 1 baitholding	Beneath collar
Cicadas	Bass	Large	2/0–No. 1 baitholding	Beneath collar
Waterdogs	Trout	Small-medium	1/0–No. 2 baitholding	Through lips
	Bass	Large	2/0–1/0 baitholding	Through lips
	Walleyes	Large	2/0–1/0 baitholding	Through lips
	Catfish	Large	1/0–3/0 baitholding	Through lips
	Pike	Large	2/0–3/0 baitholding	Through lips

predators and probably fouling your line as well. (If you snag persistently, switch to weedless hooks or use a floating jig head to keep the bait suspended off the bottom.) The technique is similar to plastic worm fishing, just slower. Retrieve 1' or 2' of line, then pause. Pull. Pause again. A couple of split-shot is all the lead you need.

Salamanders and Water Dogs

More than 100 species of salamanders inhabit North America, and at one time or another probably all have been used as bait for bass. Both terrestrial and aquatic salamanders are effective—and often account for particularly large bass.

Gathering. Salamanders are sold as bait in some locations, though usually at a dear price. Water dogs have become particularly popular as a commercial bait in recent years and are widely available throughout much of the South. Larvae of the tiger salamander are even available by mail order. If you want to catch your own, try using pieces of earthworm, light lines, and tiny hooks in areas where they're abundant, such as shallow sections of lakes, backwaters of rivers, canals, and lake overflows. You can

also catch salamanders with a seine in thin waters of lakes or rivers. Terrestrial salamanders can be caught by hand or with a net in woods near spring seeps.

Rigging and Fishing. Hook water dogs and other salamanders through both lips from the bottom up. Use a No. 4 to No. 2/0 hook, depending on the size of the bait. Where jumbo bass are present, salamanders up to 8" long may be productive. Baits 4" to 6" are normally a good choice. If you're fishing in a snag-infested area, use weedless hooks. If short strikes are a problem, try hooking the salamander through the body near the rear legs.

Salamanders can be fished with a bobber, but deep presentations are usually more productive. Simply crimp on several split-shot if the water is 10' or less. For deeper water, use a 1/4- to 1-ounce slip-sinker above a 18" to 36" leader.

Drift or cast and slowly retrieve salamanders near and over points, logjams, humps, shoals, breaklines, and other likely bass hangouts. Trolling with an electric motor set on low power is another good option. On deepwater structures you can anchor and simply freeline the bait down.

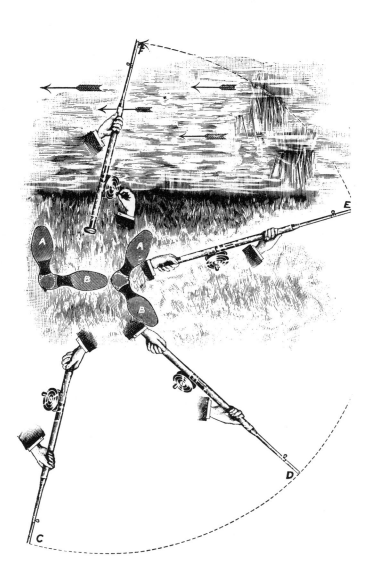

CHAPTER IV
FISHING TECHNIQUES

The "technique" of catching fish means many things to many fishermen. Ask 10 anglers what the key to successful fishing is, and you'll get 10 different answers.

Some trout anglers will insist that presentation is of utmost importance when trying to fool a wary salmonid. "No self-respecting brown trout would dare consider looking at a No. 14 Adams dry fly with just a hint of drag on the float," a flyfisherman will point out. The speed of the current, the particular lie of the trout, and its frequency of rising must all be carefully assessed before deciding which one of a dozen specialty casts should be made.

The walleye angler, however, believes that timing is everything. Prespawn, post-spawn, spring, summer, fall, morning, afternoon, evening, night—knowing when to fish is most important for catching walleyes, because different times require different strategies. "Sure," he'll say, "presentation and lure choice are essential, but they're not worth a whit if you fish at the wrong time."

Then the crappie angler will state that depth is of utmost importance, and the catfish fisherman brings up strength of tackle, and . . . well, it's not that hard to figure out what's going on. All these anglers are correct, to a degree. Whether one particular aspect of fishing technique

is more important than another depends on the species and the particular circumstance. But they're all interrelated, and if you ignore one specific link in the chain of success, you won't catch fish.

A bass angler, for example, could have the finest tackle in the world and still not catch many bass. Let's say this angler has researched the sport and filled a tacklebox with all the lures known to be the best for largemouths. The rods and reels are perfectly matched and filled with the finest-quality line. A nearby lake is filled with bass, including big ones, because other anglers come back to the docks with them. But this angler still can't catch that many bass—a couple of 1- or 2-pounders, at most. What's wrong?

It may be as simple as this: This angler isn't getting up early enough. That nearby lake also happens to be a favorite of powerboaters, water-skiers, sailboaters, and jet-skiers. All that commotion on the water disturbs the bass, but they have adapted and now confine their feeding to the quiet hours, with activity peaking right at sunrise.

So fishing "technique" does involve many things, and all of them can be important. The following chapter outlines most of those skills, and if you follow them, you'll probably catch fish. And when you're ready to go fishing, don't forget to set your alarm clock.

CASTING

There are five popular ways to deliver lures to fish: spincasting, spinning, baitcasting, flyfishing, and pole fishing. In many cases the initial exposure to a method often develops into a lifelong preference.

Each technique has its own merits and charms. Pole fishing, whether it be with a willow branch, canepole, or telescoping glass pole, possibly has more followers than the other four because of its simplistic approach. This is why it's a good method for teaching fundamentals to beginners.

Spincasting, with its closed-face, push-button reel, is the most popular method using a reel-rod combination, and is the best choice for teaching beginners because it is virtually trouble-free. Just depress the bottom on the backcast, release it on the forward cast, and the lure soars smoothly toward the target. It will handle the gamut of light to heavy lures and lines.

About the only problem with this method is line twist, which can easily be avoided by (1) never reeling against a slipping drag and (2) placing a ball-bearing swivel ahead of all lures. Best of all, there are no backlashes to pick out as with levelwind reels.

Spinfishing, with its open-face reel, is next in popularity. In addition to avoiding line twist, you must also make certain the line is rewound onto the spool under tension. Loosely wound line will form loops that squirt off the spool in a tangled gob, requiring patience to pick them out or a knife to cut them out. Like spincasting, spinning is a versatile way of handling a wide range of lure weights and lines.

Third in tackle sales and angler preference is baitcasting; an angler uses a levelwind reel in which the spool revolves as the lure pulls off the line. And therein lies the source of a problem peculiar to this reel, called a backlash. Until the caster's thumb can be educated to stop the spool the instant the lure ceases pulling off line, a backlash, or overrun, occurs.

The least popular choice is flyfishing, the only method in which the lures are so tiny they are delivered to the fish by casting a heavy line that carries the fly with it. A light terminal leader deposits the fly naturally and gently on the water. It is the choice of purists, but not those who like to catch a lot of fish. However, it enhances the challenge of catching and the pleasure in playing gamefish.

Make the Most of a Miss

Even the most proficient caster misses the target from time to time. Many anglers will reel in line quickly in preparation for another cast. There are reasons not to do this.

First, by speeding up your retrieve, you may throw off your timing and find the next cast off-target as well. More important, by slowing down your retrieve instead of speeding it up, you'll have a much better chance to catch a fish. Allow extra time for the lure to descend, giving fish extra time to move out of cover toward the bait. Slowly retrieve the lure, stopping its action occasionally. Give the fish every opportunity to get out from the cover and strike your bait. On the next cast, you will be more composed and can concentrate fully on hitting the target.

BAITCASTING

Baitcasting may be difficult for a beginner to master. The thumb must develop a fine feel and maintain a delicate contact with the line to feather it to a stop when the lure nears the target. But once this skill is mastered, it is done subconsciously like other sporting skills.

Besides, today's baitcasting reels with free-spool devices are far easier to use than the old, heavy-spooled, backlash machine of yesteryear. But let no one kid you: They can be backlashed if not properly adjusted and skillfully handled. In most situations the baitcasting outfit will (1) take more abuse without malfunctioning, (2) handle a heavier line, such as 20-pound-test monofilament, on the smallest size reel, and (3) enable you to put lures in places you couldn't reach with either spincasting or spinfishing.

Spincasting may seem easier because you go through the same minimal motions required for baitcasting. You simply bang out a cast and retrieve. But it has one serious limiting factor. You can't feather the line and ease your lure under that cut bank. (The term "feather" has been a part of fishing lingo for several decades. It means terminal control of a cast to slow a lure and ease it onto a target, or under one.

Variable thumb pressure on the line does it.)

With a mechanical thumbing button, you have stop-and-go control. The moment you push down on the button to stop the line, the internal pickup mechanism jerks the line to a halt—and the lure jerks to a halt, too. This means your lure is going to be stopped from one to several feet short of the target, unless you have the acumen to drop a cast right on target. Few spincasters have this skill. And many times a lure a foot short of the cover you aimed at will get no fish, while one feathered to within inches of the target will get you a strike. This, perhaps more than any other factor, gives baitcasting the edge over the other two casting methods. From the beginning of the cast until the end, the thumb is in positive control.

A cast is powered toward a target with the thumb caressing the line throughout the flight to prevent loose line from robbing distance from the cast. The cast is thrown to pass over the target, but as it nears the objective, the thumb imparts an increasing pressure on the line and the lure is eased onto the target with deadly effect.

Throughout the retrieve, the thumb is in constant contact with the line, lightly but alertly. When a fish strikes, the thumb locks the line so that

Practice for Casting Control

Despite the virtues of the magnetic drags and antibacklash gadgets now found on most baitcasting reels, anglers are finding that there is no substitute for an educated thumb in executing smooth casts. And, of course, the only way to develop an educated thumb is through practice. Backyard angling is an ideal way to develop that prowess. A routine backyard workout essentially consists of casting a hookless plug at a target. There are various kinds of targets, and it makes little difference which you use. Your objective is to hit any part of the target. Set up a series of targets 10' apart at distances ranging from 40' to 80'. Then practice casting the plug overhead twice at the nearest one, twice at the next one, and so on. Let your wrist and rod tip do the work.

Thumb Is Key

The thumb is the key to every cast. It should rest on some stationary part of the reel as well as on the spool. This steadies the thumb, just as the heel on the floorboard steadies the foot on a car accelerator. By removing thumb pressure on the spool at the proper instant, you will send the plug traveling toward the target. While it is traveling, keep your thumb on the spooled line at all times. Too little pressure allows the line to overrun and backlash. Too much shortens and stops the cast. Stop the spool just before the plug hits the target (or the water when you're fishing).

the barbs can be driven home with no interference from a spinning clutch, which is typical of open-face spinning and spincasting reels. And, throughout the playing of the fish, the thumb provides total control, either yielding line to the fish or stopping the lure when it nears dangerous territory.

Let's dwell for a moment on the comparative merits of cranking in line. While it's true that a spincasting and spinning reel usually brings in more inches of line per turn of the reel handle, because of a larger-diameter spool, there's more to it than that.

Spincasting and baitcasting have a reeling advantage over open-face spinning because both are done with the right hand. In spinning the rod is held in the right hand while cranking is done with the left. No right-hander can reel as fast with his left hand as he can with his right, unless he is ambidextrous.

This leaves baitcasting and spincasting in the natural right-hand-reeling category. When you need to gulp in line to catch up with a fish rushing toward you, or take slack out of a line after pumping in a heavy fish, you have to do it fast and positively.

Both reels will do this. But suddenly that big fish turns tail and drives for those tree roots. You yield line to him against the clutch of your reel, but you can sense that he's

going to run into those roots unless you add more pressure to slow him. With the spincasting reel, there is no practical way to slow him beyond the braking effect of your clutch. If you hit the thumbing button to lock the line, you not only risk breaking the line but also lose momentary control of it when you release the thumb button because it's in free-spool. It takes only a moment to crank and regain control, but that moment of fumbling can lose the big fish. This is especially true of the average fisherman, who fishes too little to do the right thing instinctively.

Now, let's recap this same situation with a baitcasting reel:

The big fish drives for those tree roots and you let him go against the drag of your reel clutch—plus the additional retarding of your thumb on the line. But as your fish nears those roots that he intends to use to break loose, you can jam your thumb on the 20-pound line and stop him, bring him to a dead halt, and guide him out of trouble. Continuous control is the answer, and that's why you can do things with a baitcasting outfit that you can't do with spincasting or spinning equipment.

However, if you have a dumb thumb, you can get into plenty of trouble with a baitcasting reel. But if you will spend time educating your thumb, you can be sure that when a big fish latches onto your lure, you will have more chances to subdue him with a baitcasting rig than with anything else available today.

Many of you are thinking: "If baitcasting is so good, why have only 15 percent of fishermen taken it up as a way to fish?" Maybe that's due to the following factors: (1) the cost of a baitcasting outfit, with free-spool reel, is far greater; (2) plenty of practice is required to develop the skill necessary to get the most out of it and reduce backlashes to an acceptable minimum; and (3) beginners start with spincasting or spinning because of lower cost and just never change.

But look around you at the fishermen who bring in the most bass, the nation's most popular gamefish. Probably 90 percent of the guides who fish for bass and most of the hardcore bass anglers use a freespool baitcasting reel. These are the 10 percent of fishermen who catch 90 percent of the fish.

Basic Baitcasting Techniques

First, be sure your spool is fully and properly loaded with line. Read the instruction booklet that comes with the reel for specifics on how much to load. Then adjust the cast-control brake or brakes for proper backlash protection. In brief,

the idea is to tighten the brake to a point where your casting plug descends smoothly and evenly from the rod tip when the reel is placed in free-spool. When the plug touches the ground, the spool should stop turning without overrunning and causing a backlash. In the beginning, it pays to err on the side of using too much brake rather than too little.

The basic overhead cast takes these steps:

Step 1. With the plug dangling a few inches from the tip, place the reel in free-spool, and keeping your thumb on the spool, turn the rod and reel sideways until the reel handles are facing upward. This position is necessary to achieve maximum flex with your wrist.

Step 2. Holding the rod horizontally, point the tip at your target. Keeping your elbow in front of your body, bring the rod tip up and back smoothly over your shoulder, letting your wrist do much of the work. As the rod bends with the weight of the plug, reverse the motion, again using your wrist, to propel the plug out toward your target. At the peak of the forward momentum, lift your thumb off the spool. This casting motion is not a slow arcing or swinging of the rod but a quick up-and-back snap that makes the rod react with a springlike motion.

Step 3. As the plug slows and begins its descent on tar-

Mastering Baitcasting
Once you feel you've mastered the baitcasting routine, see how many perfects you can make in ten casts at a single target, or two casts at each of five targets at distances ranging from 40' to 80'. When you reach a point where you can make seven hits out of ten casts, consider yourself pretty good.

With reel in free-spool and thumb on spool, dangle plug a few inches from tip and turn rod and reel sideways until reel handle faces upward.

Holding rod horizontally, tip at target. Bring rod up and back smoothly ov shoulder.

Reverse motion, using wrist to propel plug out toward target. Lift thumb from spool at peak of forward momentum.

As plug descends, thumb spool again lightly, then completely as plug lands.

Cast Farther

The best baitcasting rods are made from graphite (really graphite-fiberglass composites). Graphite rods are stiffer and stronger for their weights (compared with fiberglass), and offer a far more delicate sense of feel when you're working a plastic worm or bait. The stronger rods also let you cast farther with less effort and have undeniable advantages when there's a need for hard hook-setting and fish-fighting brawn. Nearly all the best modern graphite rods have "blank-thru" construction, which means the rod extends into (or in some cases, actually forms) the handle. This makes it easy to feel a lure's action and helps you detect light takes.

get, start thumbing the spool again, at first lightly, then completely as the plug lands. If you're too slow with the thumbing, the spool will keep turning after the plug has landed, and a backlash will result (although proper brake adjustment will minimize this). If the spool does overrun on you, pull the tangled line off slowly, reel it back in tight, and try the cast again.

Step 4. If the lure is arcing too high on the forward cast, you're releasing your thumb too early. (This often causes instant backlashes.) If the lure is zooming in too low, or hitting

ground before it reaches the target you're aiming for, you're releasing your thumb too late. It takes a little practice to gain the proper feel for the release.

Step 5. Once you have this cast under control, you can experiment by using the same basic motions sidearm and backhand (reaching across yourself and casting from the side opposite your casting hand). When you're comfortable with these three basic and useful casts—and when you can drop the plug reasonably near your target on most casts—you're ready to go out and start fishing.

How to Eliminate Backlashes

Conditions Causing Backlashes.

The first step toward controlling backlashes is to understand their causes. Some of the common ones are (1) an improperly adjusted reel, (2) line is too heavy for weight of lure, (3) thumb is not controlling spool at start of cast, (4) improper fundamentals, or just a poor cast, (5) casting a light lure into the breeze, (6) twists in the line, (7) a malfunctioning reel that needs cleaning or servicing, (8) rod too stiff or too limber, (9) having the lure's flight interrupted because it hits something like a motor, oar, gunwale, or a fishing companion, and (10) line drag set too light. There are more, but these are the main culprits you'll have to deal with.

Balance Your Outfit. A balance among rod, reel, line, and lure is important. See the chart on page 78 to guide you.

Adjust the Reel. Assuming you have a balanced outfit, which eliminates backlash causes Nos. 2 and 8, the next step is to adjust the reel properly. Essentially this means adding enough frictional drag to the end cap to stop the spool when the line ceases being pulled by the lure.

To set frictional drag, hold the rod tip high in front of you. Then lay your thumb against the spool and press lightly. Push the release lever to put your reel into free-spool. Slowly lighten thumb pressure against the spool until the lure begins descending. Next, adjust the end cap of the reel until the lure barely descends. Now give that end cap just a hair more adjustment to stop the lure from descending.

Educate Your Thumb. Cause No. 3 is one of the main inducers of backlash. And there's a simple fundamental exercise you can practice in your home. It teaches your thumb the feel of carefully controlling the line at the beginning and end of the cast.

First, loosen the end cap until the lure runs down freely from the rod tip. Lay your thumb against the line on the spool, then point the rod tip high in front of you with the lure against the rod tip. Now watch the lure as you slowly lighten thumb pressure against the spool.

With just the right amount of thumb pressure, the lure should descend slowly all the way to the floor. The instant it touches the floor, stop it so it's standing on its tail. If the lure falls rapidly, or if it falls over when it hits the floor, you can assume you had a backlash. Control is what you're after.

Once your thumb is smart enough to let the lure descend properly every time, you are ready to go outside

Line Guides

A good working baitcasting rod should have top-quality line guides. Silicon carbide is perhaps the best material—"best" meaning the hardest and smoothest, the least likely to nick or groove (a condition that can lead to line fraying and breakage). Aluminum oxide and Hardloy materials also make excellent, durable guides and are found on many of the better rods.

Buy with Care

The best way to avoid confusion is to buy rods (or rod/reel combos) one at a time, knowing beforehand exactly what kind of fishing you intend to do, then tailoring the rod or outfit precisely to that. As you learn more on the water, you'll know which kind of new rod adaptation to make. When in doubt, start with a generalist outfit.

Cast Downstream

Station yourself at right angles to the current, casting slightly upstream, and with a tight line keep the spinner turning over bottom cover. From directly above the rapids, cast downstream into slow-moving water and bring the spinner along the slot where fast downstream currents rub against slow upstream eddies. Minnows love to dart in and out of these spots in search of tiny food particles. Learn to fish spinner lures under all conditions, and you can double your usual quota. Remember, too, that evening is often the best time for catching.

and make short casts. Once you have mastered short casts, stretch them into longer and longer casts. Use a hookless practice plug for these outdoor sessions; stay with them, and you'll eliminate cause No. 4.

Be Kind to Your Reel. If you're unkind to your reel, it will give you improper conduct by malfunctioning. Kindness means periodic cleaning and lubricating. And today's reels take remarkably little care, so this isn't a chore if you're serious about your fishing.

The only care baitcasting reels seem to need is to spray the moving parts with WD-40™, wipe off the gunk when it gets too obvious, and take them to a repair center when they begin vibrating, making too much noise, or malfunctioning badly.

Casting into a Breeze. There are times when you can't avoid casting into a breeze. If you use a light lure, it and your line will hang on the breeze. The result will be either continuous fuzz-ups in your line or an occasional backlash.

The remedy is to stay with compact lures. Smaller lures weighing 1/4 ounce, made of lead or solid plastic, are compact and will cast nicely to eliminate problem No. 5.

Watch Your Backcasts. Let your lure hit something on the backcast, and you'll know what

a real backlash is—especially if a companion gets impaled with your plug. Watch behind yourself when casting and you'll obviate cause No. 9.

Control Line Twist. With a levelwind reel, line twist can occur only when a lure turns over and puts twist in the line. The remedy is never to use a lure that turns over. But if you have a pet that does, use a ball-bearing swivel. If you do get line twist, troll the line along until it is straight again. So much for cause No. 6.

Set That Drag. If your drag isn't properly set, a big fish can make a sudden dash and snatch linen off your reel so violently that it causes the spool to overrun. Then you've got a real mussup. Before each day's fishing, set your reel's drag, or brake, so the line pulls off smoothly and not jerkily, eliminating cause No. 10.

When You Do Get a Backlash. No matter what you do, you will get backlashes. The only casters who don't get backlashes are those who don't use a levelwind reel or those who lie. So here's what to do. At first, do nothing; just stare at that mess. Don't start pulling on it impatiently, whatever you do. Keep your eager fingers out of the tangled line until you have calmed down and studied it carefully.

Now take hold of the line ahead of the reel's levelwind and pull on it methodically. Do not jerk. When it stops coming, you will note that a little V, or line loop, is holding it. Get hold of the V and pull it out until the next V stops it. Patiently pull out that V, and then the next and the next, until the line pays off freely. Pull no other loops except the Vs, and you'll be all right.

Your fingers won't be able to reach some Vs because they're deep. For these tough Vs, have a handy pocket tool found in most drugstores. It usually has a sorry knife blade, a passable fingernail file, and a fingernail cleaner that has a dull hooked end. The last implement makes a wonderful backlash-picker-outer because it reaches those buried Vs without damaging the line. Use it to unsnarl those key Vs one at a time.

SPINNING

Hold the rod with your casting hand, placing the reel foot between your second and third fingers. Crank the reel handle until there's 6" or so of line between the rod tip and the lure; ideally, the line pick-up mechanism on the bail will be on the top of the reel at this point. Extend your index finger and hold the line in or just above the crook of the first joint. Then move the bail into the open position, keeping tension on the line with your index finger.

Point the rod toward the target and swing the rod

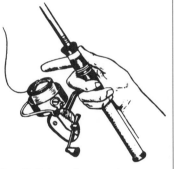

Step 1. Hold (don't hook) line with first crook or on pad of extended index finger. Open bail with your other hand.

Step 2. Release line as rod comes forward by straightening index finger.

Step 3. If necessary, slow outgoing line by laying extended index finger over coils coming off spool.

Hold on There

Holding an open-face spinning outfit with two fingers in front of the reel's "foot" or "leg" is not the only correct way to grip the rod, according to tackle officials at James Heddon's Sons. Women, kids, and others with small hands should use a different grip for greater casting control. The proper grip is actually determined by positioning the index finger of the rod hand over the lip of the reel's spool; that finger is used to "feather" the line during the cast (to slow the cast, if necessary) and is also used to apply pressure to the spool when "extra" drag is needed. Small-handed people may actually have to use three or even four fingers in front of the reel foot to allow their index finger to reach the spool lip. Conversely, people with large hands may have to place three fingers behind the reel foot.

Current Fishing

When you're fishing flow-ing water, especially below rapids in deep holes, spinners can be superbly effective because they give off flashes that resemble cavorting minnows. From below the rapids, cast upstream into the current and reel slightly faster than the flow to keep the lure barely below the sur-face. Let the current drive the spinner down so the retrieve can be just over the bottom. Remember to keep your line tight, or lures will lodge in rocks.

back over your head, until it's a bit past vertical. Then, with-out pausing, swing the rod back toward the target. The upper part of the rod should flex backward somewhat at this point; that's because the energy of your motion is being transferred to the rod (called "loading"). When the rod is approaching a 45-degree angle to the target, straighten your index finger to release the line. The lure should sail toward the target. At this point, it's possible to shorten the length of the cast by extending your index fin-ger and retarding the speed of the line coils coming off the spool. Turn the reel crank to engage the reel.

Learning exactly when to release the line from your index finger during the for-ward cast is usually the most difficult aspect of casting a spinning rod (see illustrations for details). But most new-comers pick up the basics after trying it a few times.

SPINCASTING

The spincasting technique is very similar to that of spin-ning, except that a button (usually thumb-operated) engages and disengages the reel.

Point the rod toward the target and press the button down with your thumb. This will disengage the reel, but not the line. While keeping

pressure on the button, bring the rod over your head to a point just past vertical, and in one motion bring it forward again. As the rod approaches a 45-degree angle, release the button. This will free the line, and the lure should shoot toward the target. The speed of the lure can be slowed by blocking the outgoing line slightly with your noncasting hand. When the lure reaches the target, turn the reel crank to engage the reel.

CURING CASTING PROBLEMS

Casting bugaboos beset every fisherman, expert or beginner. Depending on fre-quency and severity, they can put a pall on an otherwise enjoyable day.

The first step in avoiding casting problems is to prac-tice at home with your pre-ferred fishing outfit. Becoming thoroughly familiar with the motions of casting, as with the fundamentals of any sport, is a prime necessity.

Spincasting. The main bugaboo with spincasting is line twist, which can be caused by (1) reeling against a slipping drag and (2) using a lure that turns over and over as you retrieve. Here are the cures.

Listen to Your Drag. There is a buzzer, or click, that is activated when line is pulled off the reel, turning the spool. Listen to it. When you hear it buzzing, don't reel, or you'll add twist to the line.

There are two remedies for this problem. The first is to add more drag tension by adjusting the button, or lever. Be careful not to add too much, or a good-size fish will break the line. You should be able to judge when the line is right at the breaking point.

The second method applies if you believe the tension is set correctly. Pump the fish by raising your rod tip to relieve the tension in your line, then reel in slack as you lower the rod tip. This way you can land a large fish without acquiring line twist.

Use a Snap Swivel. If you're using a lure that twists, the best thing to do is tie on a ball-bearing snap swivel. These swivels are effective even if the lure you are using is not a twister, as the hooks on such lures can become fouled on one cast and twist your line.

The ball-bearing swivel will not permit the line to twist between you and the lure because it confines all the twirling to the lure itself. Also, should you put some twist into your line by reeling against a running fish, the swivel will be sure to take out most of it.

Practice. Because you

don't have to worry about backlash when spincasting, you can eliminate the thumb-smartening exercise. Just practice casting at a target until you attain accuracy.

One problem is achieving the same pinpoint accuracy you can get with a baitcasting reel. To do so, practice line control with your fingers. As you cast, place your left hand ahead of the reel and let the line pay out through your thumb and forefinger. To slow the progress of the lure and drop it lightly on target, just squeeze the line between your thumb and forefinger at the proper moment. Practice will make you near perfect.

ANGLING TRICKS

Many days, even experts catch only small fish, and ordinary anglers get skunked. When this happens, disregard normal methods of fishing. It's necessary to try some last-ditch tricks that can induce a fish to strike.

Reaching Impossible Places. When fish aren't in normal hangouts, they're probably in places where ordinary lures can't reach them. One such hiding place might be under overhanging branches just a few inches over the water. Fishermen often don't bother to cast into such areas.

Remember that the line-tie (where you attach the line) on

A Trick to Remember

For all those who have cast a bait or lure over a tree limb and then tried to jerk it free, there's a trick worth remembering: As the lure dangles and swings back and forth, do not wait until it moves away from you before pulling sharply with the rod. That puts the lure in line with the branch and the hooks invariably dig into the wood as pressure is applied. The secret is waiting until the lure swings toward you. Then, when you pull on the rod, the lure is cata-pulted back and over the limb.

Target Practice

To hit a target when casting, start with the tip of the rod pointing just below it and raise the rod so that the tip bisects the precise spot you want to hit. As you come forward, keep the rod on the same vertical plane and the bait or lure should find its mark. Put just a touch more energy into the cast than necessary, and then stop it in the air when the offering is directly over the target.

Fan the Area

When fishing from a bank or beachfront, most of us tend to make the longest casts we can straight from where we are standing. That's fine for the first shot, but be sure to fan the area in both directions so that the bait or lure can be retrieved at different angles. It can make a difference.

a wiggling lure is like a steering wheel. Select a floater/diver plug, such as a slim minnow or a crank-type plug. Take a pair of long-nose pliers in your strong hand, and hold the lure firmly in your other hand.

Imagine that you're looking at an overhang that will be to the left of your lure as you retrieve it (or to your right). Now hold the lure in your left hand, with its head facing you. The line-tie controls the lure's direction. If you bend the line-tie to your right, the lure will run to your right as you retrieve it.

Don't overdo it. A little bend in the line-tie gives a lot of side run to a lure. Before you cast near that branch, cast the lure into open water where you can see what it's doing.

When you have adjusted the line-tie correctly, cast slightly past that overhanging branch and reel just fast enough to make it dive. It'll swim left back under that branch where no one but you has maneuvered a lure. This technique also works well under low piers, deadfalls, rafts, anchored boats, and undercut banks.

Speed Reeling. Each of us has a certain rhythmic pace to our retrieving. This can be a problem. Each wiggling or spinning lure has a certain speed at which it works best. Study each lure and stay with that lure's best-

movement speed.

When nothing is working, though, think super-speedy. Select a lure that can be reeled very quickly without exceeding its capability to swim straight [III]. Crank lures that have no lip make a versatile choice.

What exactly is super-speed reeling? A normal reeling speed will be slightly above one turn of the reel handle per second. Super-speed reeling is about four turns per second. This allows you to pound out casts against shorelines, dropping them about 3' apart. The instant they touch down, you are super-speeding them on their way. The idea is to make a fish think something has jumped off the shore and is hightailing it away. Reflexive response compels a fish to attack the intruder, and frequently it does.

Bottom-Crawling. Use a sinking crankbait and wait for the lure to settle to the bottom. Turn the handle slowly to allow the lure to creep on the bottom in a dead drag, with no action at all. Or try bottom-crawling a sinking lure so slowly you feel silly. Though it seems strange, it works.

Ripping a Spinner. Ripping is a maneuver that requires coordinated movement of the reel and rod. Cast out a sinking spinner, and let it settle to the bottom. Reel the line taut, and point the rod tip downward. As you jerk the lure off the bottom, reel rapidly several times. The lure will hop off the bottom, the spinner buzzing like mad, like some creature trying to get away. Often a fish will nail it without knowing why.

Shock-Waving. This procedure will require some practice on your part. Timing is very important. The lure should be a slim-minnow type that floats at rest and dives when retrieved. Color isn't a factor.

You usually cast this type of lure near shore cover, then twitch it gently a few times before bringing it back. This action gives off little wavelets like an injured minnow and tempts gamefish to help themselves to an easy meal. This is frequently one of the most dependable ways to catch fish. When it fails you, try shock-waving one of these lures. Cast near cover or over weedbeds in open water.

Keep the lure motionless. As you reel slack out of the line, point the rod tip toward the lure. Now comes the critical timing. As you sharply jerk the rod tip low over the water, simultaneously reel a spasmodic, quick half-turn of the handle.

When the two motions are properly timed, the lure dives and gives off a super shock wave that travels amazingly far underwater. Once you start, keep it up all the

way to your boat. This has a strange effect on resting fish; they've been known to charge from as far away as 50'.

FLYCASTING

The Overhead Cast. Volumes have been written on the dynamics of flycasting. In brief, however, what you want to do is let out enough line so that all the leader, and its connecting knot with the flyline, have passed through the top guide of your rod. Holding your rod over your head, wave the rod back and forth from approximately the 10 to the 2 o'clock positions. Gradually let out more and more flyline by pulling it off the reel with your left hand (assuming you're right-handed), and let it slowly slip through your fingers. Make sure you let the line sail out as far on your forward cast as on your backcast. Feel the momentum of the line? That's what you're striving for. The weight of the line and its momentum are what keep the weightless fly in the air and give you a certain degree of accuracy. When you have enough line in the air to enable your fly to reach the intended target, give your arm a small snap on your last forward cast and let the line go. It should take your fly at least close to the target. The more you practice, the better you'll become.

Flyfishing Basics

The best strategy for a beginning flyfisherman is to ignore trout streams altogether. Find a pond or small lake with a good panfish population, then set yourself up on a dock or a sandbar where there are plenty of wide-open spaces all around you. Rig up with a short leader—6' is enough, tapered to 4- or 6-pound test—and use a small bluegill popper or rubber spider for a fly. Begin with casts of no more than 20' or 25', lengthening them gradually as you become more comfortable with the equipment. If the lake contains bluegills, sunfish, or crappies, your casting won't be a mere exercise— panfish are wonderfully forgiving of a beginning flycaster's mistakes. They don't mind a cast that splashes a little, or a leader that snarls up in a tangle of windknots, or a fly that skips across the water.

VITAL FLYCASTS

Slack-Line Casts

Straight casts are pleasant to make and look at, but they aren't of much use when the angler is trying to float a dry fly past a rising trout. If the fly drags on the water, the trout won't take it, and a straight cast doesn't offer much drag-free drift. The solution is to use a slack-line cast, which allows longer drifts without drag. These casts are easy to learn and can be used when fishing either upstream or down.

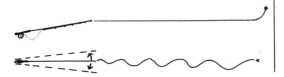

The S-Curve Cast. The easiest and most popular slack-line cast is the S-curve cast. Making one is easy: Just quiver the rod tip at the end of a regular cast just before the flyline alights on the water. This will put a number of curves into the line when it lands, and it extends the period of drag-free drift. The larger the quiver, the bigger the curves.

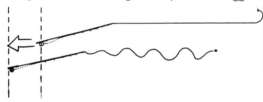

The Stop Cast. This cast is similar, but instead of quivering the rod tip, the angler simply stops the motion of his forward cast before the line touches the water and pulls back a bit on the rod. This causes the line to fall on the water in crooked loops, prolonging a drag-free drift. The stop cast may look sloppy, but it works.

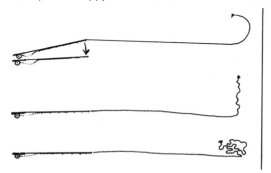

The Pile Cast. This works well when casting to small targets in broken current. Here, the angler drops the rod tip toward the water just before the flyline straightens on the forward cast. The fly line will lay down properly on the water, but the leader will pile up on the water—again, not a pretty cast, but the slack leader means a longer drag-free float.

Curve Cast

A curve cast allows the fly angler to drop a fly to the left or right of the line. Such placement can be helpful when trying to cast around obstructions or without spooking a fish by dropping the main line over it.

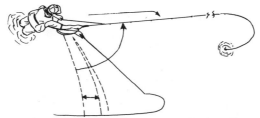

To cast a left curve, begin with a normal cast, but keep the rod angled at 2 o'clock instead of 12. Put some force into the final forward cast, and stop the rod motion before the leader straightens out. The fly should swing to the left.

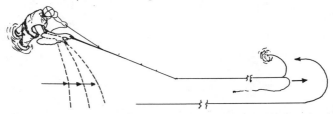

A right-curve cast is similar, except that the final forward cast should be weak and the angle at about 3 o'clock. Again, stop the rod motion before the leader straightens, and the fly should fall to the right

Roll Cast

This cast is ideal for reaching fish when nearby brush or limbs prohibit normal false-casting.

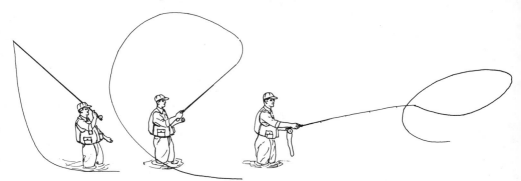

Lay a section of line out from the rod tip in front of you. Lift the rod steadily until it's angling just behind your head, and in one motion move the rod a bit to the side, away from your body. Then, without pausing, swiftly push the rod forward. The rod should "roll" out clean and straight, placing the fly on the water in front of you.

CHAPTER V

FISHING THE WATERS

W here can I fish?" is probably the question most frequently asked by budding anglers.

Actually, it's easy to find a place to fish in the United States because water, in some shape or form, abounds. Barring a very few arid areas of the country, any angler can find a spot to wet a line within a short drive of home.

And what a variety of waters to choose from! From the tiniest of farm ponds to Lake Superior, from a mountain-spring brook to the mighty Mississippi, an American angler can fish every day of his life and never have to visit the same water twice. There are freshets, runs, brooks, creeks, streams, and rivers. Sloughs, backwaters, oxbows, and coves. Ponds, lakes, reservoirs, and impoundments. Isolated beaver-dam ponds in the deepest wilderness, abandoned mining pits filled with water, streams that take on new life as the rains come.

While the amount of fishing waters, and their extreme ranges, is certainly wondrous, methods of fishing them vary widely as well and, unfortunately, may serve to intimidate the beginning fisherman. That's why "How do I fish?"

is the second most frequent question asked by neophyte anglers when they do find a place to wet a line.

For this reason, this chapter is devoted to "fishing the waters." Now that we've covered the physiology of fish, explanations of the various fish species, types of fishing gear, and many aspects of fishing technique, this chapter is where it all comes together: how to properly apply that knowledge of fish and fishing, in a particular body of water, in an effort to catch a particular type of fish.

You'll find that a body of water is like a book: It must be read to be understood. Some parts are exciting, others are dull, but they're all connected in some way. Unlike a book reader, though, the angler should be able to go directly to where the action is. This chapter will explain how to search out the best parts of a lake or stream without having to "read" the entire water. Then you'll learn how to effectively fish those areas.

And when you're reading this chapter, keep in mind that there are no dull parts—all of it is exciting!

Lakes and Ponds

COVER THAT PAYS OFF

The usual fish cover is what most fishermen pound regularly: grass, lily pads, brush, reeds, rushes, cattails, overhanging limbs, and so on. Unusual types of fish cover are those that pay off when the obvious ones don't. They're unusual because they're unobtrusive, noted only by the trained eyes of seasoned anglers.

When your favorite spots aren't paying off the way they usually do, try the following:

Flooded Willows. Early in the year, when waters are the highest, scan the shore for flooded willows. This is an area where minnow crops often hide. Fish the edges and keep scanning ahead for any movements such as shaking branches, ripples made by skittering minnows, or swirls denoting feeding fish just below the surface.

Approach quietly. Then, as you move along a shoreline, keep a sharp eye for tiny tippets of weeds sticking above the surface in open water. These can be attached to large weed patches below, where cruising fish pause to rest.

Holes. Keep a roving eye as you fish; scan the water ahead and look for darkened areas, often no larger than your boat. They indicate holes deeper than surrounding water. Fish cautiously, with sinking lures like plastic worms and grub jigs.

Muddy Shore Runoff. After a heavy rain, look for those spots where shore runoffs converge to create an influx of muddy water. A shear is formed where this muddy water pushes through clear water. This is where minnows seek shelter and protection from larger fish cruising outside. The best lures for fishing these spots include small spinners, spoons, jigs, and crankbaits.

Muddy Water. Should one section of a lake stay muddy overly long, don't shun it as other anglers do. Fish the shoreline with crank lures that rattle, others that vibrate sharply, and big-blade spinners.

Rocky Points. When you come across a rocky point, note the angle at which it disappears into the water. It usually continues under the surface. Estimate where it should be about 15' to 20' deep and fish the bottom with plastic worms, sinking crankbaits, grub jigs, and slab spoons.

Trees to Fish By

Tree overhangs have long been known as a prime source of fish fare in the form of insects that drop off into the water. The following tips will help you search out the best trees.

• Trees with conspicuous flowers. Both the insects that pollinate them and the insects that consume the pollinators, such as wasps and praying mantises, will make their way into the water and into the mouths of fish.

• Defoliated trees usually indicate the presence of moths, sawflies, or beetles in the larval stages.

• Trees cracked by lightning or severe winds provide housing for many insects.

• Woodpeckers signal the presence of tree insects.

• When angling near trees, use the wind to your advantage—fish areas where it is blowing from shore.

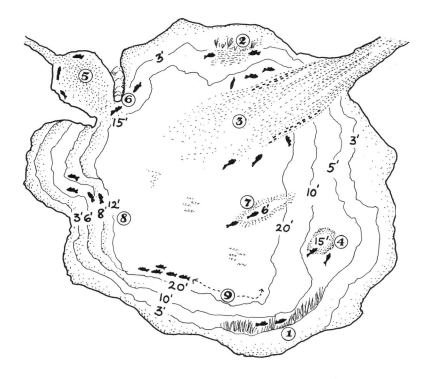

Usual Hangouts

1. Row of willows bordering deeper water.
2. Tiny weed tippets that denote a bigger mass below.
3. Muddy inflowing stream that brushes against clear lake water, forming a shear where minnows hide.
4. Deep hole on sloping shore.
5. Muddy bay where shoreline clears first and holds fish.
6. Rocky point abutting deep water.
7. Shallow shoal, or hump, in deep water.
8. Stair-step shore where fish cruise the steps.
9. Migration route along outer deepwater edge.

Shoreline Dropoffs. If a shoreline dropoff continues around a lake, you can be fairly sure that fish use it as a daily migration route. Fish it regularly to determine the migration times.

Two Final Notes. If you have a depthfinder, crisscross shorelines and look for any unusual bottom features, such as deeper holes, channels, cover patches, ledges, dropoffs, or humps. Make notes, and fish these contours regularly.

Most serious fishermen make a practice of using topographic maps to help find the best habitat. Maps reveal bottom features such as stair-stepping shores, steep banks, mid-bay holes, and old creek channels—all of which are likely hangouts. One place to acquire good, detailed maps is your county engineer's office.

Tributaries

If you're having trouble locating fish on a large impoundment, try heading up into tributaries that feed the lake. These areas ususaly have good oxygen supplies and lots of food. They're often magnets for bass and panfish.

Lead the Fish into the Open

If you hook a strong fish near a bank that has overhanging branches, thrust your rod into the water and try to lead the fish out into the open. With the rod underwater, you have a better chance of having the line clear any branches trailing in the water.

BANK FISHING

Before fishing a lake from the bank, take some time to study its makeup for potential fish-holding areas. For example, the steep bank at Location A would harbor northern pike, muskies, bass, and walleyes at any time. Location B, the shaded bank, would hold the same species at all times except winter. The rocky point at Location C is an ideal habitat for bass and walleyes. The sharp dropoff at Location D would be good during the summer and winter for perch, walleyes, northerns, and bass; year-round for stripers. Location E, with its rubble-strewn bottom, is ideal for walleyes, smallmouths, and white bass during spring and fall and at dawn and dusk during the summer. The interior of the cove at Location F would hold pike, crappies, and largemouth bass from spring through fall; the cove mouth is prime for walleyes, striped and white bass during the same period. The gradual slope at Location G would attract bass morning and evening during the summer.

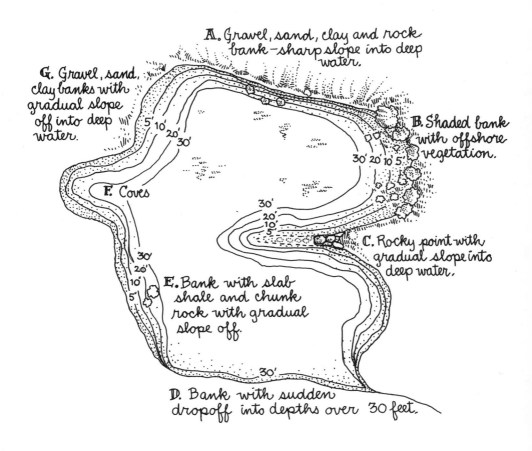

A. Gravel, sand, clay and rock bank—sharp slope into deep water.

G. Gravel, sand, clay banks with gradual slope off into deep water.

5' 10' 20' 30'

B. Shaded bank with offshore vegetation.

30' 20' 10' 5'

F. Coves

30' 20' 10' 5'

C. Rocky point with gradual slope into deep water.

30' 20' 10' 5'

E. Bank with slab shale and chunk rock with gradual slope off.

30'

D. Bank with sudden dropoff into depths over 30 feet.

WORMING FOR SHALLOW-WATER BASS

Plastic worms can be fished throughout the shallow-water bass habitat shown below. The chart indicates the best rigs plus casting distances and retrieve rate.

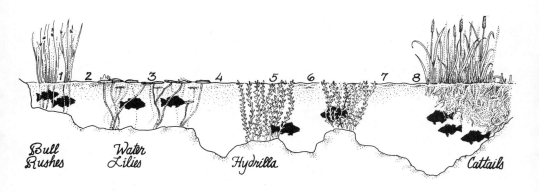

Location	1	2	3	4	5	6	7	8
Worm rigs	A, C	D, E	A, B	D, E	C, B	B, F	E, F	D, C
Cast	Flip, 10'	20', 20'	10', 30'	20', 20'	20', 30'	30', 20'	30', 30'	30', 30'
Retrieve rate	Slow jig, slow	Steady, slow	Slow crawl, fast	Steady, slow	Slow, fast	Fast, slow	Slow, slow	Steady, slow

A Texas Rig, page 112
B Texas Rig (weightless), page 112
C Texas Rig (weightless, with hook eye buried 1/2" back from tip of head), page 112
D Gyrating Rig, page 114
E Weedless Surface Rig, page 114
F Droopy Rig (without bobber), page 115

Wade Right In

When the hot summer sun melts your desire to fish on crowded lakes, try wade fishing in small ponds and streams. Get a county topographic map to locate such places. Try it. It's a see-and-feel contact you never get from a boat.

Remember that smaller bodies of water usually contain smaller fish than big lakes, so scale down the size of your lures and use light casting rigs. Keep notes on the best times of day and season, and you'll soon be reaping a bonanza!

FISHING AT NIGHT

To fish a lake from a boat at night, first determine the route you'll take and mark it earlier that day with fluorescent-colored ribbons on shoreline points. Such blazes can be picked up easily at night with a weak flashlight beam and will guide you to your course (Site A). Hang the markers near fish-holding areas near shore and around small islands, with two markers indicating a change in direction (Site B). Fish slowly and methodically around points of land, which attract fish after dark. Keep the point in sight at all times to stay on course (Site C). Be sure to work all sides of any partially submerged timber, another night-time hotspot (Site D). It's important to mark the end of your course. Do so by hanging a double ribbon (Site E).

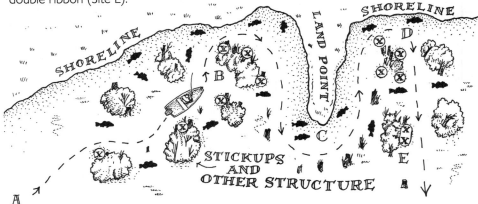

SHALLOW OR DEEP?

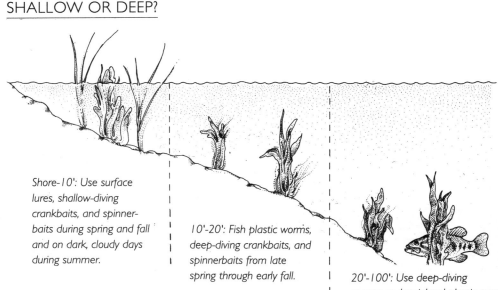

Shore-10': Use surface lures, shallow-diving crankbaits, and spinner-baits during spring and fall and on dark, cloudy days during summer.

10'-20': Fish plastic worms, deep-diving crankbaits, and spinnerbaits from late spring through early fall.

20'-100': Use deep-diving spoons and weighted plastic worms during the hottest days of summer and during the winter.

Reservoirs and Pits

RESERVOIR TACTICS

A high percentage of the freshwater fish caught each year are taken in reservoirs. When water levels remain normal over a period of time, fishing stabilizes, but when the levels go up or down, fishing is affected. The problem isn't normal fluctuations of a few feet up or down. What you need to cope with are those periods of extreme rises or drops—and with reservoirs, 20' to 40' rises or drops are not uncommon. It varies depending on the usage/need of the impounded water, be it for households, making power, or irrigation.

But there are ways you can cope. In fact, if you make it a point to study these up-and-down periods, you can enjoy fishing bonanzas unknown to those who give up in disgust. Here are tactics of reservoir fishing that have paid off over the years.

Low-Water Period

Think deep, because that's where the gamefish usually stay. Normally, when the water level rises or falls a few inches, nothing changes. But if the water drops enough to begin moving out of coves and backwaters, things vary.

The food fishes (minnows, shad, and fingerlings) usually are first to follow the receding waters. The sportfish follow them to deeper water.

Since the shore cover they normally inhabit becomes high and dry during low-water periods, fish move to offshore structures and cover of various types. Look for sharp dropoffs along now-barren shores. Such spots attracts all species.

Other good places are indentations in rocky cliffs based in darker, deeper water. Fish cruise in and around these seeking food. They are disoriented, away from their normal shoreline habitations, and seek new havens. In the meantime, they must cruise, examine, and eat.

Rocky shores disappearing into deep water are good areas to fish, as are bridge abutments or the riprap along roadbeds. Also try fishing above a dam and over old roadbeds. These are deep-water areas that offer some sort of security to fish.

Sonar will help you find these areas, but make notes, sketches, and triangulations in order to find them again. Predator fishes such as bass, catfish, white bass, crappies, bluegills, striped bass, pike, walleyes, or muskies might use one end of a midlake structure

Fish below Dams
Freshwater stripers often bite best below dams for the first hour after water is released from the gates. Phone the dam office before your trip to learn when water will be released. You can then plan to arrive just in time for the best fishing. Bucktails and live shad are the top offerings for this tailwater sport.

as a resting place and the other end as an ambush spot [II].

Seek out creek entrances when water levels are low. As you view their bottom structure (which is normally obscured by water), be sure to make sketches so you'll know better how to fish them when the water level rises again. On days when you can't find fish in usual shore cover, fish over these hidden havens. They can be terrific.

High-Water Period

When reservoir waters ascend, think shallow. Rising waters spill out over surrounding flats and backwater areas. These high waters open up vast new feeding areas for minnows and gamefish, and many of them are only a foot or so deep.

Rising water can result from excessive rains or the backing up of the normal flow of rivers and streams feeding the reservoir. If it's from rains, murky or off-colored water can result, especially where flowages enter the lake.

Many times a shear of wall-like separation is visible where muddy water meets clear water. This can be a hotspot where minnows dash in and out of the murky water, while gamefish hang around to feed on them.

High water may make it difficult for you to find fish, because they are scattered all over, feeding around fertile vegetation where minnows are prevalent. This vegetation can be in areas virtually impossible to reach unless you have a small boat or if you wade.

Mini-boats powered by an electric motor or paddles can be maneuvered into flooded, compacted timber where schools of predator fish have collected.

Other good places to fish are grassy or brushy hillsides, especially where you see wading birds such as herons or egrets. These birds eat the same small fish that predator fish eat. Watch for telltale swirls or moving Vs that indicate fish stalking or feeding.

Here are some general tips about lures. Low water that has been stable for some time usually gets quite clear. Fish are spooky, so keep your commotion at a minimum. Choose lures with subtle, natural colorations, and keep them about the same size as the food fishes you see. Try speed reeling. Count about four turns of your reel handle per second; this is a good reeling velocity.

One point should be emphasized. In either high or low water, try to be on the water the moment major water fluctuations take place. When the force of rising or falling water is felt, fish come out of normal hideouts and become more readily available. This is the best time to fish a reservoir.

Birds Are Bass Markers

Anglers have long watched for swooping gulls to locate schools of baitfish and the larger predators beneath them. Texan Gene Snider, a guide on Lake Palestine, uses birds to locate largemouth bass: "A great blue heron sitting on a stump low in the water is almost always feeding on baitfish. I motor in to check a bird, and if he lets me get really close or flies only a few feet before landing, it's a good guarantee that there are fish in the area, especially if he returns to the same stump when I back off. But if a bird just flies on down the lake without protesting, there probably wasn't enough food there to hold him."

Pit-Fishing Chart

Water Condition	Lures	Tactics
Clear	Resembling types: minnows, crankbaits	Best times: at night, during rain
Cloudy	Bright colors: metallics, yellow, orange, chartreuse, white	Work lures slowly, rapidly, spasmodically and steadily to see what attracts bass
Muddy	Noisy types: crankbaits with rattlers, lipless vibrators, spinners with large blades	Work lures loudly and give bass time to hit them

FISHING THE PITS

Anglers often look for alternatives to their regular fishing haunts, places to go when their standbys don't produce. Many fishermen are finding success in the pits, diggings once used to mine gravel, phosphate, lime, and other minerals.

The key to fishing the pits is to solve the water clarity problem. The water can range from clear to cloudy to downright muddy. Here are some effective tactics.

Clear water is the toughest of all conditions. If fish can clearly see both you and your lures, they become wary. Get upwind of your target area and move in quietly to avoid alerting fish. If you fish afoot, stay low. Try making longer casts than usual.

Watch for typical food around cover, then use resembling lures. The two best times to fish are during a rain and at night. If it's very dark, use black patterns. If moonlit, use white, yellow, or silver to reflect the light.

Cloudy water usually has visibility of 1' to 3', so more brightly colored lures are needed to entice fish. Try silver and gold metallics plus yellow, orange, chartreuse, and white.

Muddy water has visibility of only a few inches, so sound becomes most important. Try crankbaits that have BBs or rattlers inside and lipless vibrators that give off noise from hooks shaking on metal hangers. Use spinners with large blades for heavy pulsations. Work your surface lures more noisily than you usually do and pause longer between manipulations to give fish time to come to the lure.

JIGGING

The art of jigging is one of angling's deadliest yet least pursued fishing methods. One misconception about jigging is that it is done only with a jig. Not so. There are four popular ways fishermen jig for a variety of species.

Don't
Overlook Docks
Among the overlooked hangouts for many fish are the docks and piers on most lakes. You should fish not only under these but also probe for brushpiles most dock owners have planted nearby.

Jigs

These lures have a common lead-head jig hook that is animated with various bodies such as soft-plastic grubs and worms, plastic skirts, and porkrinds.

Many fishermen cast the lure out and retrieve it over bottom cover, much like the plastic worm retrieve. This is not jigging. Jigging is done with a straight line suspended below the tip of a rod or pole so that direct contact can be maintained with the jig.

Without this contact it is very difficult to detect that all-important instant when a fish sucks in the jig. With direct contact an alert angler is aware of more or less tension on the line, or lateral line movement, and knows it's time to set the hook. Later can be too late!

There are two ways to work jigs. One is with a rod-and-reel rig. The other is with a long pole. The techniques are dissimilar except for the direct contact.

Rod-and-Reel Technique. The object is to keep the jig directly below the rod tip on a taut line. It is also important to keep your boat moving slowly in order to determine what cover the fish are in. One basic rule to remember: You must match the weight of your jig to the pace of your boat's movement. The faster you move, the heavier the jig must

be to remain directly below your rod tip.

As you move along (and slower is better), keep the jig swimming, not dancing, smoothly over bottom cover such as that found on weedy shores, reefs, rocky points, around islands over midlake humps, and in and around brushy areas bordering deep water.

Long-Pole Technique. This is a time-proven method still used by many Southern fishermen. The new graphite telescope poles are better because they can be compacted for portability and provide a sharper feel.

Poles 10' to 12' long are ideal for reach and should be equipped with a 10-pound monofilament of equal length. Some anglers prefer 20-pound mono so they can straighten out the jig hook and recover the lure from snags.

Move in and out of shore cover, slowly swimming the jig over bottom, around tree roots and lily pads, and in weedy lanes. Keep in mind one of the mysteries of jig fishing: Fish prefer a presentation with as little movement as possible.

Spoon Jigging

This calls for any kind of spoon, such as a single-hook weedless, slab, or traditional treble-hook type. Instead of the usual "chuck 'em out and

---

Trigger Strikes

Most people feel a jig should be twitched and jerked on the retrieve. This sometimes elicits strikes, but often as not you'll draw more hits by simply retrieving the lure slowly and steadily. If you want to give more action, simply pause midway in your retrieve and allow the lure to sink several feet. That will often trigger strikes from following fish.

reel 'em back" tactic, employ the unusual direct-contact technique.

Look for rocky or weedy points, bars, reefs, or shoals in your favorite lake. Begin where the bottom is barely visible and work out into depths of 50' or more. As you move along, keep the spoon barely nudging bottom cover, raising and lowering it slowly, maintaining a taut line so you can feel the gentle pickups.

Weighted Spinner

These lures have a compact lead body, a belly treble hook, and a rear spinner. Fish the spinners as you would the spoon jigs. The only difference is you must raise and lower the lure fast enough to cause the spinner to gyrate and flash.

Let the weighted spinner settle to bottom, reel all slack out of the line, lower the rod tip until it's touching the water, then rip the lure off the bottom by raising your rod tip sharply and reeling rapidly at the same instant. This fast lure movement can trigger strikes when nothing else registers.

Flutterer

This unique lure has a minnow-shaped metal body, lead belly, and several line-attachment holes that create various degrees of wiggle. It is the only lure that can be fluttered vertically.

It should be jigged as described under the other types of lures, plus one additional method, backtrolling. This is a very effective way to bottom-fish shore weeds, reeds, lily pads, and brush.

To backtroll, run the motor in reverse so that your boat moves transom-first. With the flutterer just over the bottom, slowly move your corner of the transom in and out of shore cover where it meets deeper water.

By raising your rod tip in short, quick movements, you'll make the flutterer wiggle upward, then fall off, imitating an injured minnow. Most strikes occur during the lure's fall, so be alert to any change of feel in the lure. Stay as close to the cover line as possible because this is where the larger fish will be concealed with just their heads protruding.

Direct-contact jigging is not easy to learn because it requires patience plus the belief that it will work even on days when it doesn't.

How to Fish Tube Jigs

Tube-body jig lures may be the deadliest artificials used today. Let's look at what makes them so potent.

Compactness. Picture a soft-plastic tube about the size of your little finger, with a fluted tail end. The head is

Homemade Ice Jigs

To make ice jigs that are truly effective you need a soldering iron, acid core solder, and several No. 10 or 12 long-shanked hooks. It takes only a small amount of solder added to the shank of the hook just below the eye. With a little practice you can turn out respectable ice jigs that, when tipped with grub or wax worm, should produce some panfish action. Painting the jigs red or yellow seems to produce the best results.

Vertical Jigging

Vertical jigging is a great way to take bass, panfish, and stripers. This technique works in the middle of summer as well as in winter. Work your lure, usually a heavy spoon or jig, up and down 6" to 24" at a time. Expect strikes as the lure drops back down.

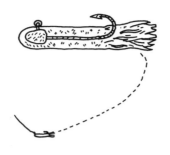

Rig the jig head forward in the tube jig for a smooth glide to the bottom.

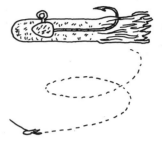

For a spiral descent, place the head further back in the tube jig body.

sealed, like a nipple, and into it is inserted a jig head with the eye on top. The lure's not floppy like a plastic worm, so it casts easily and accurately.

Buoyancy. The tube body holds air. This gives the lure buoyancy, allowing it to glide slowly toward the bottom. The slower, deliberate descent makes an easy target, as opposed to the plastic worm and other artificial lures, which move fast and hurry away.

Allure. The tube lure's tail tendrils give off multiple vibrations as the lure moves through the water. Both the appearance and the action of the lure resemble those of tadpoles, crayfish, leeches, eels, frogs, and minnows.

Preparation. Step 1: Acquire about a dozen tube-lure bodies and six 1/8- and six 1/4-ounce jig heads, with the hook-eye on top of the head.

Suggested tube colors are crawdad brown, cream with silver flecks, white, and black.

Step 2: Go to a swimming pool or fill your bathtub. With a slack line, drop the lure (with a 1/8-ounce jig head pushed all the way forward in the tube) and watch its slow, angled descent to the bottom. Then do the same with a 1/4-ounce jig head. Hop the lure off the bottom and observe its glide path. Get to know how it works; then when you fish the tube jig, you can mentally picture its reaction.

Practice. To really get to know this lure, fish nothing else for an entire day. This will help you recognize how the tube lure reacts as it contacts varied bottom contours such as gravel, rocks, mud, weeds, and brush. Because the line-tie is on top of the jig head, it will first engage and then ease over bottom cover as you gently lift and lower it when retrieving.

You'll also note the subtle feel of a take. Unlike the sharp line jerk when a bass slams a worm, the feel of a tube worm flowing into a bass's mouth is simply a gentle easing or increasing of line tension. It is therefore necessary to keep the line size small, using 6-pound test on the 1/8-ounce jig head and 8-pound on the 1/4-ounce. Learn to count down the tube jig as you lay it close to various shore covers. Say it's bottoming out on a 10 count. If your line suddenly loses feel at a count of five, set the hook; a fish has taken it on the way down.

One Final Note. Fishing tube jigs on a casting rod requires a feel every bit as perceptive as flyfishing with tiny nymphs. The more you do it, the keener your perception will become, and your totals will soar.

Vertical Jigging

The best artificials for vertical jigging must meet two main requirements. First, they must sink fast—to efficiently get down to the fish's holding level (usually between 15' and 50'). Second, they should have a seductive, fish-attracting action when worked up and down. Stocking several of the varieties described below, in different sizes and colors to match the forage found in your local

waters, you'll be set to catch many species of gamefish.

Spoons. These lures are first on the list of most verti-cal-jigging experts. Spoons drop quickly to the fishing zone and flash seductively as they fall. Shaped like shad, they imitate wounded baitfish. Best sizes for bass are 1/2 to 1 ounce; trout, 1/4 to 1 ounce; stripers, 3/4 to 2 ounces; panfish, 1/8 to 1/2 ounce. Stock a selection in white, chartreuse, chrome, and gold, with and without feather or bucktail dressings on the hook, and use a quality ball-bearing snap swivel.

Jigs. Marabou, bucktail, feather, and plastic-tailed jigs can all be effective worked vertically, with sizes ranging from 1/32 ounce for crappies up to 2 ounces in heavy tail-waters and deep lakes for leg-long stripers. Best colors to use include white, yellow, brown, smoke, and pumpkin.

Blade Lures. These heavy, slender metal lures are shaped something like a thin slab spoon but feature weight dis-tribution and line-tie holes that allow their minnow-shaped bodies to maintain a normal upright swimming posture as you pump them up and down.

Vibrators. Sometimes also called lipless crankbaits, these lures are used primarily for casting and trolling but can also be productive when jigged.

Jig/Spinner Combos. This combination includes a

Lures for Vertical Jigging
Some of the best lures for vertical jigging are slab spoons ranging from 1/8 to 3 ounces. Vary the weight according to the size game fish you're after and the depth of the water being probed.

Jig Weights

To get the most from your jigs, be sure to match jig weight to line size. Here's a helpful table:

Line Strength (pound test)	Jig Size (oz.)
4	1/16 to 1/8
6	1/8 to 1/4
8	1/4 to 3/8
10	1/4 to 1/2
12	3/8 to 5/8
14 to 20	5/8 to 3/4

Wind

Calm days can be poor for vertical jigging on clear lakes. Unless the water is a bit cloudy, your best action will come on days with a slight chop on the surface, which makes it harder for the fish below to see your boat.

Colorado spinner blade rigged just below a deerhair, feather, or plastic-tailed jig. These are excellent lures for up-and-down fishing, offering the attraction of a traditional jig plus the appeal of a silver blade that flutters seductively

Tailspinners. These lures have a heavy minnow-type body and spinner on a trailing extension shaft. They are particularly deadly when pumped up and down with 18" to 36" lifts of the rod directly over the quarry.

Tackle and Tactics

Spin tackle is useful when vertical jigging for panfish, but for larger species, baitcasting gear is preferable. Spool up with 6- to 17-pound line, depending on the size of your mark and the number of snags present. A high-visibility line will help you see strikes.

The first step in vertical jigging is finding good deepwater structure such as humps, bridge abutments, submerged islands, points, channel edges, and timber. Try to narrow things down further by pinpointing good structure with forage or gamefish showing on the depthfinder.

Begin pumping the lure up and down, moving it from 1' to 5' and pausing several seconds between lifts. Lower the rod just slightly faster than the lure drops. You want it to fall freely, but you don't want excessive

slack in the line, which can cause missed strikes. Most takes come on the drop, so be ready to set the hook at the slightest twitch, thump, sideways movement of the line, or pause in the lure's descent. If you don't draw strikes within 15 minutes, relocate.

Jigging Wrinkles

Terminal Tackle. Spoons work best with a split-ring and swivel; jigs and plugs work better when attached directly to your line.

Jigging Depth. If jigging at one level doesn't pay off, try pumping the lure, reeling up a foot or two, then jigging again. Repeat this all the way up to the surface. Often this trick will turn on reluctant gamefish.

Strip Bait. If strikes are slow in coming, add to your lure a thin piece of porkrind, a nightcrawler, a strip of white belly meat from a freshly caught fish, or a preserved minnow.

Snags. If your offering hangs on brush or a stump, don't pull tight trying to yank it off. Rather, jiggle it gently to allow the weight of the spoon or jig to work the hooks loose before they become embedded.

FOUL-UPS

Snags are one of angling's major banes. Yet there are ways to reduce the aggravation and expense of lure-eating foul-ups.

Rattling a Plug. If an overzealous cast lands a multi-hooked plug into bankside trees or brush, there's more hope than may first meet the eye. The first step is to refrain from jerking back on the rod as you try to haul it back or loosen it by force rather than finesse. Instead, relieve all tension for a moment, then gently tighten the line. Now start rattling the plug by undulating your rod tip up and down evenly. As long as the hooks rattle, you're in good shape. (A lure that won't move or rattle is one that has all hooks sunk deeply into the obstruction.) Keep rattling, increasing the speed of the rod tip. Nine times out of 10 the lure will suddenly free itself.

Hairpinning. This method works especially well with light lines, but it's also effective with stouter tackle. Keep tension on the line, then reach the rod out toward the snag. Grab the line with your left hand below the first guide and pull it back and out, as far as it will go. Then let it snap back hard, at the same time flicking the rod tip forward and down. Done properly, this makes the line crack hard against the rod, shooting enough force down the line to dislodge the lure.

Gadgets. Lures that remain snagged when these other techniques fail can often be retrieved with the aid of a "plug-knocker," easily made by sliding a spark plug (or similar weighted and easily attached object) down the line until it hits the lure, which can then be jiggled free. Be certain, however, that the sliding surface is smooth, unable to nick and fray your line.

One Final Comment. Sometimes it's best to simply break off quickly, sacrificing a snagged lure. Losing a lure, even an expensive one, may prove wiser than disturbing a prime lie or interrupting a brief spate of peak activity.

ICEFISHING BASICS

It surprises summertime fishermen to learn that more fish are caught by icefishermen, per angling hour of effort, than during any other season.

Species Available. It varies among states, but these are the most popular species sought by icefishermen: bluegills, yellow perch, crappies, bass, whitefish, pike, walleyes, and catfish. For all these fish, you've got to switch your mind and tactics from mainly horizontal summertime presentations to strictly vertical fishing.

Pretrip Presentations. Keeping comfortable is important; if you become an icefishing addict you won't stay home just because it's zero outside. The tackle used differs radically from summer rigs.

Clothing. Wear light insulated pants and jackets or jumpsuits. This "layer system"

Snap Judgment

A snap swivel is best when fishing a lure that has line-twisting tendencies like most jigs. The snap allows a lure to swim with the motion it was designed for. Knots cinched down in different locations on the line-tie can inhibit the action of sensitive lures. Some snaps will weaken with constant use and pop open under stress, so it's best to choose the type with a locking hook at the end.

Ice Safety

Ice is thicker than water, but you better make sure it is thick enough to keep you alive. The state of Colorado conducted some research and came up with the following measurements for lake ice:

• *2" of ice will support one person on foot.*

• *3" of ice will support a group walking in single file.*

• *7 1/2" of ice will support a light automobile.*

• *12" of ice will support a heavy truck.*

Remember: *Slush ice is about half as strong as clear, blue ice. River ice is about 15 percent weaker than lake ice. New ice is generally stronger than old ice, but repeated travel over the same route weakens any ice, as do underwater springs and currents.*

starts with insulated underwear, then pants, shirts, jackets, and coveralls. Feet are kept cozy in insulated boots, while hands are covered with mittens or lined gloves. Should the day turn warm, you can peel off one layer at a time to maintain comfort. Although you don't need to worry about any bugs biting your hide, wear sunglasses and lotion because you get a double dosage from direct rays of the sun and those that reflect off ice or snow.

Getting There. Most icefishermen drive cars to popular lakes. Some prefer to take off across country in snowmobiles or on snowshoes to reach remote lakes or ponds. After you arrive, gear can be carried in a rucksack, backpack, or by hand. Some icefishermen have sleds with built-on drawers and compartments that house everything from fishing gear to catalytic heaters and cooking units.

Picking the Spot. If you are a novice and on your own, look for a gathering of icefishermen and join them. Icefishermen are friendly folks; most people will show you how it's done. Good fishing spots often include beaver colonies that usually adjoin deep water, midlake springs, places where small streams flow into a lake, or deep dropoffs bordering weedy or rocky shores.

Cutting the Hole. Ice is

hard, and the only way you can fish through it is to cut a hole. This can be done with an ax if you're the Paul Bunyan type. An easier method is to use a spud—a chisel mounted on a long pipe filled with lead to give it driving weight. The best tool is an ice auger (either hand or power driven). In below-freezing temperatures, a skimmer will be needed to keep the water from refreezing once you have cut the hole.

Tackle. As in summertime fishing, the tackle varies from simple to elaborate.

Rods. A lively and limber rod is important. Many icefishermen use old flyrod or spinning rod tip sections and wrap on a rudimentary handle. To this is attached a light monofilament line, usually 4- to 6-pound test, with a No. 4 to No. 12 hook at the terminal end, and a tiny, adjustable bobber above. Thus equipped you can choose the length of line that reaches bottom where you fish and adjust the bobber to hold the bait just over bottom cover.

Another alternative is a mini-rig, which is a lively tip with wooden handles and a tiny reel filled with monofilament. These can be purchased or custom-made.

Live Bait. A wide variety of live bait is used according to state and area, such as grubs, worms, maggots, mealworms, minnows, leeches, mousies, catalpa worms, hellgrammites, and many kinds of larvae. These are kept in coffee cans or boxes filled with sawdust or leaves. Between trips they are kept in refrigerators so they are dormant but unfrozen.

Artificial Lures. Tiny jigs, spoons, and flies are the old standbys for the smaller panfishes. For larger species, larger jigs, spoons, and some sinking-wiggling lures that lend themselves to up-and-down manipulation are used.

Methodology. There are two general types of icefishermen: the sitters and the seekers. Sitters bundle up and squat beside a hole waiting for fish to bite, or they bask in short sleeves inside canvas or wooden shelters warmed by ministoves. The seekers spend five or ten minutes at a spot. If fish don't bite, they move on.

Special Tips. Here are some tips on lures, depths, and structure to fish for the most popular icefishing targets:

Bluegills. Use tiny ice spoons (1/32 to 1/80 of an ounce), ice flies, or No. 10 or 12 gold hooks. Tip them with gallworms, cranefly larvae, mousies, mealworms, waxworms, or maggots. Fish the offering with a light tremble or quivering movement. Try levels from 1' to 3' off bottom, over depths of 10' to 20'. A mucky or weedy bottom is best for bluegills. Inlets and outlets are often hotspots.

Crappies. Use a pimple jigging spoon, icefishing plug, or live minnows fished on No. 2 to 6 hooks. Crappies can suspend at just about any depth, from a few feet below the ice to just off bottom, in water from 5' to 20' deep. Move often and try a variety of water levels to pinpoint roving schools. Best bets include dropoffs, rockpiles, deep coves, creek channels, and points.

Yellow Perch. Use the same baits as those you'd use for bluegills and crappies; also try jigging spoons sweetened with the eye from a freshly caught perch or a tiny strip of meat sliced from a perch or bluegill. Concentrate on weedbeds early after freeze-up, then on rocky waters from 15' to 40' deep later in the season.

Trout. Shoal areas, the mouths of inlets, and points are known to produce the most rainbows, browns, and brookies through the ice. They have been caught on just about every kind of bait or lure you could dream up, too. Wet flies and nymphs with a split-shot crimped a foot above for weight are good, as are minnows, spinners, and jigging spoons.

Pickerel, Pike, Muskies. Live minnows or dead ones rigged to hang horizontally in the water are the best producers for these gamefish. Tip-ups allow you to spread your bait over a wide area in weedy coves and on points where

Tip-Ups

Tip-ups are also common in icefishing because they don't need constant holding like a rod. These teeter-totter devices span the hole. When a fish takes the bait, the rod tip teeters downward while a flag teeters into the air to signal "fish on."

Action All Day

Unlike lakes, where surface lures are best early and late, rivers offer potential topwater action all day long. The reason is that rivers are seldom deep. Bass are within striking distance of the surface and used to feeding there at all times. Try chuggers, propeller lures, buzzbaits, wobblers, and stickbaits—any time of day.

these predators rove under the frozen lake's surface searching for prey. Use a thin, black wire leader to avoid cutoffs when dangling bait.

Walleyes. Reefs, points, inlets, and outlets are good spots for ice walleyes. Live minnows, jigs, spoons, and blades are consistent producers. Right before sunset is unquestionably the top time for taking frozen-water walleyes.

Rivers and Streams

MOVING-WATER HOTSPOTS

Rivers and streams offer an abundance of food—crayfish, minnows, frogs, and insects, to name a few—and many types of cover. The following is a list of the best places to look for fish in small rivers, with lure choices and tactics. Remember to approach stealthily and keep an easy-cast distance away. Use oars and anchors as quietly as possible.

The Top 8

Riffle. Beach the boat above the deepest riffle run. Fish afoot with these lures with a mini-tackle kit: crankbait, vibrator, spinner, grub/jig, and plastic worm (III). Cast from the head of the riffle and cover every square yard downstream.

Pool. Anchor an easy cast from shore and work the shoreline cover as well as midstream bottom. Use plastic worms and weedless spoons inside the weedline, crankbaits

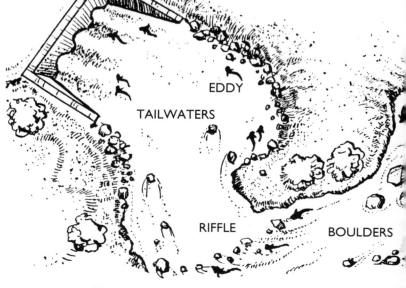

DAM

EDDY

TAILWATERS

RIFFLE

BOULDERS

and vibrators outside cover, and ply the surface with slim minnows, chuggers, buzzbaits, and surface spinners.

Dropoff. Fish deep-diving crankbaits parallel to the dropoff edge and slim minnows where water is flat, and hop the bottom with grub/jigs and vibrators. Move slowly and fish quiet-water areas; anchor and position the boat to work fast-current holes.

Fallen Tree. Cast crankbaits, plastic worms, and weedless spoons in and around all deadfall branches. Using spinners and jigs, fish the dark water below submerged branches and the main tree trunk.

Bridge Buttress. Anchor the boat parallel to eddy water below the bridge support. Use slim minnows and surface lures in the flat water behind the buttress, grub/jigs and sinking vibrators in deep water, plastic worms and spinners on the bottom.

Eddy Current. Below rapids or a dam sluiceway, there is usually an eddy where the fast water rubs against water flowing upstream, called a counterflow. Fish from the head of the eddy using crankbaits, plastic worms, and grub/jigs.

Inflowing Creek. This is where minnows feed and, of course, where bass feed on minnows. Fish from your boat and from shore, using plastic worms, grug/jigs, spinners, crankbaits, and vibrators.

Islands. Fish the upstream edge from your anchored boat using crankbaits, plastic worms, and grub/jigs on the bottom, covering both banks. Then anchor the boat intermittently along each shore, probing deep water. Finally, use slim minnows and surface lures in the calm downstream counterflow.

Incoming Water
In tidal rivers, incoming water is usually best for shad fishing. The fish are moving upstream and are active during this stage of the tide. In freshwater stretches, dawn and dusk are generally the peak fishing periods.

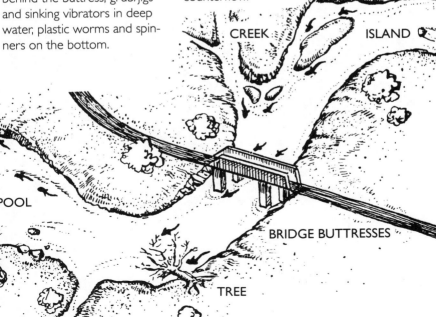

CREEK

ISLAND

POOL

BRIDGE BUTTRESSES

TREE

Practice Casting

Practice casting to specific locations like stumps, weedbed edges, and partially submerged rocks. When a fish pops at the fly, or swirls near it, practice lifting the fly and line cleanly from the water, backcasting once, and casting it back to the same spot. The shorter the cast, the easier it will be to do this gracefully. Learn the basics first, and enjoy the lessons: Those bluegills fight like demons on a flyrod.

Moving Water Tactics

Energetic fish are constantly bucking currents, moving from one hole to another, seeking whatever food is available. They leave the mainstream only to rest or digest.

As you might expect, moving-water fish are more powerful than their less active counterparts. There is never a doubt when one takes a whack at a lure, and the ensuing battle is explosive and long lasting.

Fighters are found in the currents below dams and rapids, outside the ends of streams and in lakes at the inflows of feeder creeks. Their behavior patterns set them apart from other fish, so you have to change your tactics to catch them.

To begin with, a favorite rig is a 6', long-handled rod with a large-capacity baitcasting reel. The best lures are big-lipped deep-divers, plastic worms, jig-and-grub combos, lipless vibrators, weighted spinners, and floating slim-minnow types with small lips for surface antics. Once you're set with tackle, try these strategies:

Riffles. Position yourself on the eddy side, at the head of the riffle. Cast deep-divers and jig-and-grub combos across and downstream, nudging bottom. Try various sizes and colors. Retrieve floating minnows slowly, jerking them with the rod tip. Hurry vibrators across the current.

Undercut Banks. Cast deep-diving lures close to the

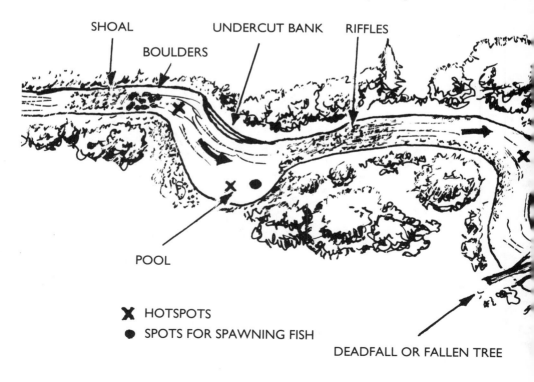

SHOAL BOULDERS UNDERCUT BANK RIFFLES

POOL

X HOTSPOTS

● SPOTS FOR SPAWNING FISH

DEADFALL OR FALLEN TREE

bank, let them lie momentarily, and then animate them into fast action. Crawl the bottom with plastic worms and jig-and-grub combos. Swim floating lures slowly along the bank lip, pausing, twitching, and jerking them into action, making them behave like feeding minnows.

Deep Holes. Weight the floating lure to take it to bottom and let the current wiggle it down slowly. Swim a lipless vibrator close to bottom, pausing occasionally to make them look as if they're feeding. Try spinners and grubs at all depths, with both dawdling and hustling retrieves.

Boulder Hole. Some boulders protrude; others can be spotted by the slick water

behind them in fast-flowing current. Gently drop fast-sinking lures—including grub/jigs, plastic worms, and spinners—into the slick spots. Let the lure touch bottom, then retrieve slowly into the current.

Tailwaters. This is the name fishermen apply to the flowing waters below a dam. It's a classic holding spot for many species because of the abundance of food being washed over the dam. Find the nearest spot to the dam where you can wade out and make a cast upstream into the deeper flowing water. Tie on a grub/jig, add a bobber 2' above it, and lob this upstream. No need to work the grub/jig; the bobber will do it nicely.

The Downstream Cast

If the angler is forced to cast downstream to the trout because he can't reach the fish from the left bank, and the trout would spook if he fished cross-stream from the right side, the angler must cross well downstream from the fish, then walk upstream well away from the bank, which also helps hide the angler's silhouette. If the fish don't take, the angler can move into the water, making sure not to stand in the feeding lane.

UNDERCUT BANK

LAKE

POOL

FLOATFISHING

Floatfishing can indeed be an enriching experience, but each trip must be planned and executed in a level-headed, thoughtful manner. If not, floatfishing can turn into a disaster.

Listed below are 12 tips that can go a long way toward making your floatfishing successful.

Choose Productive Fishing Water. Consult your state's fishery department, a local warden, or sporting-goods and bait-and-tackle stores to find out which rivers near your home are productive for floatfishing. But don't stop there. Press your sources for specifics on which stretches are particularly good.

Choose a Short Drift. Choosing too long a stretch to float can be dangerous, and it can also hurt your fishing. Instead of carefully probing prime water, you'll be rushing through it, throwing out quick, haphazard casts as you go because you're worried about being late.

The distance to choose for a trip varies with the speed of the river and how productive the water is. As a general rule, plan on one mile of river per hour of fishing if you want to cover the water thoroughly. If the river is swift, and you want to probe it lightly as you drift, 1 1/2 to 2 miles can be covered in an hour. But always err on the side of shortness, particularly for your first drift down an

unfamiliar stretch of water.

Buy a Topographic Map. Buy a topographic map from the Distribution Branch, U.S. Geological Survey, Box 25286, Federal Center, Denver, CO 80225.

First request the state index map you need, then order the topos that cover the section of river you're interested in floating. Topos show all the loops and turns a river makes, as well as waterfalls, rapids, and dams. These maps also depict landmarks along the river that will allow you to gauge the progress of your float and arrive at the take-out point exactly when you want to—not half a day early or a couple of hours late. Finally, topos are also useful for showing the backroads and river crossings where you can launch and take out a boat.

Choose the Right Boat. The best bets are canoes, johnboats, and driftboats. A canoe should be chosen only if you've had some practice in one. Pick a 16' to 18' model with a shoe-keel. Canoes are excellent for paddling through long, slow stretches of unproductive water and for negotiating narrow chutes and tricky rapids. They are not the stablest craft in the world, though, and you should know how to handle weight distribution and movements before a long float (see page 181).

Johnboats are simple, humble boats, and many anglers

successfully float hundreds of river miles in them each year. Stability and comfort are pluses of these craft. You can use either oars or paddles to propel them, and you don't have to be as cautious as in a canoe. Johnboats are also roomier than canoes, letting you stretch your legs and move about. However, they are not easy to maneuver in riffles and rapids (see page 186).

Pay Attention to Boat Handling. To have a successful and safe day on the water, someone has to be in charge of maneuvering the boat around obstructions and keeping it on a reasonably straight course. If your boat careens downstream out of control, you'll be continually banging into rocks—and that does a great job of scaring fish. It's also highly unsafe. Trade off with your partner in this boat-handling role to keep things fair.

When you approach rapids, dams, or other dangerous areas, both people in the boat should put down their rods, forget the fishing momentarily, and devote themselves to boat handling.

Choose Safe Water. Check beforehand with someone who has fished the stretch of river you're planning to float to find out if there are dangerous rapids that should be portaged or avoided. It's also wise to let someone know where you will be fishing and

when you expect to be out, so authorities can be notified if you fail to return on time.

Pack Basic Emergency Gear. You may be drifting miles from the nearest road or habitation. An accident may happen, or you may find the float takes longer than you anticipated. If the sun sets, it may well be safer to camp out for the night instead of continuing downstream on water you've never seen before.

Keep a pair of space blankets, waterproof matches, cooking and eating utensils, and drinking water on hand for just such an event. A good first-aid kit is also worth bringing on float trips, as is a spare paddle, duct tape, raingear, a flashlight, canned food in case the fish aren't biting, and of course, life vests.

Line Up an On-Stream Information Source. If you live some distance from the water you plan to float, try to find a local source on the river. This source may be a boat livery, bait-and-tackle store, or someone who lives near the water. By calling just before your trip, you might save yourself a long, useless drive. Ask if the water is high or muddy; few species bite well in a high and discolored river.

Bring the Proper Equipment. The proper fishing equipment will vary according to the species you're after and the nature of the river. For trout, bring flyfishing tackle and a

Life Preserver
Safety does not require that you wear a life preserver all the time you are fishing, especially on a hot day. Put one on when you are running from place to place, or when you approach what you think might be a hazardous situation.

Overnight Float Trip
When you plan an overnight float trip, here are some of the items you'll probably want to pack: sleeping bags and extra clothes in a watertight bag, cooking gear, lantern, flash light, waterproof matches, candles, ground tarp or tent, first aid kit, extra paddles, food, camera, and, of course, fishing tackle.

wide variety of wet and dry flies, streamers, and nymphs. For bass, pack a selection of streamers, nymphs, and poppers, as well as spin tackle and a variety of lures. If you plan to try for pike, walleyes, or bass, it may be worth taking along a seine and bait bucket. That way, if artificials prove ineffective, seine some lively minnows for bait.

Both spin and fly tackle for floatfishing should be on the light side, since river fish are often spooky. And when selecting lures and flies, always bring several of each offering.

Search for a Pattern. Use a variety of lures or flies in the early stages of the trip to determine which ones generate the most action. Also be sure to cast to different types of habitat. The deep midsections of pools may pay off one day. The next day riffles, rapids, eddies, tails of pools, or undercut banks may hold the most fish. By probing all of these areas with a variety of lures, you can usually key in on one combination of lure, retrieve, water depth, and stream location that is most productive.

Stop Often. It's wise to stop occasionally as you float. On a trout river, you might want to stop at a back eddy or side slough where fish are rising. Beach or anchor the boat, hop out, and have at those fish with a careful dry-fly presentation. On a bass river, you might come to a particularly choice-looking rapids or pool that demands extra attention. Either pull the boat ashore and wade, or anchor and cast from it. Such stops let you cover prime areas more thoroughly than you can by simply tossing out casts as you drift along.

Try Overnight Trips. Most anglers realize that the hours of dawn and dusk are prime times to catch trophy gamefish, so plan overnight float trips. Set up camp an hour or two before dark along a choice stretch and enjoy the evening fishing. It makes for much more enjoyable, unhurried, and productive sport.

FISH ON!

CUT DOWN ON LOST FISH

Losing fish now and then is part of the game. Study the following checklist to guard against it.

Put the Bite in Your Hooks. Keen points are a must, especially for hard-mouthed fish. Use a 6" tempered file and hold the hook firmly with broad-nose pliers when you file it. When the hook point bites into your thumbnail, you know it's sharp enough.

Keep Your Line Fresh. When mono line begins chalking and lying on the water in curlicues, it needs replacing because it has lost some of its natural state. Such line will impede casting, and its knot strength is suspect. It's better to fish with total confidence by using fresh line.

Know Your Knots Are Dependable. A simple way to check your knot's strength is to tie it to a screweye fastened to the middle of a section of broom handle. Tie the other end of a 6' piece of mono to a spring-type fish scale. Note the poundage registered when your knot breaks. If it approximates the pound test of your line, it is a good knot, so stay with it. If it doesn't, switch knots.

Set the Hook Properly. Efficient hook setting depends on two factors: a taut line and speed in your rod tip as you set the hook.

Reel all slack out of the line quickly, as the rod tip is lowered and arms are extended toward the fish. The instant you see the line tense, whip the tip over your head with all the speed you can muster. If it doesn't have a solid feel of resistance at the moment of impact, quickly set it again to be sure.

Play a Leaping Fish. When a fish is about to jump, watch it leap—you will remember its brute strength and gill-rattling sounds for a long time. This moment is also when many trophy fish are lost because it is easier for a big fish to throw the lure when airborne than when underwater.

Both tactics work depending on the fish. For all hard-mouthed fish, such as tarpon, muskies, pike, bowfin, and gar, yield the line because the hook point is frequently barely holding against bone or toothy plates. A taut line can jerk the lure free when one of these leapers opens its jaw.

For all softer-mouthed fish, such as bass, trout, salmon, and crappies, keep the line totally taut because the tensed lure is much tougher to disengage with violent headshakes.

Keep Your Line Tight
Before setting the hook on a fish, reel up all the slack and point the rod directly at your mark, with the tip near the water. Unless you strike with an absolutely tight line, it's difficult to exert enough pressure to drive the hook into a fish's mouth. If you have any doubts, try it with a scale on dry land.

Setting the Hook

Every angler has his own style of setting hooks. Sometimes the best technique is simply reeling faster and harder when you feel a strike. After you've done this, then pull back on the rod to drive the hook home. You can often exert more force by turning the reel handle quickly than you can by pulling back with the rod, and this starts the hook-setting process immediately.

Maneuver Your Fish. Once the fish is hooked, do the following things: If the fish is near brush or weedy cover that might allow it to foul line or lure, slowly move your boat and fish into open water where there are no obstructions.

Don't be in a hurry, either. Play the fish against a bent rod until it tires sufficiently to be led to you. Most trophy fish are lost at this juncture because the fisherman gets overeager and does not allow for the reserve power a big fish can suddenly exert.

If you plan to kill the fish, play it until it turns belly-up. Then you can land it one of four ways: (1) leading it headfirst into a net; (2) gripping it over the head and compressing both gills to paralyze it; (3) grasping its lower jaw if it has no teeth; (4) easing your forefinger into its gill slot and lifting.

Above all, don't rush things, keep your cool, and take all the time you need to wear it down.

Concentrate. This is the single most important item for not losing fish. Your mind must continually be thinking about what's happening, or what could happen, at the end of your line. This is especially true if you're fishing live bait or a subtle-feeling lure such as a jig, plastic worm, spoon, or fly.

When the normal feel of these offerings changes even a tad, then you know to set the hook, pronto. Most of your takes will be so gentle that the feel at your end of the line will be a minute decrease or increase in tension. It might be a slight sideward movement of the line, or it might just stop sinking.

If you aren't watching your line where it enters the water, or keeping constantly attuned to your lure's feel, you can lose dozens of fish.

On a long cast a fish can inhale your lure, swim toward you, and blow it out without your even sensing it. The more line you have out, and the heavier that line, the less feel you'll have from that vibrating lure. Be extra alert on lengthy casts with heavier lines.

If you keep these fundamentals in mind, and if you review them before each trip, the number of fish you lose will hit a new low.

HOW TO LAND FISH

Here are options for landing fish. Become familiar with all of them so you'll have alternatives. Just choose the one that best suits where you're fishing, how well your mark is hooked, equipment you have on hand, and whether the fish will be released or kept.

Netting

This is probably the surest method of all—if it is done properly. The angler, rather than "chasing" the fish with the net, should lead the fish over a submerged net and then lift both out of the water.

When choosing a net, favor one that may be too large over one too small. Choose a net that has a strong, rugged handle and dark-colored mesh. Several companies offer nets with black handles. These are preferable to bright, shiny ones since they're less likely to spook fish.

Don't try to net a fish that is still green and fighting hard. You're likely to touch the line with the net as the fish makes one final lunge, and that might pop the fragile monofilament. Or you may accidentally hook the plug on the net mesh or knock the fish off the hook.

Instead, remain calm and keep the net out of the way, but in your hands and ready until the fish is exhausted. When your mark is worn down enough to land, hold the net motionless near the water. As the fish comes up to the surface and is led toward the boat or shore, slip the net quietly into the water just deep enough so that the quarry can be led over it. As the fish comes more than halfway into the net, scoop forward and hoist the net and fish out of the water. Never sweep the net toward the fish while it's still fighting, for this will spook it and may cause it to thrash around and escape with one last lunge.

In lakes and slow rivers fish should be netted headfirst.

With this approach, if the fish lunges or dives, it's actually going into the net. In heavy river current it's best to position the net below you, meaning downstream. Lead the fish above the net, pump it up to the surface, then relax tension slightly on the line, and allow the current to carry the fish back down into the waiting mesh.

Nets are especially useful for lightly hooked fish. Many hooks seem to fall out of fish's mouths the instant they're netted. Most of these fish would have been lost if the angler had attempted to lift them into the boat. Nets are also useful for sharp-toothed gamefish such as pike, pickerel, and muskies and for thin-mouthed species such as crappies and shad.

Swinging Aboard. It's fairly simple, but it can't be done if you're using a light-action rod or light line. It's best when heavy tackle is employed for fairly small fish.

To execute this tactic, get the fish coming toward the boat by reeling fast. Then, when it's a few feet away, continue its momentum by sweeping it upward through the air and into the boat with two hands on the rod. Don't reel the fish all the way up to the rod tip, but rather within 3' to 5' of it.

This isn't the prettiest landing technique, but for bassing with medium and heavy tackle, it's a quick and efficient way to

Net Results

There's an art to netting fish that many anglers never seem to learn. The most common mistake is working a big fish up to the side of the boat and then repeatedly jabbing at it with the net. All this accomplishes is spooking the fish, causing it to about-face and streak way on another run. A better way is to have on board a net that's large enough to handle the biggest fish you're likely to encounter. Then, when your partner begins working his trophy in close to the boat, lower the rim and bag of the net into the water on the opposite side of the boat and hold it still. Now, your partner can lead his fish around the bow or transom to your side and guide it headfirst into the open bag. When the front half of the fish is safely through the rim of the net, you can now simultaneously move the net toward the tail and lift the whole works.

Collapsible Landing Net

Carrying a standard land-ing net over your shoulder when fishing streams crowded with bushes or when walking to water through undergrowth can be frustrating—especially when the net snags on a branch and tears. Try a collapsible landing net. You can carry the folded net on your belt in its plastic case or attached to your creel with thin wire passed through the case's belt slits and the top of the creel. Either way, it is snag-proof.

boat fish before they shake the hooks free or something else goes wrong. If your rod is too limber for this technique, you can use a variation of it by grabbing the line and then swinging the quarry aboard.

Beaching. This is a variation of the above method and is particularly useful for shore fishing where there's a gently sloping bank. Play the fish until it's tired, then lift the rod as the fish nears the shore. When you've pumped it to the surface, back up and reel, gradually sliding the quarry up on to the bank as you move away from the water.

Lip Landing. This method is good for landing black bass, but it also works on certain other species with large mouths, such as striped bass and large crap-pies. The tactic doesn't work well on small-mouthed fish, and it should never be used on fish with lots of sharp teeth, such as northern pike or pick-erel, unless you want a severely lacerated thumb.

To successfully execute the lip-landing method, you must exhaust a fish. Work it up to the side of the boat or shore and reach down, slipping your thumb inside its mouth and down against the lower jaw. With your index finger, tighten up against the outside of the lower lip. As you lift with this grip, the fish is almost totally immobilized, allowing you to bring it into the boat or onto shore and remove the hook.

Don't use this technique if a nasty set of treble hooks is hanging menacingly from the fish's mouth. When single hooks are used and the fish is well played out, however, the lip hold is highly efficient.

Belly Lift. This little-used technique works well on virtu-ally all species and does not harm the fish. Play the fish out and then slowly slip your hand around its belly. Don't squeeze the fish, as this can cause inter-nal injury. Instead, simply lift slowly, allowing the fish's weight to press down on your palm as you raise your hand from the water. This pushes the fish's organs up against its spinal col-umn, temporarily immobilizing it. Be sure to lift at the center of balance, so its weight will be evenly distributed and you can easily work your lure, hook, or fly free.

HOW TO RELEASE FISH

Returning fish alive to the water after catching them is a practice that's increasing every year. But releasing a fish in a healthy state is not simple. Returning a fish so that it sur-vives and thrives demands some forethought about your angling methods, choice of tackle, fighting tactics, and landing techniques.

Artificial lures or flies should be used whenever pos-sible. Since fish tend to swal-low natural offerings, internal injuries are more common when fishing with bait. If you do use bait, set the hooks quickly after a strike. This will result in lip-hooked fish most of the time, allowing you to release the quarry in good health. If a fish swallows a baited hook, its chances of survival are still on the order of 60 to 80 percent, according to most studies. Simply clip the line close to the target's mouth and release it with the hook inside, rather than trying to work it out of the fish.

Another preliminary step that will facilitate releasing fish is to use barbless hooks. You can buy barbless hooks, but most anglers who choose this approach simply flatten the barbs down on their lures by using needle-nosed pliers.

Releasing fish in good health is possible if you use light tackle, but it's best to avoid extremely light line and rods that require long, drawn-out fights. This type of gear can exhaust the quarry, severely reducing its chances of survival. The quicker they can be brought to the boat and returned to the water, the better the shape they're likely to be in.

Most fish that die after release are actually injured by improper handling by the angler. Fish should never be picked up by the eye sockets, lifted by the gills, squeezed tightly around the body, or thrown roughly back into the water. If you avoid these com-mon mistakes, most of your fish should swim away healthy.

Nets tend to remove protective slime from fish and can split fins, making the fish vulnerable to infections. Avoid using a net whenever possible if the fish is to be released. If you feel you must do so, choose one with a rubber mesh, since these are not so likely to damage the fish. Lip-landing large-mouthed fish such as bass, crappies, and stripers is a better alternative.

Handle fish as little as possible, and wet your hands before touching the fish. Using a wet glove is even better, since it prevents caustic amino acids on your hands from contaminating the fish and causing bacterial fungus infections later. Another approach is to dip your bare hand into non-iodized salt before handling the quarry, to neutralize the amino acid.

Often it's not even necessary to remove fish from the water to release them. Toothy fish such as pike and muskies can be handled by gripping them just behind or on top of the gill plates. Leave the rest of the fish in the water, which will help support its organs. Reach down with your other bare hand, or use a pair of pliers or surgical forceps, to grasp the lure or fly and work it loose. With bass and trout, it's sometimes possible to simply hold the line or leader in your hand and use the pliers

Mount or Release?

Modern taxidermists are so efficient they have fiberglass molds of almost any size for popular sporting species. Fiberglass is far more durable than a natural mounting, yet some say, "It's not real." The new mold is far better than the real thing for three reasons: (1) it looks just as natural, (2) it is impervious to moths and bugs and is more durable for handling or moving, and (3) you didn't need to kill a prized specimen to get your mount. How much more sensible to weigh and measure your trophy fish and release it to live on. Then, just tell the taxidermist the dimensions of your whopper and he can duplicate it for you.

or forceps to remove the hook without handling the fish at all. When feasible, this is the best release technique.

Livewells in boats can be very damaging to fish, mostly because too many fish are often crowded in and not given sufficient fresh water and oxygen by aeration.

An angler wading a river might put a fish on a stringer in the current for a few minutes so it can revive after a long battle. But if you plan to release them, there's no excuse for dragging fish through the current or taking them out of the water as you walk to other spots.

If you haven't removed a fish from the water, chances are it will dart away as soon as you twist the hook free. If you must take the fish out of the water, hold it by the lower lip, or if it has teeth, cradle it gently under the belly to support its weight as you unhook it, then slowly lower it into the water. Hold the fish level, and wait until its gills are working regularly and it appears healthy enough to swim away freely. If a fish fought for a prolonged period, it may take a few minutes of reviving before it's strong enough to swim away. In rivers, try to release fish in an area with some flow, which will provide the fish with more oxygen than backwater areas. But don't release it in a heavy current.

Releasing fish is one of the most important steps an angler can take to put something back into the world of sportfishing.

Fish Clean-up
Next time you have a mess of fish to clean, get some salt and tooth-paste. Before you start, wet your hands and dip them in the salt. It will help you hang on to those slippery little devils, especially the smaller ones. When you are done, wash your hands with the toothpaste to remove the fish odor.

Cleaning and Preparing Your Catch

Clean Fish the Easy Way

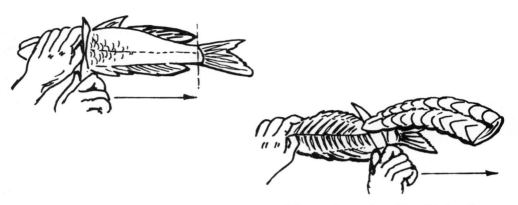

If you do it right, you can clean a 5-pound bass or a 1/2-pound crappie or bluegill in less than a minute—and end up with skinned and boneless fillets. The trick is to slap the fish down on a board without bothering to scale, skin, or even gut him. Hold his head down with one hand, and with a sharp knife in the other, cut behind his head and side fin down to the backbone; then slide the knife forward along the backbone to the tail, but don't cut through the skin at the tail. Flip the upper fillet you have just cut away from the backbone over the tail so the flesh side is up. Now, hold the section with the backbone firmly with your free hand, insert your knife between the skin and flesh of the exposed fillet at the tail end, and work the knife forward between the skin and flesh. This gives you a skinned fillet with only rib bones. Cut these away with your knife. Now, flip the other section over so the exposed backbone is down, and do another fillet in the same manner.

Dressing a Fish for Baking

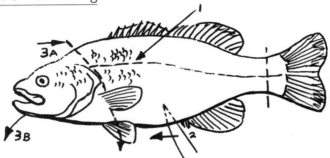

Bass, stripers, walleyes, large trout, and other large fish can be prepared with this method.

    1. Scale the fish at a 45-degree angle from belly to back. To avoid a mess, hold the fish underwater in a large sink.

    2. Carefully slit the belly skin, from the vent to the gills. Do not pierce the organs.

    3. Cut down behind the head, severing the backbone. Remove the head by pulling out and down from the body. The internals organs should come with it.

    4. Remove the kidney (which lines the spine inside the body cavity) with thumbnail or spoon. Rinse the fish well. If the cavity is to be stuffed, salt it first and close it with thread or skewers.

2

Skinning and Filleting Sunfish

Cleaning sunfish using this method is much quicker and simpler than either the traditional filleting technique or scaling and gutting, especially if you follow these instructions. First, lightly make the outlined cut shown in diagram I with a small, razor-sharp knife. Next, use a small pair of pliers to peel back the skin gently but firmly, scales and all, from point A to point B. (Don't use needle-nosed pliers; they tend to puncture and tear the skin.)

Remove the skinless fillets, as in diagram 2, by sliding your knife first along the backbone and then down and out at point C. Now turn the fish over and repeat the steps. After a stringer or two, you'll be cleaning a fish a minute. This method makes even a 4" bluegill worth keeping. The fillets will freeze readily.

Fragrant Fish

Trout stored for one or two days in a refrigerator can create a problem: The smell just takes over the whole refrigerator. To avoid that, be sure to wash fish thoroughly after you clean them to remove all slime. Put the fish in a self-closing plastic bag and add three or four generous slices of fresh lemon. The citrus will keep the smell of your fish from overpowering the refrigerator.

Fish Care

If fish are mishandled, a single bacterium, given the correct conditions, can increase to 17 million in just 12 hours. Low temperature and moisture levels keep bacteria at bay, so that's why it's necessary to kill fish immediately and place on ice in a cooler. Clean the catch as soon as possible after the day's fishing, and pack it in plastic bags on ice or in the refrigerator.

If the fish cannot be eaten within two days, freeze it. Double wrap the fish in plastic wrap or bags to prevent freezer burn, and spread fish packages out near the cooling elements for quick chilling.

Thawing, and not freezing, is actually where much flavor loss and texture deterioration occur. Decide at least a day ahead of time if you want to have fish and thaw the package out slowly, in the refrigerator, for 12 to 24 hours.

Ice crystals should melt slowly. Rapid defrosting at room temperature causes these crystals to break down the delicate fish flesh. The result: mushy, tasteless fare.

Sweet Tasting Fillets

Veteran anglers have learned that bass from waters regis-

Filleting a Catfish

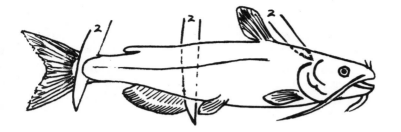

1. Lay the fish sideways on a cutting board. Hold its head firmly by inserting your index finger into its mouth and pressing your thumb on top of the skull.

2. With a sharp fillet knife, slice down and back from the head, following the spine. Cut over, not through, the ribs. Continue cutting to the base of the tail.

3. Cut down and in from behind the gills to the spine. Turn the blade out, keeping the side of the knife on the ribs as you cut.

4. Pierce the skin with the knife point above the bottom fins and slice back. The fillet is now freed from the carcass.

5. Turn the fish over and repeat steps 1 through 4.

6. To remove skin, lay fillet skin side down and hold the front end against the cutting board with your thumbnail. Insert the knife blade and slice back between the skin and flesh, keeping the blade horizontal.

tering 40° to 50°F have a stronger smell—and flavor—than those from 60° to 80°F waters. This could be due to an acid buildup from less frequent elimination. Try soaking fillets in a mild sodium bicarbonate/water

solution for 20 minutes, kneading them lightly to remove some fluids. Then air-dry for 30 minutes on paper towels. Dip into buttermilk, roll in flour seasoned with salt and pepper, and fry until crispy-brown.

Camp-Cooking Hint
Half a can of beer heated with an equal amount of tomato paste makes a good sauce for strong-flavored fish.

BOATS AND BOATING

Boating Rules to Live By

There are a dozen boating rules that should never be broken:

1. Know how to swim.

2. Don't overload— the more people, the more risk.

3. Each passenger should wear an approved life jacket; check the law in your state.

4. Position boaters carefully to prevent falls.

5. Carry a first-aid kit, and know proper first aid.

6. Carry all required safety equipment such as fire extinguishers, bailing bucket, magnetic compass (and know how to read it).

7. Obey all boating regulations such as courtesy to other boaters. Accidents are caused by clowning and drinking.

8. Don't smoke while refueling.

9. Stay out of swim areas.

10. Don't overpower.

11. Don't second-guess the weather. If it looks bad, head for shore fast.

12. Don't make high-speed turns.

HOW TO BE SAFE IN A BOAT

Here's a list of what you should know about small boats, in declining order of importance. You might use it as a test to see how you measure up.

Safety. Have a good flotation jacket and use it in any kind of potentially dangerous situation—such as running your boat alone. Also, good preservers should be at hand for every person aboard—not stowed in a locker. Anyone who can't swim and does not wear a personal flotation device (PFD) is nuts. A kill switch when running the boat alone is mandatory.

Gear. Carry all legally required gear: flares, running lights, horn. Not legally required (usually) but all-important is a bailing device: bucket or scoop or both. Not legally required—though it should be—is an anchor for the kind of bottom you'll be over and a line 7 times the depth of water you'll be in.

Shear Pins. They are rapidly becoming extinct, but if your outboard has a shear pin, have spares aboard and the knowledge and tools to pull the prop. Pull the prop annually and grease the hub, so you can make an emergency pin change easily.

Capsize. Overloading and capsizing are the chief boating killers. For fishermen, add falls overboard. Therefore it's important to know about the stability of your boat and how much weight it can carry under what conditions; even then, it helps to act conservatively.

Seamanship. You should have some knowledge of how to handle your boat in rough waters: how to heave to or when to run for it; when and how to slide down seas. For river running, you should know how to follow a swamped boat and/or how to float downstream, raised feet first.

Weather. Be alert to the patterns of weather changes and look for them. Anyone who lives within range of the government's 24-hour continuous weather broadcasts should have a battery-operated radio aboard or a CB with weather bands.

Water Conditions. A knowledge of how currents, tides, and wind affect your boat is important. Where will you drift? If you do river running, know how to scout and read whitewater.

Charts and Maps. Almost every body of water—all our rivers and coastal and deep-sea waters—is mapped or charted. Have copies of charts and maps appropriate to your area and know how to read them. Not only will they keep you off rocks and sandbars, but they are also great fishing tools.

Compass. You should have a compass aboard your boat if you do any big-water boating. You should know how to chart a course and how to run on it. Also, you should have some idea of boat speed at various throttle settings, so you can figure out approximately where you are.

Alcohol. Almost 60 percent of boating fatalities involve alcohol abuse. Impairment of faculties starts with the first sip.

Hypothermia. Be aware of the stunning effect of cold water, and act accordingly. River rafters/canoeists should wear wet suits.

Knots. Can you weave a bowline, and tie a square knot or two half hitches? Every bit of knowledge helps.

Flammable Fuel. If you have an I/O motor or inboard, you will recognize the danger of gasoline fumes. Before starting the engine, you must lift hatches and smell the bilge. Also, inspect and tighten fuel line fittings on a regular basis and treat fueling with the respect it deserves.

Rules of the Road. You should know that boats coming from your right quadrant have the right-of-way; that sailboats have right-of-way

over powerboats, except in tight channels; that boats meeting head to head steer to the right to pass; that a boat being overtaken has right-of-way. You should also be aware that most other boaters do not know the rules of the road, and go out of your way to keep dangerous situations from developing into something nasty.

Safe Clothing. You aren't okay if you're uncomfortable, so have good foul-weather gear aboard, with hood, hat, and gloves if it's cold. Wear boat shoes with squeegee soles. Bassboaters traditionally go with insulated coveralls.

Adages. "Stick with the ship" and "One hand for you, one hand for the ship" are two old safety slogans that are as meaningful now as they were in the days of the clipper ships.

FLAT-WATER CANOE GUIDE

In any outdoor activity, matching the equipment to its intended use is of utmost importance. A canoe designed for whitewater use isn't a good choice for lakes, ponds, or slow-moving streams. There are numerous subtle differences between whitewater and flat-water designs, but the primary distinction is the amount of hull in the water. In rapids, you want a canoe that will turn

Carpet for Boats
Carpet samples and swatches made of synthetic fibers, like those left over from recarpeting your home or purchased from carpet stores for nominal cost, are ideal for boating use. They serve well under tackleboxes and gas cans to reduce noise and protect the boat bottom. Shag or other fluffy carpeting helps flyrodders since it will hold the coils of flyline that fall on a deck and prevent them from blowing around. Carpet swatches can also serve canoeists as knee pads, and they help deaden noise from an anchor in the anchor locker or in the bow of the boat.

quickly and even move sideways when necessary. On a lake, however, you want a canoe that will track straight without constant course corrections. A whitewater design includes rocker: The hull curves upward from amidships to the ends. On a lake, a canoe with pronounced rocker will spin like a leaf. A good flat-water canoe will have little or no rocker, putting the entire length of the boat in the water and thus making it more resistant to turns and more likely to track straight, even in a wind.

Most canoe designs are compromises. A design that is very fast will not hold much equipment. A side canoe is stable, but it requires more energy to paddle. Lightweight materials cost more. Longer models carry more equipment but are heavier. If you understand the choices in materials and design, you can find a canoe with an acceptable mix of features—a suitable compromise.

Shop by Category

As you shop for a canoe, remember that you don't have to look at each one of the hundreds currently on the market. Instead, focus on the category that fits your needs.

Recreation canoes are the most stable. Often they are shorter and wider, and while

that makes it possible to stand in them (if you are careful), it also makes them less efficient than longer, slimmer models that slice through the water.

Touring canoes represent a middle ground. They are longer and narrower than recreation canoes, allowing them to track straighter and carry more of a load. They feel less stable but really are harder to capsize than recreation canoes. (It's the difference between initial stability and final stability. A canoe high in initial stability feels rock solid. Once it rocks too far to one side, however, it might just keep right on going until it is upside down. A canoe with high final stability might feel a bit "tippy," but it is much harder to overturn. Also, a model with high final stability is safer in high waves.)

Cruising canoes aren't for most sportsmen. They are fast, efficient, and beautiful, but it takes a skilled paddler to use one. They have less capacity and even less initial stability than touring models.

Expedition canoes are long and deep for carrying a heavy load. Most are designed for fast water. Unless you plan to spend a week at a time in your canoe, look at one of the other categories.

For fishing with two or three people in the canoe, look for a model between 16' and 18' long. All things being equal (which they never are), lighter is better (and almost always more expensive).

Material Concerns

You can still buy canoes made of traditional materials, including wood, but today most are made of aluminum, polyethylene, Royalex, fiberglass, Kevlar, or a combination of materials. All have advantages and disadvantages. Let's look at each:

Aluminum. *Pros:* Rugged, not affected by ultraviolet light, relatively inexpensive, easily repaired. *Cons:* Heavy, loud, cold to the touch,

can't be shaped into sleek, more efficient designs.

Polyethylene. *Pros:* Inexpensive, very rugged. A zero-maintenance material that will bounce off rocks and keep going. *Cons:* Heavy, requires internal bracing, generally rounded ends, less efficient.

Royalex. *Pros:* Rugged, quiet. *Cons:* Heavy, difficult to repair. A canoe made of Uniroyal's Royalex material can be bent severely, straightened out, and suffer little if any damage. That's a wonderful feature for whitewater paddling, but not important to flat-water canoeists.

	STIFFNESS	WEIGHT SAVINGS	EASE OF PADDLING	COST	ABRASION RESISTANCE	IMPACT RESISTANCE	FLEXIBILITY	REPAIRABILITY
	\	PERFORMANCE			DURABILITY			
POLYETHYLENE	6	6	6	6	6	2	1	6
KEVLAR	3	2	2	2	2	3	3	3
FIBERGLASS CLOTH	2	3	3	4	4	6	4	1
ROYALEX	5	4	4	3	5	1	2	2
ALUMINUM	4	5	5	5	1	5	5	5
HYBRID	1	1	1	1	3	4	6	4

MOST ⟵————————⟶ LEAST
1   6

Mount a Motor on a Canoe

An electric motor will move a light canoe along at a good clip. Typically, it is fastened on a mount attached near the stern or on the stern itself if the canoe has a square one. But for the angler there is a better way to mount an electric motor—on the gunwale near the bow, which requires neither a motor mount nor a square stern. Located just to the rear of the bow seat, it pulls the canoe along instead of pushing it, making it less vulnerable to the wind. And it's easy to operate from the bow seat. Since most electric motors can pivot 360 degrees in their swivel, a side mount is also no problem. On most canoes it will probably be necessary to place a short piece of wooden board on the inside to provide a sturdier clamp for the motor and to prevent damage to the gunwale. To help balance the load, the battery that supplies the power can be located toward the stern.

Paddle Savvy

What's the best length for a canoe paddle? It's supposed to come to your chin, right? Forget it. That comes from the Maine Guide Era when all paddles were the long beavertail design. Today paddles come in more styles and shapes than you can imagine. So how do you fit one? Try different lengths until you get one where you can dip the entire blade in the water without having to lean out. If you are paddling with only half the blade, you have only half a paddle. If you're going for long trips pick a paddle with a narrow blade 5" or 6". But if you like whitewater work, blades of 8" or 9" grip the water better.

Fiberglass. *Pros:* Can be worked into subtle shapes, including sharp entry lines; tough, relatively inexpensive, easily repaired. Even though fiberglass will take less abuse than Royalex or polyethylene, it is plenty tough for a lake canoe. For most sportsmen, it might represent the right combination of features. *Cons:* Less rugged.

Kevlar. *Pros:* Strong, very light. Although not as forgiving as Royalex, it is extremely tough. The lightness is what makes it so desirable. *Cons:* Expensive. But if you can afford it, a Kevlar canoe can be a wondrous thing.

Wood or Wood and Canvas. *Pros:* Beauty, tradition, pride of ownership, generally good designs. *Cons:* Expensive, higher maintenance.

Hybrid. *Pros:* Light weight, strength. *Cons:* Expensive.

The Shape Is the Thing

A canoe's shape determines how it performs. A sharp entry line (at the bow) is more efficient. If the hull flares quickly to its maximum width, the canoe will be harder to paddle. If it flares gradually, it will be tippy. If you view the canoe from either end and the sides flare out at the top, that's called "flare." If they turn in, that's "tumblehome." Tumblehome allows you to keep the paddle closer to you, making your job more comfortable and efficient.

Many people think a keel is necessary to keep a canoe tracking straight. Not so. Most canoe designs that utilize a keel do so because the material used demands a keel. It is a device for canoe construction, not for performance. A properly designed lake canoe does not need a keel.

A sharply pointed bow parts the water and is easier to paddle. A narrower canoe pushes less water aside as it passes and is easier to paddle. A longer canoe is often easier to paddle (within limits).

A square-stern canoe can be viewed as really versatile or as a "does-nothing-right" design. It won't paddle well. It won't run the way a boat will. It is a shallow-draft combination, however.

Inflatable canoes are poor choices for flat water. They track poorly and require constant course correction.

Try Before You Buy

Many of the design features discussed here are difficult to imagine but easy to experience on the water. Rocker, tumblehome, initial versus final stability, tracking—they all come alive on the water. Trying them out is the best way to shop.

A good canoe shop will make arrangements for you to try the model or models you're considering. Some stores have special days when they put several models on a lake and allow people to try them. If there isn't a store nearby that will let you try out canoes, find a canoe club. Members will be knowledgeable and usually only too happy to have you try their canoes.

Getting a Handle on Paddles

What was once considered the height of simplicity—a carved piece of wood—the paddle is now the subject of much research, debate, and redesign. High-grade wood paddles are much lighter than those you'll find in department stores. Other models have aluminum shafts and plastic blades. Some are made of graphite or Kevlar for light weight.

If you are paddling tandem and plan to cover some distance, investing in bent-shaft paddles could really pay off. A bend of 10 to 15 degrees will increase your paddling efficiency by about 10 percent. That means you can travel 11 miles with a bent-shaft paddle on the same energy it took to go 10 miles with a straight one.

Remember to hold the paddle so that the blade angles toward the bow, not so that the bend "cups" the water. Efficiency is increased because the blade stays vertical further back into the stroke. If you are alone, a straight paddle gives you more maneuverability.

ANCHORS FOR ANGLERS

There are all kinds of bottoms: sand, muck, goo, mud with weeds in it, big rocks, little rocks, stumps, brush, and so on. All require different anchors and anchoring techniques.

A very popular anchor design is the Danforth (and its many imitators). Because of its flat shape, the Danforth stows well. You can put it in a bracket on deck or lay it in the bottom of a compartment where it takes up little room. Another plus for the Danforth is that it resets itself.

Use a 2 1/2-pound anchor with a 10' boat; 4-pound with 16'; 8-pound with 24'; 13-pound with 32'. There are aluminum versions that weigh almost nothing—a 4-pounder holds a 20' boat.

Another popular anchor is the iron mushroom; they have a convenient shape and are easy to store and use. Sizes range from 10 pounds on up. Better ones are vinyl covered. Most smaller mushrooms have a full bell shirt, but there are types that cut away the bell rim to gain some digging power. If you fish around a lot of brush, tie a line to a big clip and latch it onto the brush. It will hold well.

If you fish in rocky, boulder-strewn bottoms, a grapnel or the traditional yachtsman's anchor works as well as any.

Tips about Anchors
Anchors need a lot of scope, or length, in the anchor line. The longer the line, the better the hold. For overnight or long-term anchoring your line should be 6 or 7 times the depth of water you're anchoring in. If the bottom is 10' down, let out 60' of line. Use nylon because it stretches and absorbs the shock of a boat blowing back hard against it—1/4" for the smallest Danforth, 3/8s for midranges, and 1/2s to hold a big 20' boat. Some use polypropylene (water-ski line), but its floating quality reduces its efficiency. Dacron (polyester) is okay but expensive. Don't use fiber ropes—manila or sisal—because they will rot if stored wet.

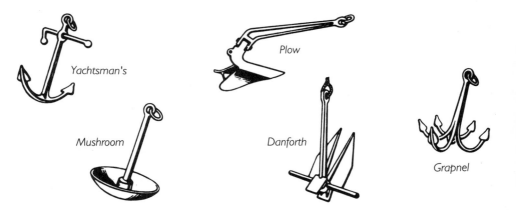

Yachtsman's

Plow

Mushroom

Danforth

Grapnel

Flat Bottom in a Pickup

A square-bow, flat-bottom johnboat can be carried in the bed of a pickup truck with the tailgate down, but loading and unloading the boat can wreak havoc on your paint job. To prevent this, all you need is a length of heavy sheet plastic as wide as your johnboat and about 2' longer. Put the plastic on the tailgate, pull the front flap of plastic up over the bow, then push the boat into the truck. It will slide easily, pulling the plastic with it. Push the boat all the way to the front of the bed and secure both sides of the stern to the truck with heavy rubber tie-downs or ropes. The boat will slide out as easily as it went in.

If you're packing in with a raft or light canoe, take along a strong bag. Fill the bag with rocks, tie on a line, and it will serve as an anchor.

Use a length of chain as a drag anchor on floats. The chain doesn't hang up on the bottom, and its drag can be adjusted: Lengthen the line, and you'll slow down; take it in, and the drag is less.

Rig a trip in case your anchor gets caught on the bottom. This is a strong line on a buoy tied to the head of the anchor. If the anchor won't break free with a straight up-and-down pull, bring the buoy on board and use the reverse pull to free it.

Other types of anchors include the popular Navy anchor, which has two wide, heavy flukes and a solid, pivoting shank. Another favorite is called a plow. It's a great anchor because it digs in well and will reset itself.

Since bottoms may have sharp rocks or shells or coral, it's customary to put a length of chain right behind the

anchor to prevent chafing as the boat pulls the line back and forth.

Every boat should carry some kind of anchor and suitable long line as a safety factor. If your boat breaks down, you'll be able to hold your position rather than be blown into more dangerous areas.

JOHNBOATS

The johnboat, a workhorse boat around the world, has been much improved in recent years. Gone is the flat, blunt bow that smacked into waves and tended to pull water aboard. Now V-bows cut the water. Yet the new bows don't sacrifice interior space the way the sharp bow of an aluminum cartopper does.

Yet the new johnboats retain all the appealing characteristics of the originals. They are wide and flat, which makes them pop on plane quickly and stay there with relatively modest power. It also makes them probably the shallowest-draft boats there are. With their wide beam, they are great load carriers.

All the johns, new or old, are made of marine aluminum. This keeps them strong but lightweight. You can easily trailer even the biggest ones with a compact car. Loading and launching are fairly simple. And relatively modest horsepower, 35 to 75 hp, is ample.

A study of the catalogs of the better-known manufactur-ers indicates that a 10' john with 55" beam is one of the smallest boats; several builders offer 20' models with 86" beams or a 14' model with a bottom width of 48".

Most johnboats are riv-eted, though a few are welded. Which is better? There isn't any good answer. It's a standoff as to which of the two is the better method of construction.

Travel Tips

Here are some helpful tips for the traveling angler.

Packing. Use soft-sided bags; they're cheaper and can't be crushed. Pack them to full capacity and use the tie-downs to keep items in place. Take lightweight, washable clothing that can be laundered and drip-dried in a bathtub. Take along several sweaters and nylon jackets to be worn in layers in case the temperature drops. The foul-weather suit is a must since it serves as both a windbreaker and a rainsuit.

Attach an eye-catcher to each bag. You can spot your luggage the moment it appears on the conveyor. Brightly colored tape will serve this purpose.

How to Avoid Lost Baggage. Rare is the sportsman who hasn't had a trip marred by having his luggage arrive late after he has traveled by air.

While there are no surefire tricks to avoid losing baggage, there are ways to reduce the likelihood of its happening. And there are ways to cut down on the negative impact the loss can have on your fish-ing expedition if it does occur.

One of the first things sea-soned travelers learn is to pack all crucial items in carry-on bags. These must fit in overhead com-partments or under the seat in front of you on the plane, but it's surprising how much you can stuff into two bags (the usual limit per person).

On fishing trips always pack at least one breakdown travel rod in an aluminum tube in one carry-on bag. Also put a few small, clear satchel-type tackleboxes in the bag with lures or flies you will need for the trip. With a couple of such boxes, extra line, reels, a pack-rod, and a change of clothes,

Foreign Travel Tip
If you travel out of the country for fishing, make copies of the two pages in your passport that contain your photo and basic information. Carry them in another part of your baggage. Should you lose the passport, the copies are invaluable in helping you get a replacement quickly.

Make a List

In your haste to get out on the water, have you ever run off and left something behind—oars, life jacket, thermos? A simple remedy to the problem is to sit down and make a list of everything you could possibly need for your outing and stick it up on the wall of your garage or in a place where it's easily noticed, such as your vehicle's windshield or door. Then, before starting each trip, just run down the checklist to be sure you haven't forgotten anything.

you can salvage a trip even if your main luggage fails to show.

Arrive at the airport early. If you show up just before departure, a long check-in line may mean your bag won't even get on to the plane. Don't check bags at curbside locations, either. They're less likely to reach their destination—and theft potential is higher.

You can almost guarantee lost luggage by scheduling connecting flights that are too close together. If you're switching planes on the same airline, you can cut it as close as half an hour, but that's risky. When you're using different airlines and flying into busy airports, an hour's connecting time is the minimum.

Fishing Tackle. If you're heading for a fishing camp, ask the owner which lures to bring. Do take along a few dozen of your pet lures in a small box. Remember that a camp always has lures on hand that have proved successful for guests.

If you carry your rods in plastic tubes, use foam plastic or rags to cushion all movement in the tube.

Boat Bag. These are necessities: insect spray; No. 15 sunscreen; a mini first-aid kit with adhesive bandages and a tube of antibiotic salve for nicks and cuts; pliers with a good hook-cutter; sunglasses; foul-weather suit; a sack of hard candy to munch on when fishing's slow; a spare hat; a roll of glass tape for repairing loose guides and

a tube of ferrule cement for securing anything that may work loose; spare line in case you need it; lightweight gloves for early and late runs against a chilly wind; and waterproof shoes or boots.

Guides. Some guides will go all out to give you a full day's worth of fishing. If you get a poor guide, tell the camp owner.

Miscellaneous Tips. If you plan to bring fish home, do not depend on the heavy paper boxes that most camps use. These offer poor insulation, and fish can thaw out in a few hours; they also break apart from rough handling. Take along your own plastic or metal insulated chest, filled with a duffel bag on the way to camp, then packed with frozen fish on the return trip. The duffel bag can return as baggage.

If you have to go through customs, be sure to open your fishing-tackle bag first and chat about your experience as the official pokes around. They probably won't bother going through your other bags. There is something trustworthy about a fisherman who smuggles out nothing but tall stories.

Keep in touch once you find a good guide, and ask him to keep you informed of any good camps he learns about.

Also, keep notes on the date of your trip and the moon phase you fished in. If you did not catch any fish, talk with the camp manager and ask him to check his log to see which moon phase is consistently best.

And finally, what kind of medicine kit should you carry around? Three standbys that are a must: (1) aspirin or suitable substitute for minor aches; (2) your favorite medication for upset stomach; and (3) something in case you get the greenapple quickstep.

Photographing Fish

Here are a few pointers to make certain your photos are as interesting to viewers as they are to you.

Pictorials—those pictures showing a favorite lake with the sun setting in the background—look better with a person doing something that leads the eye into the photo.

Try to frame your pictures. Use trees, weeds, or rocks in the foreground and midground of the picture to lead the viewer's eye. If there is nothing in the foreground, especially if the sky is cloudless, make sure to shoot a tree branch overhead so it graces the top of the photo.

Use a wide-angle lens for close-quarters shots in order to take in more information.

Try to photograph your subjects in motion. Under low-light conditions, where shutter speeds must be slow, have the subject exaggerate his motions—stretching way out to net a fish or holding a netted fish high in the air with the water streaming out. These pictures don't require the subject to move, yet they indicate action.

Catch fishing rods in motion, even under low-light conditions, by snapping the pictures just as the rod stops one motion and begins another, as in the transition between forecast and backcast.

Photograph jumping fish by bringing them to the boat as soon as they are hooked, never allowing them the chance to fight. When the fish is close enough to focus on, let it have some line. It will still be lively and put on a show.

Capture a flyline in midcast by placing the fisherman between the photographer and the sun. The sun will reflect off the airborne line.

For a still life, arrange the fish on a plain background and have some fishing gear near the fish to indicate its size. Use a fishing creel, the butt section of a rod with the reel showing, or perhaps a landing net. Wet the fish with water to give it a freshly caught look.

A polarizing filter cuts through the surface glare when photographing fish in the water. This filter is very effective in photographing a fish coming into the landing net.

Video Your Hotspots
A video camera can improve your fishing success on some lakes and streams. During periods of low water, take shots of likely fish-holding cover and structure that would normally be hidden from view. Such cover would include sunken logs, stumps, and rocks. When filming, be sure to include a landmark in the scene so that you can locate the structure in high water. Also, making notes will help you tell what's what, where, how far, and so on. Ordinary water-level fluctuations of many streams and lakes can reveal quite a lot, but the real payoff comes when manmade impoundments are drawn down for one reason or another. And new impoundments under construction, including farm ponds, offer a unique opportunity to film the entire bottom.

Cartopping

Cartopping eliminates the hassles of cumbersome trailers or the inconvenience of sharing the car seat with unwieldy equipment. Boats, kayaks, canoes, and excess luggage can go on the roof. Some systems even allow you to carry multiple items.

There are disadvantages to cartopping. The racks don't carry everything. Smaller items such as clothes, paddles, and outboard motors have to go inside the vehicle. What's on the racks and even the racks themselves may be subject to theft. (This applies primarily to old-fashioned carriers. All the modern systems offer elaborate locking devices.) And finding the right rack for your vehicle is often troublesome.

The simplest racks are soft-plastic pads that hold the gunwales of a small boat

Brackets for under $30 can be bolted to crossbars made of two-by-fours. Sears and a variety of other stores offer

inexpensive racks on which the tower foot seats in the gutter and a clamp is positioned underneath the gutter to hold the rack securely in place.

If you're wondering how much you can carry up there, remember that the roofs of most vehicles are strong enough to take whatever load you can lift on to them. You are limited only by the weight you can lift and position safely and securely. For boats, about 100 pounds is tops for a one-man load and 200 pounds is all that two people should try to handle.

A nifty device that is seldom seen but works great is a rollbar. This connects to front and rear crossbars and enables you to load sideways. Lean the bow of the boat on the rollbar, then pick up the stern. Since the rollbar absorbs some of the weight, lifting is easier. Balance the boat on the rollbar, swing it around until the bow rests on the front crossbar, and jiggle it into position.

To be safe, you should always secure cartopped loads two ways. Tie the load (or use strong shock cord) to the crossbars. Then lash it fore and aft to the vehicle itself. There are usually holes in the bumper areas to tie to, but you may have to use S hooks or even drill holes to accommodate eyebolts.

Anchor Transport

An old bowling ball bag is perfect for storing and transporting a small boat anchor. Built with a reinforced bottom, it can take and carry the weight of an anchor easily. It also has plenty of storage space on top that can be used to pack an anchor line. Secondhand bowling ball bags can often be bought at garage sales and flea markets for just a few dollars.

Basic cartop mounts (from left): Bracket clamped to car gutter and canoe gunwale; foam pad on gunwale and bungee cord; clamp bracket on gunwale and bungee cord.

Off-Season Maintenance

To enjoy your angling more in the coming season—and to catch more fish—consider devoting a few hours to sprucing up your equipment.

The first step is to reorganize all lures, putting spoons in the trays where you keep them, crankbaits all together and categorized by the depth they run, their body shape, and so on. While working on this organization, clean off any debris and clip off knots of line left in eyelets. Examine the lures and set aside those requiring further attention. If your tacklebox itself is dirty, scrub it with a good household cleanser.

Here are the types of repairs you may need to perform:

Polish spinner blades and spoons. You'll be better off if your spoons and spinners give off the most flash possible to mimic swimming baitfish. Dulled blades and bodies can be refurbished quickly with a quality metal cleaner.

Straighten spinner and spinnerbait shafts. If your spinner shafts are crooked, doctor them with pliers so they run true when the season starts.

Check the eyelets on crankbaits to make sure they're straight. If they're bent, realign them carefully with needle-nosed pliers.

Examine split rings connecting hooks to lure bodies and replace any that are deformed, rusted, or partially opened.

Check for hooks that are bent outward; straighten with needle-nosed pliers or replace them.

Touch up chipped or dulled paint on jigs, spoons, and plugs.

Repair holes or cracks in hollow plastic crankbaits with epoxy cement.

Revive flies by steaming them. You can use a pair of tweezers, and a tea kettle is especially handy for this job.

Sharpen hook points. More fish are lost due to a dull hook than to any other cause. A fine hook file or stone works well for creating a triangular point.

Knife Maintenance

Knives don't take much maintenance, but without any, they can self-destruct quickly.

First, wash your knife with soap and hot water. Then rinse in hot water and dry (the hot water will heat the steel, which aids in evaporation of moisture from crevices). Spray the whole knife with WD-40™and wipe down the blade. On a folding knife, oil the hinge pin. On sheath knives, clean the sheath with saddle soap if necessary, and wax with shoe polish. If the sheath is in truly sad shape, warm it in an oven at a very low temperature and rub in beeswax mixed with a touch of neat's-foot oil. Store a sheath knife out of the sheath.

Good-bye to Frayed Windings
Frayed windings on fishing rods can be made to look new and last years longer by coating them with plastic. Mix up a two-part resin and hardener according to directions. Then use a pipe cleaner to flow this material onto the windings at guides and ferrules. Allow to harden several days. The new covering is almost indestructible, and it lasts much longer than varnish

Acknowledgments

Our thanks to the Field Editors of *Sports Afield* as well as other contributors to America's widely read outdoor magazine, whose scores of articles and features were compiled and edited for this compendium of helpful angling techniques, facts, and tips:

Anthony Acerrano	George H. Harrison
Gerald Almy	Jerome B. Robinson
Jay Cassell	Mark Sosin
Homer Circle	Mike Toth
Tom Gresham	

Our thanks also to talented artists John Flagg, David Kiehm, Ed Lipinski, Steve Tozzi, and Glenn Wolff, whose informative and helpful illustrations added to the fundamental understanding of, at times, complex techniques. Their diagrams go a long way toward clarifying situations that may be difficult to grasp by word alone.

We regret if a contributor was inadvertently overlooked in the process of combining a wide variety of sources and creating a cohesive, highly informative text. Your thanks come from knowing that your expertise is inspiring readers to knowledgeably wet a line and enjoy the fullest pleasure of the great sport of fishing.